The Halloween Handbook

The Halloween Handbook

Written and Illustrated by
ED MORROW

CITADEL PRESS
Kensington Publishing Corp.
www.kensingtonbooks.com

CITADEL PRESS books are published by

Kensington Publishing Corp.
850 Third Avenue
New York, NY 10022

All Kensington titles, imprints, and distributed lines are available at special quantity discounts for bulk purchases for sales promotions, premiums, fund raising, educational, or institutional use. Special book excerpts or customized printings can also be created to fit specific needs. For details, write or phone the office of the Kensington special sales manager: Kensington Publishing Corp., 850 Third Avenue, New York, NY 10022, attn: Special Sales Department, phone 1-800-221-2647.

Citadel Press and the Citadel logo are trademarks of Kensington Publishing Corp.

First printing: September 2001

10 9 8 7 6 5 4 3 2 1

Printed in the United States of America

Library of Congress Control Number: 2001091784

ISBN 0-8065-2227-5

CONTENTS

INTRODUCTION

My favorite Halloween was when I was ten. In the 1960s, I lived in a small Vermont town where every kid went trick-or-treating with few of the modern fears of abduction, poisonings, or occult murders. Our only fears were the fantastic, spooky ones we could conjure in our imaginations as we raced around in the dark in hideous disguises. That year, my costume was a sheet to which my mother had stitched the rubber skull mask I'd worn the year before. The skull was nicely ghoulish, with rubber nails driven into its forehead and deep black eye sockets that made my eyes seem fiendish as they darted back and forth from behind. I had verified the effect in the bathroom mirror but had stronger evidence of the mask's hideousness—my mother had raised an eyebrow and sighed when I had chosen it at the store.

There was a full moon in the sky that night, with a high wind that sent dark-bellied clouds sailing fast and grand against a bright-starred sky. It was very cold, and my mother had made sure I had on my long johns and red flannel winter coat under the ghostly sheet. What cold bit through this armor only set a nice shiver along my spine, quite in keeping with the holiday.

Our town swarmed with costumed kids at Halloween. We'd form up into groups of friends and start the evening by gathering treats. These were all completely worthless by current nutritional standards. Word of who was giving out good treats, such as candy bars or gum, spread quickly and brought mobs of supplicant kids. Some houses in the center of town got hundreds of callers. One pair of elderly sisters got so many callers that they had children sign in to discourage trick-or-treaters from collecting twice. This wasn't a foolproof system. Often a kid would discover that someone with exactly the same name as his had already visited the old ladies. He'd look up from the ledger like a John Smith trying to register with a Jane Smith at a motel and swear that someone else had skunked him by stealing his name. The kindly ladies would look skeptical, but they never turned a kid away.

After filling our sacks with candy, we'd turn to tricks. Soaped windows and toilet-papered trees were about as wild as my friends and I ever got. We'd also try our best to surprise girls, popping out from behind bushes or the corner of a house. They'd always shriek, but they seemed to enjoy it, especially when the boy yelling "Boo!" was someone they liked. An older eye might have noticed that the same girls somehow managed to be surprised over and over by the same boys behind the same bushes.

For us grammar school boys, the heroes of Halloween were the high school boys who executed spectacular pranks. They did things like hang a dummy from a telephone pole or put a dress on the statue of a Civil War soldier in the town common. One year, a couple of farm boys put a manure spreader to rather spectacular use that made the park lawn much greener the next spring.

The fun always seemed to end too soon. Parents would call from their porches, jack-o'-lanterns would flicker and die, and the streets would empty. We lived on a farm at the edge of town, and I remember feeling a wonderful, wild thrill as I ran home with a pillowcase full of candy across the cow pasture. The dark woods came down from the hills to edge the pasture, and I could imagine all sorts of things hiding in them, peering out at me. I should have been nervous, but, as the wind cast my sheet around me and I gazed out of my rubber mask, I felt quite different. I felt that whatever was crouched out there under the evergreens should be afraid of *me*. Then I crested the stone wall that topped the hill above our house. I could see the barn, dark and huge, like a monstrous creature snoozing a bit before moving on to crush Tokyo. Across the road was our house. My folks had left the porch light on for me. It cast a small circle of yellow warmth matched by the shaded windows of the house. The wind had grown icy. It pushed heavier clouds overhead that suddenly began to spit snow. Winter comes early in Vermont. I should have wanted to run down the hill and into our warm kitchen, but instead I almost ran off into the woods. Of course, I didn't. But every Halloween since, I've wondered what I would have found there.

PART I

Halloween History and Traditions

1

THE ORIGINS
OF HALLOWEEN

The Gauls are extremely superstitious.

Julius Caesar (100 B.C.–44 B.C.), *The Conquest of Gaul*, speaking of the people of Northern Europe, including the Celts

Halloween is a curious idea—a celebration of the dead marked by children running through the streets dressed as demons and monsters to extort candy by threat of practical jokes. To understand why we would find entertainment in such a dreadful thing—according to the National Retail Federation, Halloween is the fastest-growing holiday in the country—we must go back to the ancient Celts.

More than two thousand years ago, while the Mediterranean and Near East were hosting the classical civilizations, a more primitive but equally complex civilization dominated Northern Europe in places now known as Ireland, England, France, Wales, Brittany, and Scotland. These people were the Celts. One of several Indo-European peoples, they lived in Central Europe before moving westward in pre-Roman times. They took their name from the *celt,* their favorite weapon and tool: a thin, sharp-edged stone wedge that was used in axes, hatchets, chisels, and knives. Classical mythology ascribes a more romantic origin to the Celts. Celtina, the daughter of Britannus, bore a son, named Celtus, by the Greek hero Hercules. Celtus became the progenitor of the Celtic people. Hercules was an extremely popular mythological figure; many peoples liked to include him in their family tree.

The details of the Celts' own version of their origin are largely lost to history, for the Celts had no written language. Even their art lacked a narrative element and was primarily decorative. This doesn't mean they had no stories. The Celts had a rich oral tradition, which included elaborate, heroic tales of kings and queens, ancient gods, and a lively spirit world. Unfortunately, as with most oral traditions, the bulk of their tales were lost or greatly corrupted over time. Nearly all that is known of them comes from the written accounts of their conquerors, the recordings of Celtic myths by Christian monks beginning in the eighth century, and folklore passed from generation to generation. Despite these limitations, historians, anthropologists, and folklorists have put together a fairly clear view of Celtic life.

The Celts were herders and hunters who, on several occasions, proved to be terrifying warriors. Roman historians recorded several wars fought against the Celts, noting in particular the Celtic battle tactic of ferocious yelling and trumpeting meant to unnerve their foes. If successful in their first assaults, they often overwhelmed their opponents. If unsuccessful, they just as often fell into chaos and were slaughtered by the more disciplined Roman army.

The Celts worshiped deities that were personifications of the forces of nature and aspects of the natural world—the sun, the sky, mountains, rivers, and the sea. Celtic gods could be beneficent or harmful. The Celts lived in dread of the vagaries of their gods and goddesses and routinely made sacrifices to appease them, invoke their blessings, and gain their support in important activities, such as making war, bearing children, and hunting. Julius Caesar, whose *Conquest of Gaul* described the Celts, claimed that human sacrifices using fire were common among the Celts. These sacrifices and all religious activities were conducted by Celtic priests, known as Druids.

THE DRUIDS

The word *Druid* is thought to be related to the Sanskrit word *veda,* meaning "to foretell" or "to know," and to the Greek word *drys,* meaning "oak tree." Oak groves were sacred to the Druids. A massive tree is a natural meeting place, and a grove of trees can form an imposing natural cathedral. The oak may have seemed special because it doesn't lose its leaves in winter and supports mistletoe, also deemed sacred.

The Druids weren't the first to believe that oaks were special. The pre-Druid, Bronze Age people of Britain built circles of upright oak logs with an inverted oak stump at the center. It is believed that the builders used the trees to mark sight lines to celestial events so that these could be predicted in the future and celebrated with religious rituals. One of these circles of logs, dated as at least four thousand years old, was discovered in 1998 off the coast of Norfolk, England, under a layer of ancient, waterlogged peat. Remnants of such circles are located all across England. In time, oak logs were replaced by monolithic stones. The most famous of these stone circles is Stonehenge (see below). Although far older than the Druids, the circles were later attributed to them because they used the sites in their rituals.

Druids were divided into three classes: prophets, bards, and priests. All were male; female prophets and sorcerers assisted the Druids but were not given the same status. The leader of the Druids was the Archdruid. Druids spent twenty years learning the rituals of their religion before being allowed to conduct them. Because of this long education, they were considered the most learned members of their society. According to Caesar, "The Druids officiate at the worship of the gods, regulate public and private sacrifices, and give rulings on all religious questions . . . they are held in great honor by the people. They act as judges in practically all disputes, whether

Stonehenge

between tribes or individuals. . . . Any individual or tribe failing to accept their award is banned from taking part in sacrifice—the heaviest punishment that can be inflicted." Because of their social importance, Druids were exempt from taxes and military service.

The Druids practiced astrology, studied the powers of plants and animals, and executed magical rituals. The Romans reported that the Druids believed in the immortality of the soul, which entered the body of a newborn child upon the death of its earlier host body.

THE FESTIVAL OF SAMHAIN–OCTOBER 31

Two times of the year were most important to the Celtic way of life—spring, when the herds were sent to their pastures in the hills, and fall, when the herds returned to their stables (often the same building as their owner's home). The Druids marked these moments with festivals. On May 1, they celebrated Beltane, the beginning of spring. On the evening of October 31 and the day of November 1, they celebrated the festivals of Samhain and Taman. *Samhain*, pronounced "sao-in," was the Gaelic word for "November." It was dedicated to the Celtic Lord of the Dead and marked the beginning of winter and the new year. Taman was dedicated to the Celtic sun god. Samhain was the greatest Celtic festival. Its celebration could last a week, overlapping Taman.

According to Celtic myth, at Samhain time, the goddess Cailleach hit the earth with her hammer, locking it into the iron-hard embrace of icy winter for three frigid months. In February, Brigid, goddess of healing, smithing, and poetry, broke the spell with her white wand, turning the frozen earth soft and warm and ready for planting,

October 31 and November 1 were natural times to stage Samhain and Taman feasts. Keeping cattle through the winter required storing forage. To minimize the amount of forage needed, it was common to slaughter any cattle thought superfluous or unlikely to survive the winter. Because meat couldn't be stored for long without spoiling, it was a matter of "eat it now or throw it out." The fruits and crops of the field had also just been harvested and were handy for feasting. Abundance made it a pragmatic time for ritual sacrifice. One could give something to the gods without undue pain.

Secular events were tied to this time of year, the end of the old year and the beginning of the new. Laws took effect or lapsed. Rents and taxes were due. Making payments in crops or cattle was easier because of harvesttime abundance and surplus cattle.

The hard work of summer, managing the herds and harvesting crops, ended with fall. Handicrafts, the lesser work of winter, began. Cloth was woven, tools were made and repaired, and furniture might be fashioned. These tasks took less time to complete than the more laborious work of summer. There was leisure time to fill. The character of life also changed, from the sunny, warm, airy summer to the dark, cold, housebound winter. At the end of a good harvest, winter could be a cozy time of gossip and busywork. After a poor harvest, it could be a season of want and starvation. There was always the fear that winter might outlast the supply of stored food. The sun itself seemed diminished and fearful as it ran a short course low in the sky, bringing a gloom that, with the growing barrenness of the scenery, evoked thoughts of death and of the dead.

CELTIC VIEWS ON DEATH

The pagan Celts didn't believe in Heaven or Hell. After death, a person's spirit moved on to Tir nan Og, a land of eternal youth and happiness. Tir nan Og wasn't as remote a location as the Heaven and Hell of Christianity. The Celtic dead could, and regularly did, reach from their afterlife into the world of the living. This was especially easy for them at Samhain time, a turning point in the Celtic calendar.

For the Celts, transitional points—such as the shore, where the land meets and becomes the sea, or midnight, when one day becomes another—were considered to have magical power. At such places or moments, things were in flux, belonging fully to neither one side nor the other. Chaos had the upper hand. A small action might push or pull you to either side. Samhain, when one year became another, was the most important turning point. Many legendary battles and crucial moments in the lives of Celtic heroes were said to have occurred at Samhain. It was believed that at this time of the year, the boundary between Tir nan Og and the world of the living was at its thinnest. Spirits could communicate with those they had left behind.

The Celts had a generally positive view of spirit visitations. In Northern Britain, *geist,* the word for "ghost," was also the word for "guest." The Celts invited their dead relatives to the feast of Samhain.

Some Celtic mountain villagers issued invitations impossible to refuse. They would take the skulls of their dead relatives from their graves and bring them to the feast, after giving them a decorative painting. Food or milk was often left outside the home as a hospitable way to share the feast with wandering spirits who had no relatives to stack their parti-colored skulls in a corner to watch the fun. Spirits who were left out of the festivities could turn mischievous and dangerous. Wary Celts took precautions. Cows, for example, were protected by hanging blessed bells from their necks.

At Taman, the sun god was thought to be at a low point in his battle with darkness. Druids believed that the sun god could be aided in his contest by lighting bonfires. The hearth fires of the Celts were also purified at this time of year by relighting them from a fresh source. In Ireland, according to legend, all the hearth fires were extinguished, including the central fire kept by the Druids at Tlachtga, a spot near the royal hill of Tara, the seat of power of the ancient kings of Ireland. The Tlachtga fire would then be rekindled by rubbing sticks from a sacred oak together to produce "new fire." The new fire was carried from house to house to relight hearth fires. The extinguishing symbolically mimicked the coming of winter and the lack of warmth. The relighting corresponded with the promise of summer returning and the renewal of warmth. It must have been a dramatic moment, with winter looming and all the fires in the land extinguished. Survival through the coming cold would depend upon the success of what has, for us, become a Boy Scout trick.

According to Caesar, the relit fires weren't put to Boy Scoutish use by the Druids. Ritual sacrifices of animals, especially horses thought sacred to the sun god, and human beings were made in the flames. Caesar wrote, "Persons suffering from serious disease, as well as those who are exposed to the perils of battle, offer, or vow to offer, human sacrifices. . . . Some tribes have colossal images made of wickerwork, the limbs of which they fill with living men; they are then set on fire, and the victims burned to death." Captured Roman soldiers were sometimes the unhappy victims of these toasty services.

The convulsions of sacrificial victims and the remnants left behind were studied by the Druids to predict the future. Sacrifices made at Samhain were thought to give information valuable for the new year. In some Celtic regions, in a milder rite, people would place stones bearing their names in a bonfire, then search for them the next morning. Those who couldn't find their stones in the ashes were thought doomed to die in the coming year. This custom, in a reduced form, continued in Scotland until recent times, using small marked stones placed in the hearth.

Sacrifices were also used to aid the dead. The dead of the Celts were not guaranteed an eternal reward in Tir nan Og. On Samhain, during what was called the Vigil of Samhain, the Lord of the Dead would review the souls in his possession and decide whether they should be allowed to remain in the comfort of Tir nan Og for the coming year or be punished by being returned for one year to the world of the living in the form of animals or insects. It was thought that the Lord of the Dead could be bribed to give a favorable review, so Celts commonly made sacrifices to prevent their dead relatives from being punished. Those souls punished by being returned in lowly forms were given aid in the form of food left outside. Since they were unpleasant souls, as certified by the Lord of the Dead, such aid was prudent lest they injure the living.

In addition to appeasement, the Celts sometimes resorted to ruses to confuse the returned evil dead. They would dress in strange outfits mimicking their lowly forms and loudly parade away from the homes they hoped to protect. The evil souls were supposed to mistake the costumed Celts for other evil souls and follow them. They might be encouraged to follow by the paraders, leaving gifts of food a safe distance from the households being protected.

Alternatively, the fearful costumes worn by the paraders combined with ferocious, menacing actions might frighten away evil spirits the way a big dog frightens a smaller dog. This menacing survived into modern times in rustic parts of Europe that had been Celtic lands. In a link to Celtic fire customs, shouting peasants would march about with pitchforks bearing burning bundles of straw. The flames were meant to singe the bottoms of low-flying witches and scare them away.

It isn't hard to imagine the Celtic costumed parades becoming moments of frivolity as peasants, heavy with feasting and drinking, danced around in the strangest disguises they could assemble. The connection to trick-or-treating in these customs is readily apparent.

There was also a more religious form of Celtic tribute gathering. To finance their temples and priesthood, Druids led a masked parade of

peasants door to door gathering contributions for the Druid god Muck Olla. The leader of the parade was called the Lair Bhan, the "white mare." As mentioned earlier, the horse was sacred to the Druid sun god. It was also a Celtic symbol of fertility. The Lair Bhan would demand tribute from each household the peasants visited in return for Muck Olla's continued favor. Those who failed to pay tribute or pay it sufficiently were punished. Livestock might be stolen or farm buildings damaged and even burned. Again, a link to modern trick-or-treating is apparent.

The Celtic peoples didn't include devils or demons in their religious tradition. While the evil spirits cast out from Tir nan Og served this role in part, the Daoine Sidhe, later called the Fairy Folk, were seen as the ongoing agents of evil in the world. The Fairies were thought to be the original, magical inhabitants of Celtic lands who had been displaced. They resented their displacement and seized any opportunity they found to take revenge. Rarely, a Fairy might be friendly or perform a boon, but there was nearly always some terrible price for any gift they gave, or the gift itself was worthless.

The Fairy Folk were believed to live in the mounds, or *sidhe*, that dot Scotland and Ireland. Undoubtedly, the legends of Fairies had roots in the real contest that had occurred when the Celts' ancestors took the land from the prehistoric people who had built the mounds. The former owners were driven into hiding in the woods, the domain of the Fairies, where they continued to resist until they dwindled into extinction or assimilation. Tales of the conflict and warnings of the dangers that could be encountered in the woods at the hands of the supplanted people were transformed into the legends of the Fairies.

Samhain, because of its chaotic, neither-here-nor-there nature, was a time when it was easiest for the Fairies to injure their enemies. The food and milk left outside for wandering spirits were also offerings to Fairies to win their favor. Just as with the spirits thrown out of Tir nan Og, the Celts would sometimes impersonate Fairies to confuse them and, in their impersonation, demand tribute. To lend spookiness to their impersonation, they carried lanterns made from hollowed-out turnips. They cut fierce faces into the turnips and lit them with candles to present an otherworldly appearance. This practice survives today in the jack-o'-lantern. Over time, after Christianity supplanted the Druids' faith, the wandering evil dead of Samhain were largely replaced in popular superstition with Fairies.

ROMAN AUTUMN CUSTOMS

In the first century A.D., Rome conquered Britain. The Druids couldn't successfully unite their peoples to resist. The Romans had already taken much of Northern Europe; only the remote, hostile regions of Scotland and Ireland were left beyond their control. Even there, however, the unconquered peoples felt Rome's influence as they interacted with the Romans and the Romanized Celts. Roman religious beliefs began to blend with Celtic beliefs. Such mixing of Roman and Celtic beliefs was made easier because there were similar elements in their mythologies. The Romans had pastoral ancestors who celebrated with seasonal feasts, much as the Celts did. As the Romans became an agricultural people, the importance of seasonal events grew. Crops had to be planted at propitious times; errors could bring famine. Care also had to be taken that the crops were diligently tended. The turning of the seasons and agricultural care met in the Roman legend of Vertumnus and Pomona.

Vertumnus was the Roman god of the revolving seasons. Pomona was the goddess of orchards and harvest. Vertumnus, a youthful god, fell in love with the beautiful Pomona, who rebuffed his advances because she was more interested in tending her fruit trees and grapevines than in male company. Like the changeable year, Vertumnus could assume many guises. To sneak glimpses of Pomona, he would transform himself into an apple picker or vine pruner. One day, Vertumnus disguised himself as an old woman to approach his love object. Considering the old woman no threat,

Pomona chatted with her. Vertumnus-as-old-woman pointed out that grapevines needed support to grow upright and be fruitful. He suggested that Pomona herself was much like the vines. Vertumnus then revealed his true form and offered to be her support. Swayed by his argument, Pomona fell in love with Vertumnus. Together, the couple worked to ensure that the Roman harvest would be bountiful. Because of this romantic alliance, the festival of Pomona was celebrated at a time important to Vertumnus—when the seasons were turning from harvesttime to winter, November 1. The feast was called Pomona, for the goddess. When Romans mingled with Celts and the Celts adopted Roman agricultural methods and customs, the feasts of Samhain, Taman, and Pomona blended.

ROASTING NUTS AND BOBBING FOR APPLES

To celebrate Pomona's festival, Romans laid out the bounty of the harvest in her honor. Apples and nuts were associated with Pomona. Under the Romans, they became part of Celtic Samhain celebrations and were often used in divination rituals. In northern England, one rite was performed by placing two nuts side by side on the hearth to serve as stand-ins for a would-be married couple. If the heat of the fire made one of the nuts pop and fly, the couple would part because of that person's failings. If the nuts simply sat and cooked, the couple would remain happily married. The rite can be seen as a mild echo of the horrid Celtic fire sacrifices. Curiously, in southern England, the rite was interpreted in exactly the opposite way:

> If he loves me, pop and fly;
> If he hates me, lie and die.

Ducking and peeling are examples of the use of apples in divination at Samhain time. In ducking, single young people would compete to retrieve an apple from a tub of water using just their teeth. The first person to succeed was believed to be the first person who would be married in the coming year. In the peeling rite, a celebrant would carefully peel an apple under the belief that the longer the peel produced in a single piece, the longer the peeler would live. This had the bonus of producing a lot of peeled apples ready for cooking. These rites survive into modern times as party games. In Scotland and northern England, ducking and peeling are sometimes combined, with the ducked apple being peeled and the length of the peel predicting the length of the marriage. The peel is then thrown over the shoulder. The shape it takes upon the floor is said to form the cursive initial of the person the thrower will marry.

When not playing with their food, the Celts and Romans utilized apples and nuts in holiday recipes. Lamswool, for example, was a popular holiday drink that was still served in Britain as late as the nineteenth century. It was a mixture of ale, sugar, and roasted apples. The bits of roasted apples in the drink resembled lamb's wool.

Apples and nuts—eaten or used for fortune-telling games— continued to be important in English Halloweentime celebrations until the nineteenth century. Indeed, the association with apples and nuts was so strong that Halloween was sometimes called Nutcrack Night or Snap Apple Night.

ROMAN VIEWS ON DEATH

The Roman festival honoring the dead was called Feralia (the word *feral*, meaning "wild," is related to Feralia). Like Samhain, it was celebrated in late October. Roman attitudes toward the dead were different from those of the Celts. The Roman afterlife was based on the Greek classical view, in which good people who were properly buried might be rewarded with a pleasant afterlife in the Elysian Fields. Those who were deemed evil or who weren't buried correctly wound up in Hades, an unpleasant place of dim, gray, ghostly half living. The misery of Hades is described in *The Odyssey,* the Greek epic by Homer that tells the story of the long voyage home of Ulysses after the fall of Troy. At one point in his journey, Ulysses meets the ghost of the great Trojan warrior Achilles. Achilles, who was sent to Hades, bitterly complains of its dreariness. When Ulysses tries to comfort the warrior by telling him that he lived a glorious life, Achilles replies that he would rather be the humblest slave alive than the most glorious ghost in history.

While the Greco-Roman afterlife was much gloomier than the Celtic, Roman and Greek spirits were more securely bound to the other side. Unlike the Celtic dead, Roman ghosts weren't as likely to come rattling your roof tiles on dark and stormy nights.

THE END OF THE DRUIDS AND CELTIC TRADITIONS

Celtic traditions had their appeal to the occupying Roman soldiers, whose terms of enlistment required them to spend decades hundreds of miles from home. Some began to adopt Celtic beliefs. The Roman authorities feared they would lose the loyalty of their legions. Since the Druids were perceived to be the exploiters of such disloyalty, they came under increased suspicion. There was also a philosophical conflict between Roman and Celtic traditions. Despite the grisly pleasure the Romans took in gladiatorial combat, Roman religious leaders frowned on human sacrifice and worried that the Romans might be induced to accept the practice by persuasive Druid priests. Because of these worries, the Roman authorities did their best to exterminate the Druid priesthood and obliterate Celtic ceremonies. The Druids relied upon an oral tradition; when the priests who knew the old stories disappeared, then their religion faded into legend and superstition.

THE CHRISTIAN ABSORPTION
OF PAGAN PRACTICES AND HOLIDAYS

When the Roman Empire became Christianized during the fourth century, the Roman state began to impose Christianity on its subjects. Christian missionaries bravely traveled to distant lands to preach. Bluntly trying to replace pagan beliefs with Christian beliefs met resistance. The common folk had great faith in the deities they and their ancestors had worshiped for centuries. The Christian clergy thus developed a clever tactic to turn this faith upon itself: Instead of denying the powers of the ancient gods, they labeled them demons who had used lies to portray themselves as beneficent gods. Pagan faiths also considered the gods capricious, and some outright evil. It wasn't too great a stretch to suggest that all pagan gods had nothing but their own amusement at heart. Christ was advanced as the all-loving defender of man against the demonic old gods. Those gods and goddesses whose reputations for beneficence were too great for twisting into malevolence were subsumed into the saints or angels of the Catholic Church. A prominent example of this among the Celts was the Christianization of the goddess Brigid into St. Bridget of Kildare.

Another example of the Church incorporating earlier gods is the Archangel Michael, the commander of God's army of angels. He inherited some of the associations that had formerly been given to Mithras, the Persian god of light. Mithras had been a favorite deity of the Roman military, and his military associations were readily transferred to Michael.

Another effective tactic of Christian missionaries was to take over a pagan holy site and convert it to Christian usage. Sites sacred to Mithraism often became sites of Catholic churches dedicated to Michael. The spectacular fortress-island Mont-St-Michel on the coast of Normandy, for instance, is a former Mithraist holy place. The conversion of pagan holy places neatly pushed out the older gods. You couldn't go to the temple of Jupiter to sacrifice to him if there were a bunch of Christian priests busily performing a Mass there when you stuck your head  inside. The pagan who found the property of the old god under new management couldn't help but speculate that the new god was stronger than the old.

The famed cathedral of Chartres was built on a Celtic sanctuary. The Celtic sanctuary itself had supplanted an earlier pagan holy place. A prehistoric "Venus"—a pregnant goddess statue—was venerated at the spot by the Druids who had inherited it from still earlier, non-Druidic worshipers. The Catholic Church also venerated the figurine, identifying it as an image of the pregnant Virgin Mary. It remained at Chartres till the French Revolution, when less religious-minded revolutionaries destroyed what was probably one of the oldest continually venerated religious figurines in history.

An extension of the physical co-optation of pagan sites was the absorption of pagan festivals by the Christians. The pagans loved their festivals just as we modern people love our holidays, and becoming a Christian seemed unappealing if you had to abandon all that fun. The Church thus decided to rededicate the old festivals to the new religion. Rituals associated with the Celtic and Roman deities were adapted and reassociated with Christianity. Persecution of early Christians had produced numerous martyred saints who could be honored by revamped pagan festivals.

ALL HALLOWS' DAY AND ALL HALLOWS' EVEN

In A.D. 610, Pope Boniface IV consecrated Rome's great pagan temple, the Pantheon, to St. Mary and the Martyrs, designating May 13 as a feast day for saintly martyrs not otherwise memorialized—sort of a Miscellaneous Saints' Day. In the eighth century, Pope Gregory III moved the feast day to November 1 and extended it to all saints so that every church in Christendom, each of which had its own patron saint, would have reason to celebrate the day. The feast day was now known as All Saints' Day or All Hallows' Day—from *hallowed*, meaning "honored." Gregory also added All Souls' Day, celebrated on November 2, to the holy calendar to extend the honors given to the saints to a remembrance of all the souls of the dead. The Church urged the faithful to use the day to pray for and honor the dead—something well in keeping with the old traditions of Samhain, Taman, Pomona's festival, and Feralia. All Hallows' Evening, October 31, was celebrated with the activities very similar to Samhain. In time, All Hallows' Evening became All Hallows' Even, then Halloween.

After the Romans left Celtic lands and the Dark Ages overwhelmed Europe, the Catholic Church endured. The absorbed traditions of the Celts and the pagan Romans were preserved in Catholic traditions and Halloween became a part of the Catholic calendar.

GOING A-SOULING

The custom of marking a holiday by going door to door demanding tribute isn't unique to modern Halloween celebrations. Other holidays incorporate what anthropologists call "ritual tribute solicitation." In Cajun parts of southwestern Louisiana, where Mardi Gras is celebrated in its traditional form, rowdy parties of men disguised in masks and costumes go from home to home collecting tribute before the main celebrations begin. Even the Christmas caroling tradition, wherein carolers go door to door, sing, then receive a reward of eggnog, cocoa, or other libation, is similar to trick-or-treating. As described above, the tradition of gathering Halloween tribute can be traced to ancient Celtic times. When Christianity replaced paganism, the tribute gathering was transferred to All Souls' Day and other holidays.

In England and areas that came under English domination, "going a-souling" became an All Souls' Day tradition. Poor people would go door to door seeking soul cakes—sweet buns with currants. The cakes were remnants of an old fall tradition of distributing to the poor bread made from the first grain harvested. In return for the soul cakes, the eaters promised to pray for the household's dead relatives. It was believed that all of the dead spent time in Limbo just after death and that prayer, even prayer bought with baked goods, speeded their movement on to Heaven. Children, in particular, enjoyed souling and often received coins as well as soul cakes. They sometimes carried turnip lanterns, called punkies, direct descendants of the turnip lanterns carried by the Celts. In Shropshire and Cheshire, children gone a-souling would sing:

> *Soul, soul, for a souling cake*
> *I pray, good missus, a souling cake*
> *Apple or pear, plum or cherry*
> *Anything good to make us merry.*

Adults who went souling wanted stronger tribute. Farmworkers souling during Victorian times sometimes sang: "All that we soul for is ale and strong beer."

The money gathered from souling was commonly used by children to buy fireworks and by adults to buy liquor. Both added to the rowdiness of the celebration.

Prophecy by Indigestion

In the Hebrides Islands of Scotland, cakes made with meal and salted herring were an All Souls' Day treat. It was believed that if a person ate one of the salty cakes before bed without drinking any water, the thirsty sleeper would have a dream in which his or her future spouse would offer a drink.

In some parts of England, souling blended with seasonal mumming rituals that reach back to the Druid's Muck Olla. Townspeople dressed in strange costumes, repeated verses, and paraded with a mock horse called Old Hob. The paraders performed a rustic mumming play with the horse—usually just a horse's skull set on a pole with a sheet attached to cover the pole's bearer. The bearer cavorted with the skull, making its jaws snap at bystanders. A man dressed as a huntsman played the driver. He mockingly tried to sell the horse to the audience, insisting (like a modern used-car salesman) that it was a very valuable item while admitting that the creature was a bit old. The last was an ironic comment on the fact that the horse was so old it was just a skull.

Some mumming plays have been revived in recent times and are performed in country pubs. In East Kent, the horse was called the

Hooden Horse and carried from house to house at Christmastime seeking tribute. A rider tries to ride the animal, and the Hooden Horse makes much of trying to buck him off. The horse was sometimes frightening to the weak spirited. In 1839, a woman was said to have been scared to death by the sudden appearance of a Hooden Horse,

and outraged authorities attempted to suppress the custom. While many villages lost the tradition, some retained it; today interest in folkways (and tourism) has brought revival of the mumming plays.

One notable revival of mumming occurred in Philadelphia in 1900, when community members staged a New Year's Day mummers' parade. It is still celebrated, with great fanfare, today.

Another contributor to the custom of dressing up at Halloween was the old Irish practice of marking All Hallows' Day with religious pageants that recounted biblical events. These were common during the Middle Ages all across Europe. The featured players dressed as saints and angels, but there were also plenty of roles for demons who had more fun, capering, acting devilish, and playing to the crowd. The pageant began inside the church, then moved by procession to the churchyard, where it continued long into the night.

During the Protestant Reformation, many folk customs were spurned as being linked to the Catholic Church and the Pope. Martin Luther rejected the notion of saints, which ended All Saints' Day and Halloween. In Calvinist times, even Christmas was stripped of its festive trimmings. The Restoration brought festivity back to Britain, but as the country became more and more urbanized, rural villagers who moved into cities left their ancient customs behind. Curiously, a traitorous plot provided a refuge for many old customs.

GUY FAWKES DAY

During the night of November 4, 1605, Guy Fawkes was arrested in the cellars under London's Parliament building. He was surrounded with more than a little incriminating evidence—thirty-six barrels of gunpowder, which he was planning to detonate later that day as James I ceremonially opened Parliament. The explosion would blast the king, the hierarchy of the Anglican Church, and all the members of Parliament into tiny bits. Fawkes had hoped to replace the Protestant government of England with a Roman Catholic one; Catholics were at that time subject to harsh penal laws drawn up by the Protestant government. For his crime, Fawkes was executed by the horrific practice of drawing and quartering before a huge crowd of spectators. After his torturous death, his body was burned. November 5 was declared a day of thanks by Parliament and became popularly known as Guy Fawkes Day.

Because it occurred near the now-forbidden All Souls' Day, many of that day's customs were transferred to Guy Fawkes Day. The authorities were happy to encourage a patriotic holiday.

For weeks in advance of Guy Fawkes Day, English children prepared dummies in the likeness of Fawkes. Called Guys, the dummies were set up on curbsides and street corners, where children would beg for "a penny for the Guy." Sometimes the dummies would be carried about town by children, who chanted:

> *Please to remember the fifth of November,*
> *Gunpowder treason and plot.*
> *I see no reason why gunpowder treason*
> *Should ever be forgot.*

The money would be used to buy fireworks for the fifth of November. The night of the fourth was named Mischief Night. To celebrate it, English children would play pranks on adults. On the night of the fifth, called Bonfire Night, the fireworks were detonated and the Guys burned on great bonfires. Children cavorting around the fires chanted:

> *Guy, guy, guy.*
> *Poke him in the eye.*
> *Put him on the bonfire*
> *And there let him die.*

Sausages and potatoes were often roasted in the bonfire, and Bonfire Parkin—a cake made of oatmeal, molasses, and ginger—was eaten.

The citizens of Ottery St. Mary in Devon still practice a rather hazardous Guy Fawkes Day fire custom. The insides of wooden barrels are coated with a thick layer of tar. At nightfall, the tar is lit, and the men of the town run through the streets with the burning barrels on their backs, streaming flames and sparks in a very spectacular display. When one man can no longer stand the heat of the burning barrel, he passes it on to another, who does the same. The barrels are passed on until they disintegrate. The barrel "rollers" commonly get burned but claim to have a good time nonetheless. The echoes of Celtic fire rituals are evident in their antics.

English celebrations of Guy Fawkes Day often included anti-

Catholic elements. The Guys burned by some English children weren't meant to represent Fawkes—they were meant to be the Pope. One Guy Fawkes children's chant went:

> *A rope, a rope, to hang the Pope.*
> *A piece of cheese to choke him,*
> *A barrel of beer to drink his health,*
> *And a right good fire to roast him.*

Guy Fawkes Day wasn't celebrated in every part of Great Britain. In Ireland, the people were Catholic. They were reluctant to join in the celebration of the punishment of a failed Catholic coup. This encouraged the older Halloween customs to linger there as substitutes for Guy Fawkes Day. Ironically, while the Celtic fall customs and Catholic All Souls' customs faded elsewhere in Europe, the traitorous Fawkes helped assure that the customs would survive in both Protestant Britain (subsumed into a patriotic holiday) and Catholic Ireland (in the preservation of Halloween as a religious and nationalist reaction to Guy Fawkes Day). As we'll see in the next chapter, a far more devastating event—the Irish Potato Famine—would also play a part in the development of Halloween.

R.I.P.

SAM B. JONES

1843-1889

2

HALLOWEEN IN AMERICA

COLONIAL CELEBRATIONS IN AMERICA

When the English settled North America, they carried their traditions with them. The hardships of the frontier, however, provided little surplus time, energy, or sustenance to divert to partying. These difficulties made the holidays that were celebrated sweeter and more eagerly anticipated. Christmas was widely marked with familial and community celebrations, with the exception of Puritan New England, where it was seen as frivolous and offensive to God. Celebrating Christmas was officially banned in Massachusetts until the mid–nineteenth century. Thanksgiving was a different matter for the Puritans. It was celebrated with feasting but not frivolity. Prayer and sermons were the entertainment.

Guy Fawkes Day was officially endorsed throughout the English colonies as a time to demonstrate loyalty to the king. As in England, it was marked with bonfires, effigies, and fireworks. Halloween, by virtue of its associations with the spirit world and Catholicism, didn't enjoy similar treatment.

New York, settled by the Dutch, was less dour when it came to holiday merrymaking. In addition to Christmas, colonists marked New Year's Day by drinking, discharging firearms, and visiting door to door, where they were treated to alcoholic drinks. May Day was similarly celebrated, complete with the maypole and dancing. Shrovetide, a period of merrymaking ending on Shrove Tuesday, the last day before Lent, was celebrated with partying, which sometimes included men dressing like women and parading, to the amusement of their neighbors. Halloween had no special significance to the Dutch—as Protestants, they had abandoned All Saints' Day and Halloween—

so after the English took over the colony, Guy Fawkes Day, with its traditions, occupied the portion of the calendar Halloween would have taken.

Pennsylvania was a predominantly Quaker colony until the mid–eighteenth century. The Quakers were a tolerant people, and those of other faiths felt free to practice their customs in the colony. This tolerance continued when German Lutherans replaced the Quakers as the largest religious group. The Lutherans had maintained many of the holidays of the Catholic Church, including All Souls' Day. They also had a rich folk history, well populated with witches. Another large ethnic group in Pennsylvania were Scots-Irish Presbyterians. They celebrated Halloween with the Scottish custom of *guising,* the donning of disguises by children, who then went door to door begging apples, nuts, and coins, another predecessor of Halloween trick-or-treating.

The southern colonies were more rural than the northern. Settled by English in the east and Scots-Irish in the interior, the South celebrated Guy Fawkes Day while keeping a few of the Halloween customs of Celtic Britain. The scarcity of people and remoteness of many communities limited partying but preserved traditions. In the rugged, poor-soiled backwoods of Appalachia, for example, many customs were preserved for centuries (just as the English spoken there retained words and forms from Elizabethan English long after they disappeared elsewhere). The tradition of storytelling was strong in the South, with tales of ghosts, demons, and witches enlivening many a Halloween night.

A second great influence upon Southern folk beliefs were the customs of Africans transported to the South as slaves. The Africans believed in a world filled with spirits that could touch the living. Voodoo was the most notable result of the blending of African and European beliefs, but countless superstitions, ghost stories, and tales of witchery came from the mix of cultures.

In every American colony, holiday customs changed and were redefined. The building of new settlements and the mixing of immigrant groups of various ethnic backgrounds invited the creation of new public celebrations and mutation of older customs. Modern historians have tended to concentrate on xenophobia and racism in American history and to ignore powerful elements of xenophilia and tolerance. Over and over again, Americans have admired some element of a for-

eign culture and adopted it, flavoring it with an American interpretation often itself constructed using foreign elements adopted earlier.
America can almost be defined by this process. One product of it was
the modern Halloween.

HALLOWEEN
IN POST-REVOLUTION AMERICA

While the Revolutionary War separated the American people from
their British forebears, British holidays continued to be part of life.
Guy Fawkes Day was a notable exception. The war had improved the
repute of those who attempted to depose kings. Occasionally, during
the war, the traditional Fawkes effigy would be replaced with an
effigy of King George; despite this, the holiday still seemed too
British, and it faded away. Some of its customs were transferred to
other holidays. The setting of bonfires was moved to the Fourth of
July and New Year's Day. The solicitation of tribute by children
moved to Christmas or, in some regions, to Thanksgiving.

Post-Revolution sentiments also favored more democratic celebrations. In rural areas, two kinds of celebrations, "work parties" and
"play parties," were common. Work parties included gatherings such
as barn raisings, corn-husking parties, quilting bees, apple-paring parties, taffy pulls, maple-sugaring parties, and sorghum-making parties.
To get a large job done quickly, neighbors collected at a work site.
Usually, while the men and boys worked at the collective task,
women and girls put together a meal that served as a reward for the
work. Sometimes all worked together, then shared food prepared earlier. Partying with dancing and games often followed the work. A
popular game at corn huskings was a search for an ear with a red
kernel. A young man who discovered such an ear could demand a
kiss from his choice of the girls. Sharp farm boys would palm the
red-kerneled ear and swap it off to a pal so that that boy could redis-
cover it and get a kiss.

Play parties weren't associated with a task; they were held just for
fun. They were often put together as a school entertainment, featuring recitals and plays. A common time for play parties was late October. The old English and Scottish customs of Snap Apple Night and
Nutcracker Night were enjoyed, especially those involving fortune-
telling. In Puritan times, divination rituals had tempted charges of

witchcraft, but now, a century later, witches were regarded by most as superstitious nonsense.

One purpose of play parties was to provide an opportunity for young men and women to socialize. Consequently, dancing was popular. Group dancing was favored; partner dancing was considered an invitation to impropriety. In some areas, dancing had to be done to the accompaniment of singing, stomping, and clapping, because musical instruments, especially the fiddle, were thought sinful. Another favorite activity was telling ghost stories. These were enjoyed for the same reason that teenagers would later enjoy drive-in horror movies—they provided an excuse for the girls to act scared and seek the reassurance of boys acting brave.

THE IRISH AND HALLOWEEN

By the nineteenth century, the potato, imported from South America, had become the main source of food for Ireland, with nearly half the Irish populace completely dependent upon it. In 1845, blight struck the potato crop, causing most of it to rot in the ground. During the next four years, each crop was spoiled by the blight. Famine killed millions. The British government took some steps to relieve suffering, spending eight million pounds and giving as many as three million Irishmen government jobs to support their families. Private funds were also sent. The measures, however, failed to meet the exigencies of the famine. By the time it passed, 1.1 million Irish had starved or died from famine-related disease, and another 1.5 million had fled their homes to find their livings in other countries. The United States received hundreds of thousands. Many more thousands would follow in later years to join their relatives.

The Irish settled in every city and every state in America. They helped fight the Civil War (on both sides) and settle the West. They worked on farms, mines, and railroads. The blue-collar laborers who made cities like New York, Boston, and Chicago manufacturing centers included large numbers of Irish. Where the Irish went, they carried their folkways, including the Irish Halloween. The throngs of Irish immigrants brought a revival of and expansion to Halloween customs already celebrated in America. There was one major change from the Old World—turnip jack-o'-lanterns became pumpkin jack-o'-lanterns.

The Irish Halloween had great appeal, especially in rural areas that

still followed the same harvest routines that had originally given rise
to the holiday. It fit in well with rustic play parties, which already featured many Halloween customs. It also served as a good substitute
for Guy Fawkes Day. The begging, bonfires, and pranks of that holiday were transferred to Halloween.

HALLOWEEN
IN NINETEENTH-CENTURY AMERICA

Pranks were an important part of nineteenth-century Halloween. A
favorite stunt was to tip over outhouses, hopefully with some hapless
user inside. A counterprank was to move the outhouse just a bit so
that when pranksters came to tip it, they'd fall in the foul privy hole.
Another favored prank was to set a buggy atop a barn. Wooden
doorsteps might be pulled away from their doors so that household-
ers risked a tumble when they stepped out in the morning. Door-
knobs might be coated with grease, tar, or syrup. A laundry line full
of clothes might be stolen and hoisted up a flagpole. Windows might
be soaped or painted black. A coopful of chickens or a few sheep
might find themselves being passed into a parlor through a pried-
open window. Tricksters might quietly tie all the doors of a house
shut, then ring the house's doorbell. This trick was considerably
improved after electric doorbells replaced old-fashioned mechanical
bells: The pranksters would jam the electric doorbell button with a
toothpick and it would ring till the homeowner managed to escape.

Another prank was performed using homemade devices called tick
tacks—small, rubber-band-powered contrivances that made the windows rattle like the Devil himself was trying to enter. Alternatively, a
bit of string, a pulley, and a rock might be strung together so that
pranksters could tap on a window like a ghost, avoid detection when
the homeowner peered inquisitively outside, then renew tapping
when the homeowner left the window. Horns, pots banged with
spoons, crank rattles, cowbells, and noisemakers of all kinds were
used to ensure that neighborhoods remained awake until the wee
hours. Gates, wooden rain barrels, and outhouse doors were often
stolen to build bonfires. Neighborhoods sometimes competed to construct the largest bonfire possible.

In some areas, the night before Halloween was named Mischief
Night, for the English pre–Guy Fawkes custom of the same name. In
other regions, it was called Cabbage Night, for the custom of throw-

ing cabbages at doors and other targets. Any farmer who had failed to get in his cabbages by Halloween was deemed fair game. Cabbage Night gave pranksters an extra evening of foolery. Adults tolerated the pranks when not joining in the fun.

ROMANTICISM AND HALLOWEEN

At the end of the eighteenth century, Romanticism swept Europe. It glorified the imagination and emotions over intellect and reason. It incorporated reverence for nature, a love of rustic ways, mysticism, the rejection of social mores, the glorification of melancholy, an attraction to the morbid, and a love of the supernatural. The Gothic novel was a product of the Romantic movement. In Europe, Romanticism began to fade in the 1840s, but it arrived later in America and lasted years longer. A good example of an American Romantic work is "The Raven," by Edgar Allan Poe.

The Romantic movement encouraged the upper classes to enjoy Halloween. The holiday's ancient folk customs and the supernatural beings associated with it suited Romantic predilections. Rural customs were revived in urban areas and strengthened in rural areas. Popular magazines and newspapers carried articles detailing old traditions and offering ways to include them in Halloween celebrations. This helped produce a uniformity in celebrations across America—which itself invigorated the holiday.

In America, some Romantic sensibilities carried over into Victorian times. The upper classes indulged themselves in neo-Gothic architecture and enjoyed reading fervid historical novels that glamorized the past. Over these interests, a new restraint emerged. Victorians wanted to enjoy the mysteries and excitement of old customs but didn't want anything too extreme. In relation to Halloween, this meant emphasizing those party entertainments that were mild enough to be acceptable in any company while discouraging the more gruesome associations with demons, monsters, and witchcraft. Reaching out to the dead, the original reason for Halloween, was ameliorated by a growing interest in spiritualism, which made dead spirits seem less horrific.

Another reason that party games were emphasized at Halloween was that they provided opportunities for courting. The old divining rituals of Nutcracker Night and Snap Apple Night, which revealed to young women the identities of their future husbands, were a coy and amusing device for flirting. Halloween costume balls gave an excuse to wear exotic, pretty costumes and masks that could also be turned to demure flirtation. Even party foods gave an excuse to demonstrate domestic talents.

Toward the end of the nineteenth century, theme Halloween parties became popular. Fairy tales, King Arthur's Court, and Mother Goose were typical themes. It was also common for hosts to construct elaborate haunted houses. Sometimes a cellar would be used to simulate a catacomb. Ghostly drapery, mysterious sound effects, gloomy lighting, and costumed figures increased the spookiness of the setting. Outside the ballrooms, children and rural folks continued the rowdier traditional Halloween.

The 1944 film *Meet Me in St. Louis,* which starred Judy Garland, contains a fine depiction of Halloween as celebrated in America in 1903. In it, a timid little girl, anxious to prove she is big enough for Halloween high jinks, sets out to "kill" a noted old grump. She rings the doorbell of the grump and, when he answers the door, she tosses flour into his face, shouting "I hate you" then running away. The little girl is lauded by the other children as the "most horrible" of them all, and she triumphantly joins in the building of an enormous bonfire.

Oddly, trick-or-treating wasn't a significant part of Halloween until the mid–twentieth century. According to folklorist Tad Tuleja, the phrase *trick-or-treating* didn't even appear in the files of dictionary publisher Merriam-Webster until 1941, and a *Life* magazine article about Halloween traditions printed in the same year didn't mention trick-or-treating at all. The old customs of soliciting tributes door to door had faded. In America, the great bulk of the populace resided outside cities in small towns or in rural isolation. Door-to-door begging would require hours of work to make much of a haul. Pranks, on the other hand, were a more immediate source of fun. You could play several on one house and a few more on another and fill your evening. You could even reuse pranks and perfect them. In urban areas, people were often too poor to pass out tributes; those better off didn't want the poor bothering them. Pranking didn't require money. It wasn't until population densities increased in rural areas and pranking began to get out of hand that trick-or-treating became common.

TWENTIETH-CENTURY HALLOWEEN CUSTOMS

As America moved into the first decades of the twentieth century, the courtly Halloween party began to seem old-fashioned. The auto-

Halloween Superstitions and Rites

- Sprinkle salt on your doorsteps to bar evil spirits from your home.

- Hang socks that have a hole worn in them in your windows to prevent evil spirits from flying in.

- Go to a cabbage patch, put on a blindfold, and grab a random cabbage. If the cabbage is fresh and clean, your coming year will be fortunate. If the cabbage is spoiled or dirty, your coming year will be similarly blighted.

- Drop two needles in a basin of water. If they come together at the bottom, you and the person you love will come together in the future.

- Take an oaken torch and visit a spring. When you gaze into the water, you will see your future wife or husband. This can also be done by taking a lit candle and a mirror into a dark cellar. The future spouse will appear in the mirror.

- Sprinkle a patch of cornmeal by your bed. In the morning, you will see that ghosts—more likely mice or bugs—have drawn your future in it.

- As a party treat and game, bake a cake with a coin, a thimble, a ring, and a china doll in it. When the cake is served, whoever finds the coin will have wealth in the future. Whoever finds the thimble will never marry. (Single women once supported themselves sewing or spinning—hence the term *spinster*.) Whoever finds the ring will marry in the coming year. Whoever finds the doll will have many children—hopefully after finding the ring on an earlier occasion.

mobile, phonograph, radio, movies, and other innovations changed the way couples got together. Manners changed. The flapper of the Roaring Twenties didn't need dainty evasions to modestly pursue a fellow. Halloween became more of a children's holiday. The party games that adults had enjoyed were passed on to children, partly as a substitute for mischievous pranking.

Small-town Halloween pranks were limited in damage because it wasn't easy for a prankster to avoid responsibility when his neighbors knew him and his parents. Prank playing in larger towns and cities was more anonymous. Windows by the hundreds would be shattered, false fire alarms would be turned in, tires would be slashed, and more serious vandalism would be done by rowdier and rowdier bands of children. The cost of damages rose. Law enforcement was strained. By the 1930s, with the social unrest of the Depression, civic leaders grew fearful of pranks getting out of hand. They set out to tame Halloween.

Organized holiday activities, parties, carnivals, games, and contests were offered as alternatives to Halloween hooliganism. Business leaders, religious authorities, and youth organizations such as the Boy Scouts helped popularize these activities. The custom of businesses staging store-window-decorating contests, for example, arose at this time under the theory that children would be less likely to break windows that bore their artwork. Trick-or-treating was promoted as part of the effort to moderate Halloween excesses.

The promotion of trick-or-treating spread across the country through newspaper accounts, journals dedicated to youth improvement, women's magazines, and word of mouth. Ironically, church leaders whose predecessors had condemned Halloween and burned witches now promoted Halloween trick-or-treating as a healthy, wholesome activity. Adults, presented with dozens of children demanding treats, felt compelled to buy candy. Once having invested in the holiday, they sought their fair, reciprocal share of the bounty by allowing their own children to trick-or-treat. Conformity and the desire to keep up with the Joneses persuaded even childless adults to pass out treats. The excitement and good feeling produced ensured that most of the community would join in the fun. It was a pleasant activity for both children and adults.

To get bountiful portions of candy, some children, in a tradition that has disappeared, would execute little bits of show biz. A child might do a jig, sing a song, tell a joke or riddle, or recite a short poem.

During the 1940s, while World War II raged, civic order was seen as important to the war effort. Halloween pranks were wasteful. Destroying property was even labeled sabotage. Despite this, many civic leaders insisted that, while large public celebrations such as parades should be suspended, celebrating the holiday in the home, in the neighborhood, and in schools was good for public morale. Sugar rationing meant fewer sweet treats, but there were other goodies available. Gathering treats was encouraged over pranking. When the war ended, Halloween was celebrated with new vigor. Sweets were again plentiful, and there was an urge to make up for past sacrifices.

During the 1950s, the rowdiness of Halloween joined juvenile delinquency, horror comics, excessive realism in movies, rock and roll, drug abuse, and premarital sex as an issue of parental concern. Parents sought to further de-emphasize tricks and promote treats as the heart of Halloween. Candy companies and costume manufacturers were happy to encourage this. Their advertising helped spread trick-or-treating.

Postwar parents had had to endure childhood during the Depression and young adulthood during the war years; now, they wanted a happy, middle-class family life for themselves and their children, the great demographic lump called the Baby Boom generation. This required participating in all the activities of the community, which, for Halloween, meant costuming your children for trick-or-treating and passing out candy to your neighbors' children. The popular media, films and television, reinforced the custom and made it seem as if all American children went trick-or-treating. By the 1960s, most of them did. This decade was the Golden Age of child-centered Halloween in America. Great masses of children enjoyed trick-or-treating in safe neighborhoods.

Trick-or-Treat for UNICEF

In 1950, members of a Philadelphia-area Sunday school class chose to collect money trick-or-treating instead of candy. The seventeen dollars they collected in decorated milk cartons was sent to the United Nations International Children's Emergency Fund (UNICEF), which had been created in 1946 to supply child refugees of World War II with food, blankets, and clothing. The donation inspired other children to do the same. Today two million children participate in UNICEF's Halloween program, and over more than a hundred million dollars has been collected since the kids from Philly turned down candy in favor of philanthropy.

Halloween as Retail Money Machine

According to the American Express Retail Index, the average American consumer spends about a hundred dollars for Halloween-associated items each year. Eight dollars of this goes for Halloween home entertainment. Eleven dollars is spent on parties. Another eleven dollars is spent on decorations. Jack-o'-lanterns take sixteen dollars; costumes, twenty-two. The remaining thirty dollars, the largest portion, goes for Halloween candy.

The National Retail Federation estimates that Americans currently spend $2.5 billion on decorations, pumpkins, and greeting cards. Another $1.5 billion is spent on costumes, and $1.8 billion on candy. These numbers are expected to grow.

"You know, I expected more than just big *feet*."

3

DEATH HOLIDAYS
AROUND THE WORLD

MEXICO'S DAY OF THE DEAD

It is common in Catholic countries for All Saints' Day and All Souls' Day to be celebrated with solemn visits to cemeteries, graveside prayers, and grave decoration. The parish priest will often lead his flock in procession to the cemetery. There, the congregation prays while the priest urges its members to reflect upon death and blesses the graves. In Mexico, Catholics celebrate with similar activities but have also incorporated Native American beliefs to create a more elaborate holiday called Dia de Muertos, the Day of the Dead, celebrated on November 2.

Mexicans, particularly southern, rural Mexicans, believe that the dead return to visit the living on the Day of the Dead. They take elaborate measures to guide the dead home and to welcome them. The holiday is strongly influenced by Native American traditions, particularly those of the Zapotec Indians of southern Mexico. The Zapotec have an accepting attitude toward death and, during the Day of the Dead, joke about it with folk art that satirizes the living by placing skeletons in scenes of everyday life. A skeleton might be getting a shave from a skeleton barber. A skeleton guitarist may serenade a skeleton señorita. A skeleton policeman chases a skeleton speeder. There are even toy coffins that, when opened, pop out a skeleton jack-in-the-box. These kinds of decorations are found everywhere during the Day of the Dead.

In Mexican homes and workplaces, altars to welcome and commemorate the dead are constructed with flowers, fruit, tinsel, elabo-

rately cut tissue paper, religious icons, candles, and incense. Photographs of dead relatives are placed upon the altars, and their
favorite foods, liquors, and objects are set by their images. The smell
of the food and incense and the light of the candles is meant to help
guide the dead home for their visit. The doors of homes are left open
to encourage visitors, both living and dead, who are served delicacies.
Visiting children receive candy and toys.

   In cemeteries, graves are tidied up and decorated with dozens of
candles and floral arches composed of orchids, cockscomb, lavender,
chrysanthemums, and *flor de muerto,* the bright orange "flower of
death." Baskets of food are set by the graves as offerings to the dead.
On the first of November, women and children stand vigil inside the
cemetery while men and older boys gather outside the cemetery to sip
pulque, a strong liquor, and sing. The mood is reflective but not mournful because the living tend to believe that the dead have gone on to a
better world. At dawn, the food baskets are offered again to the dead,
then shared out among the living as a sort of picnic breakfast.

   The food offerings are often the favorite meals of the departed.
They usually include candy skulls called *calavera* made from sugar,
chocolate, and amaranth seeds. The skulls have colored icing hair

and tinfoil eyes. Another traditional food is *pan de muerto,* "bread of the dead," small loaves formed into the shape of skulls or bodies and dusted with colored sugar. The loaves often bear bits of dough formed into crossed bones.

The traditions of the Chamul Indians of the village of Romerillo in southeast Mexico are typical of Day of the Dead celebrations. As the first fingers of light brighten dawn on November 1, the Indians, who support themselves by growing corn, gather at the cemetery. The women wear blue blouses and shawls. Tall crosses wound in pine branches, a symbol of life, are carried by the celebrants. Musicians wearing conical hats strum guitars, while hundreds of black candles set upon the graves flicker. *Cana,* a home-brewed sugarcane liquor, is shared with both the living and the dead, being sprinkled upon graves as a companionable offering. Corn tamales and peeled oranges are set out for the dead.

In Mixquic, twenty-two miles southeast of Mexico City, on the afternoon of the first, a coffin containing a cardboard skeleton is carried through the streets. As it passes, bystanders display the respect they would give a real funeral procession. The entourage stops at the doors of homes celebrating the holiday and asks to enter. Once inside, the coffin is set down and everyone kneels around it to pray. After the prayers, the homeowner gives out candy and bread. After many stops, the entourage arrives at the cemetery, where a mock funeral is held.

———————————— ✦ ————————————

How to Make Pan de Muerto

Preheat your oven to 350 degrees. In a warm saucepan, combine $2/3$ cup water, $2/3$ cup milk, and $2/3$ cup butter. In a large bowl, mix 2 cups flour, $2/3$ cup sugar, 2 packages dry yeast, 1 tablespoon anise seeds, and $1 1/3$ teaspoons salt. Add the warm contents of the saucepan to the mix and beat. Slowly mix in $4 1/2$ cups flour. Place the dough on a flour-sprinkled surface and knead for 10 minutes. Put the dough in a greased bowl then place the bowl in a warm place to rise until it doubles in size. This can take 1 to 2 hours.

After it has risen, remove the dough from the bowl and form it into 8-inch people shapes. With two small pieces of dough, make a cross upon each figure's chest. Alternatively, you can shape the dough into skulls. Form 4-inch balls. Flatten them to form a dome shape. With a small chunk of dough, form a jaw. With your thumb, poke eyes and a nose in the skull. Make vertical lines in the jaw for teeth.

Bake the figures for 40 minutes.

While baking, make a glaze by boiling ½ cup sugar, ⅓ cup strained orange juice, and 2 tablespoons grated orange peel for 2 minutes. Brush the glaze onto the figures while they are still warm from the oven. You can sprinkle the figures with colored cake-decorating sugar or put a few drops of food coloring in the glaze. White icing can be used on the skull figures.

In other urban areas, the Day of the Dead is a three-day celebration. October 31 is dedicated to the *angelitos,* or "little angels"—children who died before they could be baptized. These children are thought to go straight to Heaven because they had no time to sin. In memory of the little angels, adults give begging children candy. November 1 is All Soul's Day. Roman Catholics attend masses honoring saints, then begin an all-night, candlelit vigil at the graves of their dead relatives. At midnight, church bells are rung to guide the dead back to the physical world. Prayers are recited for the sake of their eternal comfort. Families stage reunions with picnics and music. November 2 is dedicated to the adult dead. Fireworks signal the beginning of a special holiday mass.

The American Halloween is threatening to overwhelm Mexico's Day of the Dead, especially in areas near the United States. The traditional association of October 31 with dead children has encouraged this. Halloween decorations are more and more popular, and children go trick-or-treating in such numbers that some households greet a hundred children when answering a single doorbell ring. To some Mexicans, Halloween is a sinister conspiracy to destroy their culture. They claim it is drenched in commercialism instead of the spirituality of the Day of the Dead, ignoring the commercialism associated with the Mexican holiday (at many cemeteries, tourists outnumber celebrants, and peddlers have always sold holiday food by the cartload) and dismissing Halloween's spiritual roots, which are similar to

those of the Day of the Dead. These Halloween haters turn away trick-or-treaters, placing signs upon their doors declaring that they don't celebrate foreign holidays.

Curiously, the Day of the Dead has received a better welcome in the United States. Beginning in the 1980s, Mexican-American communities have staged Day of the Dead celebrations to keep old traditions alive in a new setting.

OTHER DEATH CEREMONIES IN VARIOUS CULTURES

Reverence for the dead is present in every culture. Customs associated with the dead include:

- The Tuaregs, a nomadic, Islamic people living in the Sahara, visit the graves of their dead on the first day of Islam's month of Ramadan.

- Jews visit the graves of their dead in the month of Tishri.

- In France, on October 31, children beg for flowers or money to buy flowers to decorate tombstones.

- In the fourteenth century, in the city of Salerno, Italy, families would prepare elaborate feasts for the souls of the dead. They would lay out the meal on their dining table, then leave home for the day without locking their doors. The spirits were supposed to enter and eat the feast. If the meal went uneaten, it meant that the spirits were angry with the household members and would punish them during the coming year. Few feasts went uneaten, however, because the city's poor could be counted upon to sneak inside and dine.

- In the middle of summer, Japanese celebrate the three-day Bon festival, dedicated to the spirits of their ancestors. Families gather for the celebration much as Americans gather for Thanksgiving.

- In Hong Kong, during the seventh lunar month of each year, which falls in late summer, traditional Chinese celebrate the Hungry Ghost Festival. Food is offered up to the spirits of the hungry dead through charitable donations of food, especially rice and bread, to the poor.

- On the island of Madagascar, the Malagasy people believe that the dead become nearly godlike and have the power to bless or curse the living. Consequently, the dead receive special treatment. They are customarily buried in family tombs the size of small houses that are often more ornate than the homes of their living relatives. Once every few years, the bones are ceremonially exhumed. The remains are rewrapped in fresh shrouds, then paraded upon the shoulders of their families before being re-entombed. In recent years, the Malagasy have been scandalized to discover that grave robbers have been looting tombs of their bones. Some claim the bones are sold to foreigners for medical purposes, though the bones, ridden with disease and germs, have no medical use. Some claim the bones are used in magic. This seems likely given the power the dead are thought to possess.

  A third theory suggests that the bones may be looted in order to do injury to the family of the deceased by destroying their link to the power the dead possess. This, too, seems plausible.

- In rural Brittany, All Saints' Day and All Souls' Day are called Jour des Morts, the Day of the Dead. It is marked with church bell ringing. Eight men are selected from the parish. Four take turns tolling the church bell for an hour after sunset. The other four spend the night walking the local roadways, ringing hand bells and calling upon the houses they pass to pray for the souls of the dead. The people inside awaken, answer "Amen," then pray.

  Visits are made to the graves of relatives. Prayers are said and holy water sprinkled. At the dinner table, an extra seat is set. The food that would be served to that seat is given to the poor.

- In Hungary, before the Communist occupation, All Saints' Day and All Souls' Day were marked with Halottak Napja, the Day of the Dead. In addition to praying for the dead, Hungarians invited orphan children to dine with them, giving them toys and clothing. They also took care to tend and decorate the graves of those who had no relatives to mind them.

HALLOWEEN ABROAD

From its earliest days, America and American ways have been interesting to the rest of the world. Our republic inspired others to revolution. Our industries have been imitated. Our music, films, and television programs have entertained billions. During the World Wars and the Cold War, our armies carried notions of equality and freedom wherever they ventured. Not all nations like Americanization, but it has become so powerful a cultural force that even nations other than America are exporting it through their own American-style movies, foods, clothing, and so forth. The custom of Halloween is no exception to the Americanization process.

As mentioned above, Halloween is making inroads in Mexico. It is also celebrated in Japan and extending a few skeletal fingers into China. In Britain, it is apt to become a rival to Guy Fawkes Day. In Ireland, where it faded, it is being reinvigorated by Irish who have returned from America.

Halloween has even established itself in France. In towns and villages across the country, you can see costumed children trick-or-treating, along with jack-o'-lanterns, witches, ghosts, and monsters decorating more and more homes. Defenders of France are appalled at what one newspaper called "The Great Yankee Invasion," decrying it as part of an American commercial conspiracy that includes fast food, movies and television.

The Catholic Church in France has campaigned against Halloween. "We should have something else to offer children besides a macabre festival," Father Louis-Marie, a priest leading the protest, pronounced in October 2000. "Imposing on them only that which is cold, dark, and morbid is not good." One Protestant group joined the Catholic protest, declaring "Our lay society . . . must not focus its attention on the death cult that surrounds Halloween." They also claimed that Halloween was "not harmless for the psyche of children and fragile people." Many French people are concerned that Halloween will gradually take the place of All Saints' Day, a day the French traditionally devote to remembering the dead by visiting the graves of loved ones.

But Halloween has triumphed, nonetheless. In part, this was because

French companies joined in on the "commercial conspiracy." Costume and candy makers delight in heavy sales. Halloween-themed marketing promotes services. Bakeries offer up Halloween goodies. Bars serve Halloween cocktails made with blood oranges. Even those bastions of French culture, French restaurants, serve elaborate dishes based upon the humble pumpkin. One French restaurant chain, the Chez Clément, even claims that "Halloween is a festival of Gallic origins that the Americans borrowed from us." They argue that Halloween is a Celtic holiday and that the French are a Celtic people. Unfortunately for this soothing argument, nearly all Celtic traditions died out in France, with the exception of Brittany, centuries ago.

If the French find Halloween irresistible, we can confidently believe that Halloween, itself a composite of many nations' customs, will find celebrants in other cultures all around the world.

4

THE JACK-O'-LANTERN

With its fiery, leering grin, no object is more closely identified with Halloween than the jack-o'-lantern. It originated in ancient Celtic superstition. Rural people, whose nights were undiminished by artificial luminance, commonly saw mysterious, dim nocturnal lights. They were most often reported darting around near swamps and graveyards. Today these might be identified as UFOs. Most scientists prefer to believe that such lights are produced by marsh gas—methane gas naturally generated by vegetable and animal decomposition. They call such light *ignis fatuus*, Latin for "foolish fire." Some scientists believe that the lights are an as-yet-unidentified electrical phenomenon created by seismic activity. They note that seismically active areas are often "haunted" by unexplained lights. In the past, country folks had more magical explanations. They believed the lights were Fairies or evil spirits who were trying to lead night travelers dangerously astray.

The malevolent lights were given many names: will-o'-the-wisp, corpse candles (when appearing in a cemetery), lantern men, hob-o'-lantern, and jack-o'-lantern. A wanderer might see a light, think it to be coming from a country home's window, and walk toward it, only to find the light moving away or off in another direction. He might find himself mired in a swamp or tumbling down a hill. To wander aimlessly after one of these lights was to be led *willy-nilly*, a term that survives in modern speech.

When confronted by a jack-o'-lantern, superstition decreed that you must put out any lantern you were carrying and toss it aside, or the jack-o'-lantern might come swooping in to destroy it. If it got close, you must throw yourself to the ground and crawl away while holding your breath. This bit of folklore might actually be good advice. If the jack-o'-lantern is being produced by a form of ball light-

ning, then discarding a metal lantern—which might attract the electrical phenomenon—and lying flat lessen the danger of it hitting you.
And if the jack-o'-lantern is produced by marsh gas, it is a good idea
to hold your breath until you can crawl away from it. The gas might
otherwise stifle you. Also, since methane gas is explosive, it might
detonate if you leave your lantern lit.

As with many holiday customs, there is a legend associated with
the jack-o'-lantern.

THE LEGEND OF THE JACK-O'-LANTERN

It seems that in days long gone by, there was a gentleman in Ireland
named Jack, who had a great fondness for whiskey. He spent every
coin he could scratch up or steal upon his vice. One day, he was stum-
bling home from his favored tavern—always the closest one—when
the Devil appeared before him in a great flash of sulfurous smoke.

"I have come to take you to Hell, Jack. All your old drinking bud-
dies are waiting there for you."

The appearance of the Devil had a miraculous effect upon Jack.
While just a moment earlier he had been barely able to sing off key
and had just managed to walk a crooked line, fear now cleared his
mind to crystal. His thoughts raced like fire through dry leaves.

"Mr. Devil, I've heard condemned men are given one last boon."

"That is so."

"I find myself thirsty and would like to have a wee nip before I go.
Could I have one last drink at the tavern?"

"Feel free to satisfy your thirst, Jack."

"I'm afraid I'm a bit short of funds. Could you lend me a sixpence?"

"I don't carry money. I board all the tax collectors down below,
and it's not safe to have a coin in your pocket."

"I've heard the Devil can change himself into anything."

"That is true."

"Then change yourself into a sixpence. I'll buy a drink and you
can change back after."

This appealed to the Devil, who enjoyed the idea of cheating the
tavern keeper.

"Very well," said the Devil. He disappeared with a puff that ended
with the tinkle of a coin falling to the stones of the roadway. Quick
as he could, Jack scooped up the coin and put it in his coin purse,

which he closed with a snap of its iron clasp. He pocketed the purse and resumed his way homeward.

"What's this?' demanded the Devil in a tiny voice muffled by the purse and pocket.

"I've decided I'm not so thirsty. I think I'll save you for later."

"Let me out!"

"Is that bit of iron bothering Your Infernalness?"

"You knew I can't undo an iron clasp!"

"I suppose I might have."

Jack and the Devil argued for hours. Finally, the Devil agreed to let Jack live another year, if he would let the Devil go. Jack did so and the Devil, with a fiery glare, turned to smoke and disappeared into the earth.

Jack spent the next year at his usual pursuits, drinking, carousing, and sleeping off the resulting hangovers. One year to the minute, the Devil reappeared in front of Jack, who was once again staggering home.

"Oh, 'tis yourself."

"I've come to fetch you. And I won't be turning into anything you can pocket."

"Of course not. I wouldn't think to ask. But I do find myself hungry and would like to have a bite before I go. Could I have one of those apples hanging from that tree over there?"

"Feel free to satisfy your hunger, Jack."

Jack made his way to the tree, weaving and staggering precariously as he did so. Indeed, someone familiar with his after-drinking perambulations would have remarked that he seemed to be far clumsier than he had ever been seen before.

"Are you sure you can find the tree?" the Devil sneered.

"Of course, Your Lordship. It's right over there," Jack said, pointing eastward. He took one step south then two north. The tree was to the west.

"Stand aside, you worthless sop. I'll get your apple for you."

With a clip and clatter of his cloven hooves, the Devil strode to the tree. With a burst of sparks, he transformed himself into a serpent and, just as in the Garden of Eden, swiftly twined his way up to a nice, plump red apple, which he delicately plucked. Unlike Eve, however, when the serpent extended the apple, Jack ignored it and dashed to the base of the tree. He whipped out a pocket-knife and slashed a cross in its bark.

"There, now, Mr. Devil, you can eat that apple yourself. That cross will keep you in that tree till the tree tumbles over in a hundred years or so!"

The Devil sputtered and struggled, but he couldn't leave the tree. The mark of the cross kept him prisoner.

"You've tricked me, Jack, I'll admit it. What will you have to let me go?"

"I'll take your promise to never take my soul."

"Very well. You have my word."

Jack sliced the cross from the apple tree, and the Devil, with another burst of sparks, resumed his demonic form and jumped down. He growled, searching in vain for an oath that didn't involve himself or his home, then, failing, disappeared in less than a blink.

"There!" Jack declared and went back to the pub for another drink.

Jack spent many years drinking and telling the tale of how he had beaten the Devil until he grew so old and gray that he seemed just a wispish shadow of a drunken man. Finally, at the age of 101, after celebrating a merry Halloween with as much whiskey as three other men could stomach, he died. He shortly found himself at the gates to Heaven, where St. Peter reviewed his life and told him, "There's no room in here for the likes of you."

Jack glumly turned away and found himself at the gates to Hell.

"Hello, Your Lordship. Do you remember me?"

"Yes, I do, and I remember my promise, too. I won't take your soul."

"But where will I go?"

"That's your lookout!"

Jack turned away again but there was nowhere to go except the dark night world where lost spirits wandered.

"Go on!" the Devil bellowed.

"But it's dark out there."

The Devil reached into Hell, plucked up one of Hell's orange-hot, forever-glowing coals, and tossed it to Jack.

"Light your path with that!"

With bowed head, Jack took a half-eaten turnip from his pocket and placed the coal in it to form a lantern. To this day, in the dark of night, whenever and wherever the spirits aimlessly prowl, the fiery gleam of the Hell coal in Jack O'Lantern's turnip can be spotted, wandering this way and that with no place to go.

More mundanely, the jack-o'-lantern is a descendant of the turnip "punky" of Ireland that was carried by revelers. The lighted face was a neat bit of country trickery meant to frighten with its demonic appearance. In Scotland, the lighted turnips were called bogies. In England, beets were used, and the lighted beets were called mangel-wurzels. In America, pumpkins, which make much better lanterns, were especially plentiful at harvesttime and replaced turnips.

THE PUMPKIN

Pumpkins are members of the gourd family, which also includes muskmelon, watermelon, and squash. More specifically, pumpkins belong to the family Cucurbitaceae. There are a number of varieties, all of which are long-season, long-trailing varieties of *Cucurbita pepo*. Squash is closely related. The fruit of the pumpkin vine commonly weighs as much as eighteen pounds. In 1999, a pumpkin nicknamed Moonie, of the "Atlantic Giant" variety, set a world record, weighing in at 1,131 pounds.

Pumpkins range from pale yellow to rich orange. The skin of the pumpkin is lightly furrowed. Pumpkins are planted upon small hills about ten feet apart. Each hill hosts one to three pumpkin plants, which mature early in the fall. Originating in North America, pumpkins are now a popular crop around the world.

Pumpkins were cultivated by Native Americans long before the arrival of the Pilgrims. The Indians ate the flesh of the pumpkin roasted, boiled, or dried. The seeds were eaten roasted or boiled. Native Americans used pumpkins to prepare medicines, too; they also cut strips of pumpkin, pounded them flat, dried them, and used them

to weave mats. When English explorers arrived in America, they were much impressed with the usefulness of the pumpkin.

The word *pumpkin* is derived from the Greek *pepōn,* meaning "large melon." The English modified this into *pumpion* or *pompion.* When the Pilgrims settled New England, they adopted the pumpkin as a crop, eating it themselves and feeding it to their livestock. They copied the way the Native Americans prepared pumpkins, adding European touches. They ate it as a side dish, mixed with other vegetables, and in soups. One recipe called for opening the pumpkin, cleaning it out, filling it with a mixture of milk, spices, and honey or maple syrup, then baking it in hot ashes for six to seven hours. The result was a crude form of pumpkin custard pie. Even a kind of beer could be made from pumpkins. The Pilgrims so loved pumpkins that they wrote poetry about them:

> *For pottage and puddings, and custards and pies,*
> *Our pumpkins and parsnips are common supplies.*
> *We have pumpkins at morning and pumpkins at noon.*
> *If it were not for pumpkins we should be undone.*
>
> Pilgrim poem, circa 1630
> *The New Pumpkin Book*, 1981,
> The Half Moon Bay Art and Pumpkin Festival,
> California (as quoted on the eHow Web page)

The pumpkin remains a New England favorite. As the New England poet John Greenleaf Whittier (1807–1892) wrote:

> *What moistens the lip and what brightens the eye?*
> *What calls back the past, like the rich Pumpkin pie?*

Pumpkins are a good source of vitamin C, beta-carotene, and potassium. They are said to discourage arteriosclerosis, which can produce strokes or heart attacks. Pumpkin seeds and their oil are rich in zinc and unsaturated fatty acids. They are said to hinder prostate disease. Pumpkin is a good source of fiber. A USDA study of subjects given a diet including significant amounts of pumpkin suggests that pumpkin fiber reduces appetite. It provides low-calorie bulk—a half cup of cooked fresh pumpkin contains only twenty-four calories and 0.09 gram of fat. Subjects of the study also absorbed fewer calories and fats from the foods they ate with the pumpkin.

Cooking fresh pumpkin is a little tricky. Select a "pie pumpkin" or a "sweet pumpkin." These are smaller than pumpkins used for jack-o'-lanterns, and their flesh is sweeter and not as fibrous or watery. A pumpkin that has a soft spot, extensive blemishes, or mold is spoiled. Remove the stem and guts. Rinse in cold water. Cut it into chunks and either steam for ten to twelve minutes or boil for twenty minutes. A pumpkin can be roasted in the oven by slicing it in two and placing the two "bowls" round-side up on a baking sheet. Bake at 350 degrees for an hour or until tender. Cool the cooked pumpkin, then peel it. Puree the cooked flesh in a food processor (a potato masher can substitute).

Once cooked and pureed, the pumpkin can be used in a pie or other baked items.

Pumpkin Pie

Pumpkin pies can be made using many recipes; this one comes from the Vermont Department of Agriculture.

⅔ cup honey
½ teaspoon salt
1½ teaspoons cinnamon
½ teaspoon ground ginger
½ teaspoon nutmeg
½ teaspoon allspice
½ teaspoon ground cloves
1½ cups cooked pumpkin
1⅔ cups evaporated milk
2 eggs

Refrigerate a 9-inch pie shell for several hours. Preheat your oven to 425 degrees. Combine all ingredients. Beat until smooth, then pour into the shell. Bake for 15 minutes, then lower the heat to 350 degrees and bake for another 35 minutes or until the filling has set. Take care, because it is easy to undercook or overcook the pie. Let the pie cool before serving it.

Pumpkin Muffins

A batch of 16 pumpkin muffins can be made using the following recipe.

¼ cup molasses
½ cup softened butter
¾ cup brown sugar

1 beaten egg
1 cup pureed pumpkin
1¾ cups flour
¼ teaspoon salt
1 teaspoon baking soda
¼ cup chopped pecans

Preheat your oven to 375 degrees. Cream the molasses, butter, and sugar. Add the egg and pumpkin. Blend. Mix the flour, salt, and baking soda. Beat this into the pumpkin mix. Fold in the chopped pecans. Fill the cups of a greased muffin pan half full with the mix. Bake for 20 minutes.

For variety, small quantities of raisins, whole cranberries, or orange zest can be added.

CARVING A JACK-O'-LANTERN

Jack-o'-lantern carving has become a minor seasonal art form. While children find great range for self-expression in cutting out jagged-toothed faces, no less a home decor expert than Martha Stewart has lent her talents to designing elaborate, stylish jacks. Science has even joined art, with elaborate designs being carved by artistically wielded laser beams. Some carving tips include:

- Select a large, firm, unbruised pumpkin. Pumpkins ripen in the field on the vine. They grow harder as they ripen. A healthy, ripe pumpkin is very hard and should sound hollow when rapped with the knuckles. The stem of the pumpkin should be intact, firm, and dry. Reject soft or blemished pumpkins. They have begun to spoil.

- If the pumpkin is to be stored before usage, it should be washed with a solution of one teaspoon chlorine bleach to a gallon of water to disinfect the skin and inhibit mold or rot. Pumpkins are best stored in cool, airy places where the temperature doesn't fall below freezing (the best range is forty-five to sixty degrees). A porch or a dry, unheated cellar is a good storage spot. If a pumpkin must be stored in an apartment, choose a cool closet or

Two Dozen Jack-o'-lantern Faces to Consider

corner. Keep the pumpkin away from radiators or any other heat source. Don't stack pumpkins; it can cause bruising, and it limits the amount of air that can reach them. An uncut pumpkin can last for a month. If stored in a refrigerator (and kept dry), it can last for three months.

- Some pumpkins are larger on one side than the other. Use the larger side for the jack-o'-lantern's face. Round pumpkins are good for happy faces and tall, thin ones are good for sad or

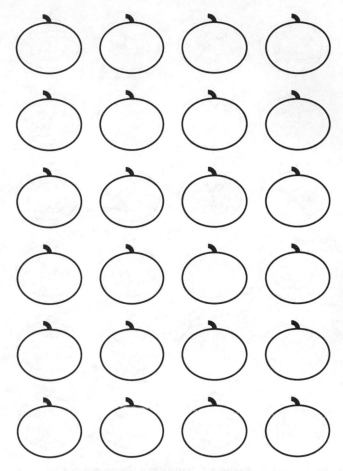

**Blank Jack-o'-lanterns
to draw your own designs upon**

scary faces. The latter have more room for downturned frowns and howling mouths.

- Spread newspapers where you will be working to catch any stray mess.

- Select a very sharp knife. It will cut more easily and require less force. Gentler cutting is less likely to be dangerous. Always cut with the blade pointing away from you. Children should be carefully supervised. Young children can participate by drawing a face, which an adult can then cut out.

- Cut a polygon- or star-shaped opening in the top of the pumpkin. These shapes are less likely than a circular shape to fall into the jack-o'-lantern. When you cut, cut at an angle, so that the top of the opening is wider than the bottom. The jack-o'-lantern's lid will shrink, and having the opening taper into a smaller opening will help prevent the lid from falling inside. Make a thumb-sized notch in the back edge of the lid so the candle you put in later will have a good supply of oxygen.

- Scoop out the contents of the pumpkin. A melon baller or an ice cream scoop makes a good tool for this. Scrape until you reach the firm shell of the pumpkin. Discard the gooey, stringy stuff, but keep the seeds to roast later.

- Dig a small hole in the bottom of the jack-o'-lantern to hold a candle cup.

- Draw a face upon the jack-o'-lantern with chalk. This will serve as a guide.

- Put the mouth above the spot where the pumpkin curves into its bottom. This will help prevent the face from falling in. Avoid locating the eyes, nose, and mouth too close together, which would weaken the face.

- You can also draw a pattern for your jack-o'-lantern on a piece of paper. Use masking tape to attach it to the pumpkin. With a toothpick or other sharp skewer, poke holes through the pattern to transfer the design to the pumpkin. Poke enough holes so that you can follow the design. Remove the paper and cut along the dotted lines.

- After you have the design laid out, begin cutting with a thin paring knife or other slim blade. A serrated knife will cut better than a plain blade. A back-and-forth, slicing motion cuts best. Don't bend the knife in the flesh to make sharp curves. Remove the blade and reinsert it. You can smooth the curve after rough-cutting it with straighter cuts. To make sharp corners, such as those needed to make teeth, remove the knife and reinsert it to form the angle. Work slowly to avoid making errors. Take care not to place your hand where you may cut it with the knife. When possible, work from the center of the face outward to avoid putting too much pressure on the carved face, which might break.

- White teeth or other white details such as eyebrows can be created by cutting halfway through the pumpkin from the outside. This technique, sometimes called scrape carving, can be done by using a knife to cut crisscross lines in the area to be scraped then using a spoon to scrape out the pieces cut.

- You can add ears to a jack-o'-lantern by cutting up some of the pieces removed and attaching them to the sides of the jack-o'-lantern with toothpicks.

- A carrot can be used to make a nose. Place the thick end of the carrot against the face of the jack-o'-lantern. Trace around it with chalk. Cut out the circle made by the chalk, cutting the hole a bit smaller than the chalk circle so that the carrot will fit tightly. Use a twisted, unpeeled carrot to get a more witchy effect.

- The jack-o'-lantern will immediately begin to dry out. This can be slowed by rubbing petroleum jelly along its cut edges. A jack-o'-lantern can be preserved by wrapping it in plastic wrap and storing it in a refrigerator.

- Place a short, thick candle in a candle cup, and place it inside the pumpkin. A votive candle is ideal. Be sure its flame won't scorch the lid. To help prevent the lid from burning, staple a circle of aluminum foil to the lid's underside. Light the candle with a long fireplace match or long-necked lighter, then replace the lid. Sometimes it may be necessary to cut extra thumb-sized notches in the lid or to leave the lid off entirely so that the candle will burn well.

- Always take care where you place your lit jack-o'-lantern. Don't place it near anything that may catch fire. This includes curtains, straw, and paper. Never leave a jack-o'-lantern unattended.

- Cut grooves in the underside of the lid, and place sticks of cinnamon in them. Cloves can be stuck into the lid, as well. This will cause an indoor jack-o'-lantern to produce a pleasant aroma. Alternatively, a scented candle can also produce a nice fragrance.

- A string of outdoor Christmas lights can be used to light your jack-o'-lantern. Follow the directions packaged with the lights to avoid shock hazard. If properly used, electric lights can be safer than candles. A battery-powered light is the safest way to light a jack.

- Adults should supervise children lighting jack-o'-lanterns.

- A jack-o'-lantern can be effectively displayed outdoors using a pole with a circle of wood nailed atop it as a platform. Drill a couple of holes in the platform so that wire can be threaded through it and into the jack-o'-lantern to firmly secure it. Sharpen the other end of the pole. The pole can be elaborately painted or a rough tree branch. Make several poles of different lengths and group them to display an assemblage of jack-o'-lanterns. Be sure to drive the poles deep into the ground so that they won't topple.

- Don't eat your jack-o'-lantern. Once cut and displayed, it can easily become contaminated.

A face is not the only thing that can be carved in a pumpkin. You might also try a silhouette of a Halloween icon, such as a witch or a crescent moon. Simple round holes made with a power drill can make an interesting design. A Halloween cookie cutter can also be used to make designs on a pumpkin.

Roasted Pumpkin Seeds

The seeds of the pumpkin are called pepitas. They can be eaten after roasting. To prepare them:

- Separate the pumpkin seeds from the stringy pumpkin goo. Wash the seeds to remove all traces of the goo. Blot the seeds with paper towels, and let them dry for 3 hours.

- Preheat your oven to 350 degrees (some prefer to roast the seeds at a lower temperature—250 degrees—for about 1 hour).

- Spray a baking sheet with butter-flavored cooking spray, or lightly coat the sheet with vegetable oil.

- If not using cooking spray, toss the seeds in a plastic bag with 1 tablespoon vegetable oil (olive oil is best).

- Place the seeds on the baking sheet in a single layer. If using cooking spray, give the seeds a very light spray. If using vegetable oil, turn the seeds on the sheet so that both sides have some oil on them.

- Sprinkle coarse salt over the seeds. If you prefer a spicy taste, sprinkle taco seasoning or curry powder on the seeds (be careful; a little goes a long way).

- Place the baking sheet in the oven and bake for 10 to 20 minutes, turning once. Keep an eye on the seeds to see that they don't scorch or burn. When golden brown, the seeds are done. Remove and let cool; store the roasted pumpkin seeds in an airtight container.

- Pumpkin seeds can also be roasted in a microwave. Follow the above preparations, using a microwave-safe plate instead of a baking sheet. Cook on high for about 7 minutes, turning every 2 minutes. Microwaves vary a great deal in power, and some experimentation may be necessary to find the best time and power settings. Again, be careful not to scorch or overcook the seeds.

Eek!

Apocolocynposis is the fear of being transformed into a pumpkin.

5

WITCHES
AND WITCHCRAFT

With my own eyes I saw Canidia, black-cloaked, barefoot,
wild-haired, go howling with the older Sagana.

Horace (65 B.C.–8 B.C.), Roman lyric poet, describing
witches in a cemetery preparing for a necromantic
ritual, *Satira*, Lib. I, VIII, V, 23

A conical hat, black rags, scraggly hair, a big nose well speckled with
warts, and a nasty cackling laugh are all hallmarks of the Halloween
witch. After jack-o'-lanterns, they are the most powerful of Halloween
icons. Any examination of Halloween must include a look at witches
and witchcraft. The subject is not an easy one to explore. There are
many conflicting descriptions of witchcraft offered from many conflicting viewpoints. This confusion is compounded by ancient bigotry
and modern revisionism.

There are at least four identifiable classes of witches:

- Sorcerers and practitioners of occult arts. Witches of this classification practice magic based upon animism, shamanism, and
  other conceptions of the natural world that exist outside formal
  religions.

- Witches practicing corrupted forms of older religions or blends
  of older religions.

- Satanists seeking a dark mirror of Christianity and the power to
  do evil.

- Modern practitioners of Wicca, a faith reconstructed from ancient pagan religions.

The first three classifications sometimes overlap, adding to the confusion.

"What'd you mean: 'Just a smidgen of cinnamon?'"

THE ORIGINS OF WITCHCRAFT

For early man, the world was a mysterious place full of unpredictable and unexplainable events. Animism was one ancient attempt to give order to the universe. This belief, which can be found in every culture's past, if not its present, holds that all things—animals, people, plants, the sky, the sea, everything—have living spirits. These spirits can be helpful or harmful and should, for safety's sake, be treated with respect and caution. Certain people with special knowledge or rare talents are thought to be able to communicate with the spirits and exploit their powers.

In prehistoric Europe, an Earth Goddess faith was the predominant religion. Small figures representing the Goddess, usually displaying advanced pregnancy as an invocation of fertility, have been found all across the continent. Such a figurine is called a Venus, after statues of the later Greek goddess who inherited some of her characteristics. The priests of this female-centered creed were predominantly women. These wise women were charged with executing the rituals that kept the earth and their tribes fertile. They led sacrificial rites, purified spiritually unclean places, cast out evil spirits, sanctified marriages, cast spells and counterspells, foretold the future, and performed other spiritual tasks. Managing the dead was one of the more important duties entrusted to the wise women. They ordered burials so that the dead would not roam the earth after death; when the dead escaped these precautions, they interceded to protect the living. Wise women also provided more immediate services, such as ensuring that the communal fires weren't extinguished, delivering babies, and treating illness. They were knowledgeable in the use of plants, animals, and chemicals to cure. They could also use their knowledge to afflict and they wielded much power in their societies.

The Earth Goddess of prehistoric times was modified by later peoples. To the Babylonians, she became Ishtar. The Egyptians transformed her into Aset and Isis, goddess of fertility. On the island of Crete, she became Rhea. The Phoenicians called their version Astarte. To the Canaanites, she was Ashtaroth. The Greeks turned her into Hera. The Romans modified the Greek Hera into Juno and gave some of the Earth Goddess's attributes to lesser female goddesses such as Diana, goddess of spring, and Venus, goddess of love.

A male pagan codeity to the Earth Goddess was the horned virility god. In prehistoric cave paintings, figures of a skilled hunter wearing horns were common. It is thought that these represent a god of hunting and virility. The many pillars of stone that can be found all across Europe are sites where the Horned God's virility was venerated (the maypole is a relic of this worship). Just as the Earth Goddess survived through mutation into similar classical goddesses, the Horned God was transformed by later peoples into gods in their faiths. The Celtic god Cernunnos, or Cerne the Hunter, for example, wore horns and was associated with virility.

Pagans often deified the bull or the goat as the embodiment of strength and virility necessary to fertility. The art of the ancient Minoan people of the eastern Mediterranean is filled with images of bulls, and the Greek legend of the Minotaur, a monstrous man with the head of a bull, remains a legacy of their faith. In ancient Egypt, sacred bulls, believed to be connected to the prosperity of the nation, were lavishly cared for and given elaborate burials upon their deaths. The Hebrew people used horns as a symbol of divine power. Moses adorned his altar with brass horns. Later Greek beliefs included the half-man, half-goat deity Pan, who had horns and cloven hooves and was noted for his playful woodland lechery and love of the flute.

The Horned God or Goat God was often paired as consort to the Earth Goddess, with their sexual congress ensuring the fertility of the soil and livestock. Modern witches continue to make this linkage, ascribing different, opposing forces to either. The Goat God, for example, is believed to be predominant in winter, and the Earth Goddess in summer.

An echo of Cerne the Hunter survives in the English ghost Herne the Hunter. According to legend, Herne was a hunter who saved the life of Richard II when he was attacked by a wounded stag. Herne was badly injured in the process, but a passing wizard managed to save his life by binding the stag's horns to Herne's skull (an echo of earlier symbolism equating horns with strength). The grateful king made Herne the royal gamekeeper in the Great Park at Windsor. The king's other keepers were jealous and persuaded the wizard to steal away all of Herne's woodland knowledge. The king was forced to dismiss Herne. In despair, the keeper hanged himself, only to return in ghostly form upon a fire-breathing horse to lead a pack of spectral hounds after those who had destroyed him. He hunted down each of his enemies and killed them.

Instead of retiring to the afterlife, Herne continued to charge through the forests on dark nights with his supernatural hounds. No less a notable than Henry VIII claimed to have seen Herne. It was reputed that those who saw the ghostly keeper were doomed to misfortune. Henry's poor luck at marriage might be viewed as a consequence of his spotting Herne on his wild, nocturnal ride.

In time, the Earth Goddess religions were replaced by what have been described as male, "sky god" religions. The sky gods were various in their guises, from Zeus in the city-states of Greece, to Odin in the Scandinavian lands, to Jehovah in the Middle East. The Earth Goddess was disdained by these faiths but often had some role in their theology. The Jews incorporated her into their tradition through Lilith, a demonic spirit who was the first consort of Adam. Some theologians see the great veneration of the Virgin Mary among some Catholics—the "cult" of Mary—as a legacy of the Earth Goddess. In Northern Europe, where paganism persisted longer, echoes of the Earth Goddess were found in the Saxon goddess Goda or Frig. The Celts of Ireland gave Brigid, the goddess of wisdom and poetry, some of the Goddess's attributes. As mentioned earlier, when Christianity supplanted paganism, the old gods and goddesses were recast as demons or had their tasks and areas of responsibility taken from them and ascribed to Christian saints.

As the sky gods supplanted the Earth Goddess, her wise women were pushed from power. Their skills were still recognized, however, and they were openly consulted in matters such as midwifery, herbal medicine, divination, interpreting dreams and omens, and casting protective spells. These wise women became witches. In addition to the positive skills, witches were surreptitiously consulted for tasks that were socially unacceptable or illegal, including making potions to win involuntary love, amulets to improve gambling skills, curses or hexes, and poisons to kill, along with necromancy. The last was communicating with the dead in order to predict the future. The word is derived from the Greek *nekros,* meaning "dead," and *manteia,* meaning "divination."

Aside from pestering the dead, necromancy was viewed as a form of blasphemy that attempted to defy the will of God. God would speak through prophets of His choice, and witches seeking to know His plans through magic were condemned. The Bible condemned witches.

> Thou shalt not suffer a witch to live.
>
> Exodus 22:18

And again:

> There shall not be found among you any one that maketh his son or his daughter to pass through the fire, or that useth divination, or an observer of times, or an enchanter, or a witch. Or a charmer, or a consulter with familiar spirits, or a wizard, or a necromancer. For all that do these things are an abomination unto the Lord: and because of these abominations the Lord thy God doth drive them out from before thee.
>
> Deuteronomy 18:10–12

The Bible contains an account of a witch conducting a necromantic ritual. King Saul, before a great battle with the Philistines, sought guidance from God, but because of Saul's sins, God had forsaken him. Saul decided he could get the answers he wanted only from a necromancer. This was a bit awkward, because Saul, in keeping with God's condemnation of witchcraft, had executed wizards and witches who performed necromantic rituals. Those left alive fled his kingdom or hid their activities. Despite this, when Saul sent his servants in search of "a woman that hath a familiar spirit," they quickly found one, the Witch of Endor.

Saul disguised himself to consult the Witch of Endor, asking her to summon up the ghost of the prophet Samuel. As soon as the ghost appeared to her, however, she recognized Saul as the king. Full of fear, she asked Saul if he were trying to entrap her into performing a forbidden rite. After Saul swore he would not harm her, she continued the ritual.

> And the woman said unto Saul, I saw gods ascending out of the earth. And he said unto her, What form is he of? And she said, An old man cometh up; and he is covered with a mantle. And Saul perceived that it was Samuel, and he stooped with his face to the ground, and bowed himself. And Samuel said to Saul, Why hast thou disquieted me, to bring me up? And Saul answered, I am sore distressed; for the Philistines make war against me, and God is departed from me, and answereth me no more, neither by prophets, nor by dreams: therefore I have called thee, that thou mayest make known unto me what I shall do. Then said Samuel: [the LORD will] deliver Israel with thee into the hand of the Philistines: and tomorrow shalt thou and thy sons be with me.
>
> Samuel 28:13–19

The next day Saul and his sons were, indeed, killed in battle, and Israel fell to the Philistines.

That Saul would consult a witch despite prohibitions has puzzled biblical scholars. Some believe the tale is included in the Bible as a warning that knowing the future can be more a curse than a gift. The dreadful knowledge Saul gained was punishment for the sin of seeking it and it did nothing to save him from his fate.

Other ancient cultures have stories of witches. Homer (circa

850 B.C.–800 B.C.) writes in *The Odyssey* of a witch encountered by Odysseus during his arduous voyage home to Ithaca from the Trojan War. The events of the tale are dated as far back as 1200 B.C. Odysseus visited the isle of Aeaea, home of the witch Circe, who, unlike many storied witches, was a great beauty with many suitors. She amused herself by transforming them into beasts. Odysseus's crewmen were transformed into swine when their table manners proved lacking. Odysseus, with the aid of an herb given to him by the god Hermes, thwarted her attempt to bewitch him. Then, after he rushed at Circe with his sword, she turned his crew back into men and hosted them in style for a year. When it came time for them to leave, she advised Odysseus to make a journey to Hades to consult the spirit of the prophet Tiresias, who would tell him of the dangers he would have to overcome in order to return home.

To find Tiresias, Circe told Odysseus that he must fill a pit with sheep's blood. The ghosts of the dead, she explained, were irresistibly drawn to feed upon blood. Odysseus would have to stand by the pit and ward off the dead with his sword till the ghost of Tiresias appeared to drink. Odysseus did as Circe bid and managed to speak not only to Tiresias but also to many other deceased heroes and heroines, including Achilles (as described in chapter 1) and Ajax.

Tiresias told Odysseus he would make it to his home, but warned him of several dangers to his crew. While they talked, more dead drew near. Eventually, so many spirits swarmed to the pit that Odysseus fled in terror. The warnings that Tiresias had given him proved true and unavoidable. Odysseus returned to his home but lost every remaining member of his crew. Just like the Witch of Endor, Circe had provided a means of communicating with the dead and, as with Saul, the fate revealed was inescapable and unpleasant.

Greek myth had a goddess who came to be associated with witchcraft: Hecate, the goddess of darkness. Unlike Artemis, whose nightly activities were associated with moonlight and night beauty, Hecate was associated with the terrors of the night. She was often depicted as having three heads—those of a horse, of a dog, and of a snake. Two ghostly, howling hounds accompanied Hecate through the dark as she wandered on moonless nights. At first a benevolent spirit (she helped rescue Persephone from the Underworld), Hecate's repute became darker and darker. She was said to have the power to control dreams and summon the spirits of the dead. She commonly frequented graveyards and other bleak places associated with death, such as crossroads, where suicides were buried. Hecate was visible only to those knowledgeable in the black arts; consequently, witches were her most faithful worshipers. They sacrificed black sheep and black dogs to win her favor.

The ancient Romans had their witches. The poet Horace described in his *Satires* (quoted at the beginning of this chapter) dark-robed witches profanely clawing up the dirt in a cemetery, preparing to invoke the spirits of the dead. The witches were fearful looking, with scraggly hair tossed by the night wind. To Horace and other followers of the newer religions, witch rituals were sinful and criminal. This pattern, of the sacred beliefs of one age becoming the blasphemy of a newer age and being subsumed into superstition, crime, and witchcraft, repeated when Christianity rose to dominance in the fourth century. Again, some of the rituals and dogma of the passing religions were carried on in corrupted form by a small subculture. Again, some of the people in the subculture were known as witches.

Forms of Magic

There are several forms of magic, which sometimes overlap.

IMITATIVE MAGIC

The sorcerer imitates the goal he wishes to accomplish. This can be done by drawing the goal or by imitating the goal. Archaeologists believe that cave paintings left by prehistoric men were a form of imitative magic. The paintings show large numbers of plump animals being successfully slain by hunters. It is thought that, by drawing this, the cave painters were magically willing the slaughter to occur or asking spirits to make it occur.

Navajo Indians in the American Southwest practiced imitative magic. They dressed in flowing costumes and performed a dance imitating rain in order to bring actual rain. In other cultures, a sorcerer might mimic a prey animal, such as a deer or a buffalo, in a dance meant to attract the prey animals. Often, after killing the prey, the sorcerer and the hunters would politely thank the spirits of the dead prey through more rituals.

Curiously, there is a modern psychological technique similar to imitative magic that is used to achieve goals. Before an event, a person imagines himself performing successfully, and this helps the person to succeed in reality. The technique has been used by professional athletes and reportedly improves performance.

CONTAGIOUS MAGIC

In contagious magic, the sorcerer casts a spell employing an object closely associated with the target, such as fingernail clippings, a lock of hair, or a bit of clothing. The theory is that an object closely linked with something retains a connection with that thing, even after the objects are separated. The possession of the object linked to the victim gives the sorcerer power over the victim. In some cultures, a person's name can serve as the associated item. To prevent misuse of names, then, people were given two names. One was used as the public name and known to all. The second name, a secret name, was the true name and was known only to the individual and a select few. If the secret name were discovered by an enemy, it could be used to destroy its owner. A folk memory of this belief can be found in the fairy tale Rumplestiltskin.

A key to the effectiveness of contagious magic is the knowledge by the victim that he or she is under magical attack. Scientists believe that the victim's own fears make the spell come to fruition.

SYMPATHETIC MAGIC

This form of magic, dating as far back as the ancient Assyrians, is based on the idea that like produces like. The Ojibwa of North America, for example, would carve a wooden image of a foe, then torment it with pins to magically injure the enemy. The Voodoo doll of the Caribbean is similar but includes a bit of contagious magic; it is made with an object closely associated with the victim. The Voodoo priest pokes the image with pins, knots a rope around its neck, or burns it, thereby inflicting parallel injuries on the victim. Witches in the backwoods of Kentucky attempted the same mischief with "witch dolls."

The most straightforward counter to image magic was to steal the image from the witch. A victim might seek to inflict his own image magic counterattack by imitating the witch's magic. A white witch might be enlisted in this effort or in composing protective charms.

A curious variation of sympathetic magic was "weapon salving," the belief that treating an item that had wounded someone would help cure the injured person. A man struck in battle by an arrow would have the arrow removed and treated with a healing salve while the wound was left untended but for cleaning and binding. The arrowhead would be frequently examined and cleaned, because any spot of rust on it would indicate death. As late as 1902, in Norwich, England, a woman named Martha Henry died of tetanus after stepping on a rusty nail. The nail had been cleaned and treated while her wound had been left untended.

Not all the injured who received this inverted medical treatment died. A wound left clean and untreated was often better off than a wound treated with the horrid concoctions common to folk medicine. One salve described in a seventeenth-century book of household remedies (and cited in *The Encyclopedia of Superstitions,* edited by Christina Hole) included bear fat, dried worms, grease from "the flick of the Boar, the staler the better," powdered bloodstone (a form of quartz), and an ounce and three-quarters of moss from a dead man's skull, "or more if you can get it." It's easy to see why rubbing this unsanitary mess on an injuring item was better than applying it to a wound.

NEGATIVE MAGIC

In *The Golden Bough,* anthropologist Sir James Frazer added the classification of negative magic. He cited the custom among South Pacific Islanders of labeling certain actions, things, or places as taboo as an example of negative magic. It might be prohibited for anyone other than a sanctified priest to climb a certain volcano, upon penalty of a deadly curse. In this case, the negative magic is a sort of inverted contagious magic in that, when the taboo is broken, the contact with the taboo item causes injury.

The distinction between negative magic and the earlier types, aside from the order of actions, may be more one of motive than of form. The earlier types can, according to believers, inflict injury and must appear negative to a victim. The "evil eye" is a subtle example of negative contagious magic—the ill is caused through the eye of the evildoer, where the victim's image is captured by reflection.

DIVINATION

Divination is the use of magic to obtain knowledge—often of the future, but sometimes of the past and of the present. The examples of witchcraft from the Bible and ancient Greece and Rome cited above are forms of divination. A diviner would commonly invoke the dead (necromancy) or a demon (demonomancy) to provide the desired information. While diviners commonly claimed to be invoking only good dead people or good spirits, the authorities usually declared any invocation as an invocation of the Devil. It was thought that, even when an invoked spirit described itself as good, it was actually the Devil lying to worm his way into the spiritual life of the invoker.

Despite the connections made with the Devil, divination has been popular with all levels of society in every culture, with many variations in technique. Examining the lines upon and shape of hands (chiromancy), casting dice (astragalomancy), gazing at the reflections formed in a basin of water (lecanomancy), and even interpreting the noises made by the stomach (gastromancy) are forms of divination. There are many, many others. Some forms in common use today include Ouija boards, tarot cards, psychic friends, spiritualism, and even fortune cookies.

One kind of divination, the examination of the entrails of sacrificed animals, was a favorite of the Romans. Before building a city, Roman priests might kill a chicken and examine its organs for blemishes that they interpreted so as to identify a location as favorable or unfavorable. Oddly, there is some scientific backing for the efficacy of this practice. An animal's health is affected by where it lives. A chicken raised in an unhealthy spot will have marks of disease or parasites on its liver.

Not all Romans venerated divining priests. The Roman orator Cato (234 B.C.–149 B.C.) said of one group, called haruspexes: "How could one haruspex look another in the face without laughing?"

DARK PLACES IN THE FOREST

The rise of Christianity in the West corresponded with the fall of the Roman Empire. Earlier faiths lost their official supremacy to the Catholic Church. At first, pagans reluctant to embrace Christianity were given a measure of tolerance by the early Church. This faded as Christians became wary of increasingly secretive pagans. After losing the shrines, temples, and holy places of their religions, pagans met in remote, lonely places. The forests were a natural location for their rituals, especially since the pagan gods they worshiped often had woodland associations. Nighttime provided safety from unfriendly eyes. Pagan worshipers often kept their allegiances confidential while following the forms of the Christian Church in public. This increased Christian suspicion and antagonism.

Faced with Christian opposition and lacking the backing of the state and an official priesthood to enforce orthodoxy, the formalities of the pagan traditions devolved into superstition, folklore, and corruption. Much of paganism simply disappeared into oblivion. The tenets of the Druid priesthood, for example, were nearly entirely lost. What we know of them (as mentioned in the first chapter) comes mainly from oral tradition, accounts of non-Druids, and the application of reconstructive theories. While stories of the Greek and Roman gods were kept alive in literate circles and later rediscovered in scrolls tucked into corners of dusty libraries, the common people, who had once made offerings in classical temples, forgot their old gods and took up the new.

Superstition transformed pagan beliefs into empty ritual. Actions that had once been part of pagan ceremony lost their original meaning and lingered on as small, stilted gestures. Interestingly, the Church wasn't unduly upset by superstitions. They might have been

viewed as trivial nonsense that did little injury; or given the igno-
rance of the times, perhaps they weren't seen as superstitions at all
but as self-evident facts of life.

Folklore also absorbed pagan traditions. An elegant bit of mythology might be blended and twisted with other stories until incidents
belonging to one mythos became part of another. Tales of Hercules,
for example, were transformed into tales about local heroes all across
Europe.

Those who attempted to maintain pagan rituals had no means to
keep their faith unadulterated. Corruption crept in and compounded
over time. Eventually, that which latter-day pagans worshiped was
far different from what had been worshiped by their ancestors. Oddly,
their dogmas began to be defined by their persecutors. The Church
said that people worshiping in the woods were worshiping the Devil.
For those dissatisfied with Christianity, this became a reason to join
them. Defectors from Christianity brought their expectations of
what Satanic worship should be with them. These views had been
drawn from the descriptions provided by the Church. In effect, the
Church was unwittingly defining Satanic rituals. The original non-
Satanic beliefs of the pagans were corrupted by Devil-worshiping
ex-Christians.

The early Catholic Church had been indifferent to sorcery, so long
as it didn't involve demonic practices. Herbal cures, the interpretation
of omens, the garnering of good luck, and other forms of positive
magic were acceptable. A person delving into grayer magic could
make amends through confession and penance. Witchcraft historian
Chadwick Hansen noted in his 1969 book *Witchcraft at Salem* that in
the seventh century the Archbishop of Canterbury prescribed just
three years of penance for those who donned skins to appear as "a
stag or a bull" in pagan rituals.

Tolerance disappeared as Church leaders began to associate magic
with the Devil. Sorcerers didn't invoke the Christian God to effect
their magic. If God's power wasn't in play, there was only one other
source of supernatural power. The growing numbers of Satanic worshipers further tainted traditional sorcery. Their activities were terrifying to the Church, which responded brutally, discarding subtle
differences between white and black magic. The heirs of debased
paganism and the new followers of Christianity's Satan became the
much-hated and much-feared witches of the Dark Ages.

The Cult of Diana

The cult of Diana is a good example of how the worship of a pagan goddess degenerated. Diana was the ancient Roman goddess of hunting, fertility, and the moon. As her worship spread across Europe, the Near East, and North Africa, it absorbed beliefs associated with earlier Earth Goddess religions. When Christianity replaced paganism, the worship of Diana declined until only a handful of followers remained. These worshiped in secret at remote spots. Corruption confused their traditions, and would-be Devil worshipers twisted them further. While not generally identified as a witch cult, by the mid–Dark Ages, Diana worshipers matched many of the descriptions later given of witches. Indeed, their customs and outsiders' fearful beliefs about them helped shape later ideas about witchcraft.

Diana was thought able to change her shape—a power later witches were said to possess. Diana favored the form of a cat, an agile, expert, nocturnal hunter. Cats were later a favorite form for witches to adopt. Cat familiars were common for later witches, and the Devil was said to appear to them in cat form. Diana cults were said to meet in the forest, by night, to indulge in orgiastic dancing around great fires. Later, witch sabbats were similarly described. Diana cultists were said to join Diana in her nocturnal hunts across the sky. Witches were also said to be able to fly.

Modern witches often claim to worship Diana as the Earth Goddess. Ironically, when the worship of Diana was at its height during the Roman Empire, it was probably as stodgy as any modern established religion. Today, it has become part of the counterculture.

WITCH HUNTS IN EUROPE

Life was cramped during the Dark Ages. Every man and woman knew their station in life and also knew that that station wouldn't change. A peasant boy could never become a knight or a merchant. He was destined to be a peasant tied to the land on which his peasant fathers had toiled for generations. Even the choice of whom he would marry would be made for him by his parents. A peasant girl was similarly bound to a limited life. She would also marry someone chosen by her parents and spend the rest of her life performing the duties of a wife and mother. Some sought escape from their circumstance by joining the clergy. A studious mind could find intellectual pleasure in a monastery or nunnery, but such lives were even more rigidly bound than nonclerical lives. Even for the well born, life was constrained by obligations that dictated behavior from birth to death. When the ordinary hardships of medieval life, such as disease, war, famine, pestilence, and harsh labor, are added to this rigid structure, it becomes easy to understand how desperately hard life could be. Witchcraft provided an escape from these limitations.

Witches broke social rules. The men and women who joined bands of witches, called covens, gained companionship that could include forbidden sexual release. Witch meetings, called sabbats, often turned into orgies. Narcotic, alcoholic, or psychoactive concoctions were sometimes consumed to increase the riotous and licentious nature of the occasion. There was a great deal of equality in the covens. Women, who had little authority in the public world, had real influence. Class restrictions fell away when witches gathered. A masked aristocrat might make merry with a peasant. As with other secret societies, members might use their private connections to help them in their more public lives. People low in life could gain command over others. When witches secretly turned to concocting poisonous potions or other mischief, they exercised considerable power over their neighbors. The aged, starving widow in a tumbledown hut could use fear to compel charity by threatening to curse those who treated her poorly.

Witches performed many tasks deemed useful. They conducted fertility rituals, served as midwives, concocted tonics and herbal medicines, treated wounds, thwarted curses, and procured luck. A witch might be consulted when someone fell prey to mental illness. Belief in witch powers was so strong that a witch could sometimes impose a cure upon a disturbed mind. With less success, witches were sought when droughts or disease afflicted the land. When the misfortune passed, as they all eventually do, the witch would be given credit for its disappearance. Witches were also sought out to foretell the future or to interpret dreams and omens. As with modern psychics, fortune-telling witches maximized their accurate predictions while minimizing their errors, and customers, anxious to participate in a supernatural event, tend to find truth in vague predictions. Generally, witches offering predictions did little harm, as they seldom provided enough misinformation to endanger customers.

Not all the tasks witches took up were beneficial, however. The temptation to use their knowledge and repute for evil was powerful. Witches were commonly accused of blighting crops, drying up cows, tainting wells, turning bread black, and provoking feuds or other mischief. They were believed to have power over the weather and were said to raise storms, ruining crops or sinking ships, or to still the wind, stopping windmills and stalling ships. With such supposed powers, it was easy for nefarious witches to exploit the fearful. This fear caused those who thought themselves victims to seek out protection. Often, as described elsewhere in this chapter, a white witch might be sought out to cast counterspells. Alternatively, victims might seek official protection through the civil authorities and the Church.

There was little separation between Church and state during the Middle Ages. The Catholic Church had its own courts that, in several areas, had jurisdiction superior to civil courts. Even when they didn't have direct authority, they were often consulted and deferred to as if they did. This was the case with witches. Because witchcraft was viewed as a sinful, antireligious activity, the Church was considered the authority best prepared to deal with it. The authorities and the Church worked together to thwart those viewed as dangerous witches. This enterprise, being a convoluted mishmash of conflicting superstitions, self-delusions, cruel judicial practices, and unrestricted power, produced horrible injustices. At first, these were limited. Witch trials and executions were few and far between. Common sense often caused spurious cases to be rejected. This slowly changed, however, as witch covens became more established and common.

The Catholic Church, and later the Protestant sects, feared that witchcraft constituted an alternative religion devoted to evil. They believed that Satan-worshiping witches were attempting to destroy Christianity, and, just as they believed in the power of Christ, they believed in the powers of Satan. As an article of faith, they knew Satan was the enemy of good. They also believed that, while the triumph of Christianity was foretold, the struggle for individual souls didn't always have a happy ending. Satan could and would delude countless souls into evil. Witches were seen as victims and victimizers in this delusion.

There was a geopolitical aspect to Church hostility toward witch-craft. The Church had a vivid history of persecution at the hands of the Romans, which had nearly snuffed it out of existence. Overcoming the classical faiths of the Roman Empire had been long and difficult. The conversion of Europe's pagan peoples to Christianity had been even longer and more difficult, marked with great sacrifices by missionaries. Church leaders feared that many conversions might be superficial, and the old faiths might return. There was also fear of sectarian strife within the Christian faith. Heretical schisms, such as the Albigenses and Cathari, had advanced different forms of Christianity that had attracted thousands of followers and held sway over large portions of Europe. The Church had defeated these offshoots only after taking extreme, near-genocidal, measures.

The rise of Muhammadanism in the East and its lightning-quick spread was also a shock to the Church. These regions had once been Christian. Islam, founded upon Judeo-Christian roots, conquered all of the Middle East and North Africa, and it threatened to overrun Europe through the Balkans or Spain. Church authorities felt compelled to take every measure to ensure the survival and dominance of Christianity. They turned to the kings of Europe to defend the faith. The savage Crusades were an ultimately unsuccessful response by European kingdoms to the Islamic conversion of the Holy Land. Islamic armies marched on Europe and were barely stopped after ferocious wars in the Balkans, France, and Spain. For protection within the Christian kingdoms, the Church turned to the Inquisition.

Established in the early thirteenth century, the Inquisition was charged with the discovery and eradication of heresy. In 1252, Pope Innocent IV gave the Inquisition the power to use torture. The Church had formerly opposed torture but became convinced that it was better for a person to suffer pain on Earth and be forced to cleanse his soul than to die polluted by evil and suffer an eternity of pain in Hell. While the Inquisition discovered heresy and sorcery, the civil courts administered punishment. (After the Protestant Reformation, the civil courts continued their work under the direction of Protestant clergy.) Witchcraft was viewed as a form of heresy, and the Inquisition sought to eliminate it.

Heresy and the rise of Islam weren't the only dangers the Church feared. In 1347, the Black Death arrived by ship in Messina, Sicily. Carried by fleas that fed upon the blood of rats, bubonic plague rapidly spread through all of Europe. It earned the dreadful name of

Black Death from the black sores that marked its dying victims. By the time it faded, one out of every three Europeans had died. Whole families and entire towns were wiped out. Frightened people, desperate for an explanation of its cause, blamed the corruption of the people by the Devil and his allies, the witches. In 1484, Pope Innocent VIII issued a papal bull directing inquisitors and the civil authorities to execute anyone who practiced witchcraft or any diabolical art. The craze to find and burn witches spread across Europe. Historians call this period the Burning Times.

To aid this activity, religious authorities concocted a profile of what they believed were the characteristic traits and activities of witches. The purported facts were often gathered through horrid torture of supposed witches. In 1486, Heinrich Institor and Jacob Sprenger, two Dominican inquisitors, published the book *Malleus Maleficarum* (The Hammer of Witches), which described witchcraft, listed methods for discovering witches, and prescribed how a witch trial should proceed. The book was quickly translated into several languages and published in many editions. Protestants adopted it, and in time it outsold all other books except the Bible.

The Three Levels of Witchcraft

The least dangerous kind of witchery was white magic—the use of charms, potions, incantations, and ritual to serve a positive purpose. A magical ointment might be used to treat a wound. A pair of scissors might be placed under a bed to cut the pain of childbirth. A bit of salt might be tossed over the shoulder to counter the bad luck produced by spilling salt at the table. White magic could easily edge into gray areas, however. A love potion, for example, produced the positive emotion of love but stole the freedom of the target to choose his or her own beloved.

The next dangerous form of witchery was black magic. Here there was no pretense of doing good. Magic was used to sicken and kill enemies. Witches knowledgeable in herbs and simple chemistry could make this kind of magic genuinely dangerous. An absurd incantation and a bit of magical powder could kill when the powder included a poison.

The form of witchery deemed most dangerous by the authorities was the pact with the Devil. Satanists would swear their eternal soul to Satan in return for power on Earth and favor in Hell. Dr. Faustus is perhaps the best-known figure purported to have made such a deal. He was a real historical figure, a self-identified wizard who studied the black arts and proclaimed his allegiance to the Devil, whom he referred to as his *schwager*, or "buddy." Faust died in 1540, but his evil reputation lingered on, serving as the inspiration for several books, plays, and even puppet shows. The most notable of these efforts were the 1604 play *The Tragicall History of D. Faustus* by Christopher Marlowe, the 1808 verse drama *Faust* by Goethe, and the opera *Faust,* composed during the nineteenth century by Charles Gounod.

The story of Faust provided writers with a framework to discuss sin and redemption and to answer questions such as "What would an invocation of the Devil look like?" and "What does Satan want with human souls, anyway?" The answer to the latter question was best given by Mephistopheles in *Faustus;* he says the Devil's pain at being cast out from Heaven is mitigated by the companionship of other unhappy souls in Hell— misery loves company.

Professional witch hunters traveled from town to town identifying witches. The most popular technique was pricking supposed "witch marks." These were said to mark the witch as a disciple of the Devil. Sometimes the mark served as a sort of nipple from which a witch fed her own blood to her familiar. The familiar was a demon who often took the form of a small animal and who served as an assistant in magical enterprises and as a link to the Devil. Witch hunters would strip suspected witches to search for any mark that might be such a witch mark. The marks were thought to be impervious to pain, so every blemish found would be tested with a needle until one was found that failed to draw a wince. An unscrupulous witch hunter could easily fake a positive result from such a test whenever he wished.

Another sign of being a witch was the inability to sink in water. Water was thought to reject unnatural things. A witch tossed into a pond wouldn't drown, because the water wouldn't close over him or her. Countless poor people were bound up in chains and tossed into ponds to test whether they were or weren't witches. Those who proved themselves innocent unfortunately drowned. The few who somehow managed not to drown went to the stake.

One technique to discover witches ironically resembled the "water-witching" or dowsing technique still in use by well drillers in America today. The witch hunter walked about with a forked branch of witch hazel until, of its own volition, it pointed out a witch. Results were certainly subjective and could be easily faked.

The few people who dared object to the witch hunts were often themselves targeted as witches or heretics and executed. Even witch hunters were suspect. The English witch finder Matthew Hopkins sent many witches to the stake during the middle of the seventeenth century until he himself was tested by being tossed in a river. He floated, was pronounced a wizard, and was executed.

Some historians estimate that as many as 82 percent of those executed as witches were women. Women were seen as more easily recruitable in the Devil's service. Women often had few legal rights and little influence, which made them easy victims for witch hunters.

Bats and Witches

One reason bats may have become associated with witches is that during witch sabbats, their fires attracted flying insects, which in turn attracted hungry bats. To an observer, the wheeling, darting bats would seem to be joining in the festivities.

SATANIC WITCHES, AS DESCRIBED BY THEIR HUNTERS

The witch hunters extracted accounts of Satanic witchcraft through torture. These narratives described wild encounters with powerful demons and Satan. The tellers made fantastic claims of magic, claiming to fly, for example, or to be able to afflict enemies. While the more fanciful elements of the narratives can be dismissed, especially since they were obtained by torture, the less outlandish parts of the accounts, which describe gatherings and rituals, probably have some accuracy. Certainly, those seeking to worship Satan mimicked the accounts in popular stories of witchcraft and, when caught, repeated them back to their examiners as descriptions of witchcraft. Secrecy, however, clouds the activities of witchcraft. Practitioners of both Satanic witchcraft and witchcraft based on pagan beliefs kept their faith hidden for fear of persecution and execution. The better they kept their secrets, the longer they lived. Keeping in mind these conflicting and confused sources, a general description of how witchcraft was purported to be practiced can be constructed.

Satanic witches were grouped into covens under the leadership of a master, usually a man. The master sometimes claimed to be the Devil himself. He might use costumes to make himself appear demonic and to conceal his true identity. Sometimes an animal was brought to the meeting and presented to the coven as the Devil. Nearly any animal would do—a cow, a cat, a horse, even a mouse or a bug—but the most favored creature was a black ram. A black ram that was deformed or could be disguised to appear unusual was a particular favorite.

WITCHES' SABBATS

Witches, as noted earlier, marked significant moments in the year with festive sabbats, which included feasting, drinking, dancing, and sexual intercourse. While the word *sabbat* is similar to *Sabbath*, etymologists do not believe it is related. Rather, it has been traced to the French *s'esbettre*, which means "to throw oneself about," a good description of the cavorting of the witches. In addition to the playful activities, sabbats were celebrated with solemn rituals in which witches were said to vow their souls to the Devil. The animal or human stand-in for Satan was given fawning respect. It was commonly said that witches showed their subservience to the Devil by lining up to bestow kisses upon his posterior. They also were said to have ritualized sex with Satan or his representative, the coven's master.

Witches celebrated eight solar sabbats that coincide with Winter Solstice, Candlemas, Spring Equinox, May Eve, Summer Solstice, the first of August, Fall Equinox, and Halloween. The sabbat coincident with Winter Solstice marked the longest night of the year, the darkest day of winter. After it, the days grew brighter and brighter. The sabbat on Candlemas, February 2, was sacred to Brigid, the goddess of fire and inspiration. Initiates were commonly brought into a coven on this sabbat. The sabbat of Eostar occurred on the spring equinox. On this day, morning and night were of equal length. Eostar marked the beginning of spring. The sabbat of Beltane came on May Eve. Pagans had long celebrated this time by dancing around a phallic maypole to cel-ebrate fertility and by leaping over bonfires for purification and luck. Witches incorporated these customs. The sabbat of Litha occurred on the summer solstice, the longest day of the year. Witches marked this date by casting into a bonfire a wicker figure of a man with a loaf of bread inside. This was an echo of ancient Druid sacrifices, in which much larger wicker figures, stuffed with horses and sometimes human beings, were set afire. August 1 brought the sabbat of Lugh-nasad. It marked the time of the year just before harvest. In agricul-tural communities, where a failed crop could mean famine, this was the moment of suspense. Would the crops survive all hazards, or would they be destroyed by some last-minute disaster? The sabbat of Mahon came on the fall equinox, when day and night are again of equal length. It marked the end of harvesttime and the beginning of winter. The sabbat of Samhain was celebrated at Halloweentime. It marked the beginning of winter and the witches' new year.

On two of the year's sabbats, covens from across a region gath-ered. The first gathering, on April 30, was called Roodmas in England and Walpurgis Night (Walpurgisnacht) in Germany. It was the evening before May Day. The second gathering was on Samhain, October 31. This date was sometimes called the Night of the Witches because it was considered the day of the year when they were most powerful. At the gatherings, the witches caroused with each other and the Devil. They danced around a great bonfire, sometimes in the nude, supposedly plotted crimes, and brewed magical potions in great cauldrons. Cauldrons had their obvious utilitarian use, but also had a symbolic significance in Celtic lore.

Moo Moo Magic

Evil witches were notorious for inflicting their spite on the cows of their enemies; it was the most commonly reported witch crime. A cow was a valuable asset for the European peasant and, later, for American settlers. If she became sick or unproductive, the owner and his or her family could suffer and might starve. A witch might use magic to kill a cow, dry her up, steal her milk, or spoil butter making from the milk. The witch might resort to disguise to do such evil, stealing milk in the form of a rabbit, a hedgehog, a cat, or even an insect. Butterflies were named for the suspicion that they were witches stealing milk.

WITCHES AND ANIMALS

As mentioned earlier, individual witches were said to harbor a demonic spirit, known as a familiar, as a companion and assistant in evildoing. Familiars took the forms of small animals, such as mice, beetles, and, most notably, cats. Witches were thought to feed their familiars with their own blood, often from an extra nipple located at some odd spot on their bodies. These were the "witch marks" mentioned above.

Blood and Witchly Power

For witches, blood was believed to be more than just the fluid of life; it was inseparably bound to a witch's magical powers. These powers were transferred to the witch's children through blood. An initiate to witchcraft was often bound to his or her new allegiance through a ritual bloodletting and mingling. The contract with the Devil signed in blood derives from this blood-as-power notion. A derivative of this belief was the idea that witches could be attacked through their blood. One anti-witch rite was "scoring above the breath." A witch's influence over a person could be broken if that person managed to inflict a bleeding wound upon the witch above the mouth and nose. Another use of blood to defeat a witch was to secure a vial of the witch's blood and, with a snip of the witch's hair and some of the witch's urine, boil the blood over a fire at midnight. The heat was supposed to be magically inflicted upon the witch, killing or so injuring him or her that further attacks would be prevented.

Perhaps because of the link between their power and blood, witches were thought to have magical control over bleeding. They were said to be able to stop or start bleeding in people and animals. Curiously, this was a skill that blacksmiths were also said to possess. Iron was a powerful weapon against black

magic and evil spirits. Consequently, ironworkers were sometimes considered magical. Some smiths set themselves up as
"blood charmers," stanching bleeding wounds for money.

Witches were also thought able to transform themselves into
animal forms. Again, cats were a preferred form, but witches were
said to turn into owls, toads, wolves, goats, ravens, and snakes as
well. In the Basque regions of the Pyrenees, in 1525, a women was
arrested as a witch and forced to confess that she and several
acquaintances had transformed themselves into horses, then had
flown off into the night sky.

A GRIM REAPING

During the sixteenth and seventeenth centuries, witch hunting and
burning exploded across Europe. No one knows how many died, but
the estimates range from as few as fourteen thousand to as many as
two hundred thousand. About five thousand died in Scotland, and
approximately one thousand were killed as witches in England.

The hunts were particularly harsh in Germany, with half of all executions occurring there. In Bamberg, Germany, nine hundred witches
were burned in the years 1609 to 1633. In the small town of Quedlin-
burg, also in Germany, 163 were executed on a single day. So heavy
was the smoke of their burning that buildings were covered with
sticky, human soot. German authorities were allowed the use of torture to extract confessions, and the estates of the condemned were
confiscated by the state. This gave them the tools and the motivation
to use them. In England, where torture was not allowed, the hysteria
was more limited. Still, English witch hunters, using examinations
that approached torture, long confinement in wretched jails, and the
threat of execution, managed to convict thousands.

By the end of the seventeenth century, the witch-hunt hysteria was
subsiding. As the middle class grew in size and influence, education
and skepticism spread. Knowledge itself grew more systematic, practical, and scientific. Intellectual pioneers, often risking charges of being
witches themselves, utilized the scientific method to explode magical
explanations for natural phenomena. Misfortunes that had once
seemed the result of witchery could more and more be explained or
avoided by reason. Medical science began to offer cures that worked

better than magical potions. Even for those who didn't understand science, the products of technology—great edifices, powerful machines, and abundant goods—were more impressive and persuasive than the furtive, often silly, unverifiable results of magic. Eventually, only the isolated and backward believed witchcraft was anything more than crude chemistry and superstition glamorized by fanciful folklore. By the middle of the eighteenth century, the witch hunters were gone. Official accusations of witchcraft and witch trials became rare.

Maybe It Was Something They Ate?

Scientists offer a microscopic explanation of some of the illnesses attributed to witchcraft. Until the nineteenth century, microfungi commonly contaminated grains that were improperly dried or stored. These fungi produced mycotoxins, which produced dreadful illnesses. They suppressed the immune system, inhibiting the body's defense against disease. The poisoning reduced fertility. Ergot, the most unpleasant of the microfungi, produced numbness, feelings of suffocation, bizarre hallucinations, seizures, and death. It destroyed blood circulation, leading to twisted limbs and gangrene. On occasion, whole villages, having eaten bread made with ergot-tainted grain, went into manic frenzies. The ergot-afflicted were said to be suffering from holy fire or St. Vitus' dance.

In 1989, Mary Kilbourne Matosian argued in *Poisons of the Past* that microfungal contamination was linked to outbreaks of witch hysteria. Many of the afflictions supposedly created through witchery are identical to ergot poisoning symptoms. Matosian pointed out that, ironically, because there were herbal treatments for ergot poisoning, it was believed that the symptoms were consciously inflicted by evildoers. Illnesses such as the plague, which had no treatment, were seen as afflictions from God. The result was that an herbalist who could help the sufferers was often blamed for causing their afflictions and executed as a witch. The superstitious linkage of cure with disease greatly hindered science. Still, while the witch hysteria was undoubtedly horrific and irrational and the superstitions that served as the basis of accusations are ridiculous, there is the possibility that some herbalists, knowing the effects of ergot poisoning, might have used it, instead of black magic, to do evil. It certainly would be more effective than a mumbled invocation of the Devil.

Baba Yaga

Eastern European folklore contains the story of a witch, Baba Yaga, with an unusual home. She was a little, skinny, ugly old crone (*baba* is Hungarian for "old woman") with a huge nose and long, yellow teeth. She lived in a hut in the deep woods. The hut was supported by a pair of gigantic chicken legs. When Baba Yaga spoke a secret rhyme, the legs would bend, lowering the hut for the witch to enter or exit. Baba Yaga had a penchant for cannibalism. She was a hard bargainer and ate those who failed to keep their word. Around her hut was a picket fence, which she decorated with the skulls of her victims. Baba Yaga magically transported herself in a giant mortar and pestle, which rushed her through the forest at terrific speeds. She steered the mortar by turning the pestle with one hand while using the other hand to drag a broom behind her, obscuring her trail.

WITCHES IN AMERICA

The European settlers of America carried their religions and superstitions with them. They believed the Devil was anxious to steal their souls, and they believed witches, who voluntarily gave their souls to the Devil, were his helpers. These spiritual fears were heightened by the everyday terrors of living in tiny, precarious colonial villages on the edge of a vast, unknown continent. Indians, far greater in numbers than the settlers, lurked in the dark forests, where they worshiped their own strange gods and visited fearful tortures upon their captives. In league with the hostile French in Canada, they commonly attacked vulnerable settlements or lone farmers in their fields. The seaward side of

Salem Village

the colony also posed dangers. In addition to French, Dutch, and Spanish warships, ruthless pirates raided merchant ships, making the link to the mother country precarious. Support and defense of the settlements were further diminished by political and religious turmoil in England.

Human dangers were compounded by natural threats. Friendly Indians had helped the settlers develop the crops necessary to survive, but the settlers routinely starved when their crops failed. Disease also decimated them. Smallpox killed entire families. Despite these many dangers, which might have tempted superstitious authorities to seek supernatural scapegoats, witches and witch hunts were few in the American colonies. The most notable incidents occurred in Massachusetts in the late seventeenth century.

There were witches in America. Deluded and malicious people sought power through witchery. We can dismiss their efforts as ridiculous, but they sincerely believed that if they carefully followed the rituals of black magic, they could do harm. Lawyers use the term *a guilty heart* to describe this malicious intent to injure. Their victims just as sincerely believed that black magic could harm them.

The famed theologian Cotton Mather detailed an incident involving a woman who truly believed herself a witch. Mather wrote of the event in his memoir, *Memorable Providences* (the incident is recounted by Hansen in his history). In 1688, in Boston, the four children of mason John Goodwin began to suffer strange fits. These fits had begun after one of the children, a girl, had quarreled with an Irish washerwoman. That woman's mother, Goodwife Glover, had joined in the argument, cursing the girl. Glover, "a scandalous old woman," had proved less than a good wife to her husband. Before his death, he had told his neighbors that he thought she was a witch.

The Goodwins were urged by their neighbors to seek out a white witch to counter Glover's magic. John, a religious man, refused. He took his children to a series of doctors. They could do nothing to cure the fits and they, too, suggested white witchcraft as treatment. Reluctant to resort to magic, John took his children to the clergy. A day of prayer was held, and one of the children was cured. The other three, however, remained afflicted. John finally turned to the authorities.

Goodwife Glover was arrested. She gave such a "wretched" account of herself that she was immediately jailed and her home searched. There, "several small images, or puppets, or babies, made of rags and stuffed with goat's hair and other such ingredients" were discovered. When Glover was confronted with these in court, she admitted that they had been devised to magically inflict the fits upon the children, "by wetting of her finger with her spittle and stroking." The children were present in court and, when Glover was handed the dolls, they fell into fits.

Glover's case was further injured when she tried to call the Devil as a character witness. He failed to appear at her bidding. Later that night, she was overheard scolding her demonic friend for his lack of support. She vowed that she would now confess all to the court.

The court appointed a panel of doctors to determine Glover's sanity. She gave every evidence of not being "crazed in her intellectuals," answering all questions with seeming reason. When one doctor asked what she thought would become of her soul, she evenly replied, "You ask me a very solemn question, and I cannot well tell what to say to it." After the doctors labeled her sane, the court ordered her hanged.

Glover didn't go to the gallows meekly. She ominously declared that the Goodwin children would continue to be cursed with fits after her death. The children were. It took months of prayer by Mather and other neighbors to cure the children, who went on to live normal lives.

Interestingly, the Glover incident shows that while black magic was vigorously condemned in New England, white magic was tolerated. The doctors consulted by Goodwin, among the more learned men in the colony, thought nothing odd in recommending a magical treatment for a magical affliction. In a society where magic was taken seriously, such treatment could be effective. The beliefs that made a curse work could also make a cure work.

As strange as it might seem to modern sensibilities, the judgment of the court was legally correct by the law of Goodwife Glover's time. She was what the law defined a black witch to be. She believed this herself and confessed. She had, in her own mind, struck a bargain with the Devil in return for the power to do evil. The punishment for witchcraft was well known; she couldn't have been surprised at her sentence.

While the Glover case had a horrific conclusion, it is an example of a case of witchcraft handled in a legal and methodical way typical of New England witch trials. Only fifty people were executed for witchcraft in all of the American colonies during the entire seventeenth century. American witch trials more often ended in acquittal than conviction. This wasn't the case, however, with the Salem Witch Hunt, where superstition, hysteria, and common maliciousness ran wild, carrying nearly all before them.

THE SALEM WITCH HUNT

The Salem Witch Hunt began in 1692 in the home of the Reverend Samuel Paris, a Puritan minister in Salem Village (now Danvers), a tiny settlement of just five hundred people in Massachusetts. Paris had a daughter, Elizabeth. While the minister was out one day, Elizabeth and her cousin Abigail Williams persuaded the family's Carib Indian slave woman, Titubah, to try a little fortune-telling, something that was forbidden by Puritan custom. Titubah had been entertaining the children for some time with lurid supernatural stories, also forbidden. Now, she cracked a raw egg into a glass of water. The girls were instructed to gaze into this amorphous mix, where they would see the forms of objects associated with the men they would one day marry. A hammer shape, for example, would indicate that the spouse-to-be would be a carpenter. It seemed a harmless game, but the girls didn't see any objects belonging to future beaus. One of them instead saw the shape of a coffin. Terrified, the girls fell into hysterical convulsions that astounded onlookers. The girls suffered from choking, temporary loss of sight and speech, and horrific hallucinations.

At first, the Reverend Paris tried to cure the girls with prayer and fasting. When this proved ineffective, he consulted local doctors.

They couldn't offer any treatment or explanation, until one doctor declared that the girls were the victims of witchcraft. The diagnosis added to the spreading hysteria; soon, nine young girls were throwing fits that they claimed were caused by witches. Under questioning, they began to name their tormentors.

Sarah Good, Sarah Osborne, and Tituba were the first to be denounced by the girls. A tribunal was set up to investigate. Others were accused. Those who confessed and named others were treated leniently. Those who insisted upon their innocence were relentlessly examined. If convicted, they were executed.

One major difference between the Salem cases and the Glover case was the admission of "spectral evidence." It was believed that a witch could send out a spectral self to do mischief. The specter was invisible to all except other witches and the victims of spectral attack. The ability to project spectral selves could allow witches to attend a distant sabbat while remaining physically at home. Before the magistrates, with the accused present, the afflicted girls claimed that the supposed witches were using this method to torment them right then and there. To this kind of charge, the accused could make no defense. How could they prove that something invisible didn't exist? The magistrates also believed that the children couldn't possibly make up such fanciful charges or fake the fits and other bizarre behaviors that they displayed. For the magistrates, the only explanation was spectral attack, and they allowed the girls to testify as to who was invisibly assaulting them.

Spectral evidence was controversial, even in the seventeenth century. It was an open-ended weapon that could place anyone in jeopardy. After the trials, it was realized that some of the condemned had been innocent, even though the accusers had blamed their specters for their torment. A person attending church services, for example, could hardly be using the powers of the Devil to appear elsewhere. God surely wouldn't permit His house to be used as an alibi for evil. Defenders of spectral evidence claimed that the Devil must have disguised himself as the innocent person and done the evil they had been accused of doing. In the past, it had been held that the Devil could take the form only of those who were in service to him. Now, if the innocent could be imitated, it seemed that no one was safe from accusation, no matter how godly. Some of the more reflective witch hunters realized that if an alibi had been lacking, an imposture by the Devil would have caused the innocent to be convicted. This prosecutorial dilemma helped raise doubts. Spectral evidence fell into disfavor. It was too dangerous and was not allowed in future witch trials. This was, unfortunately, too late for the accused at Salem.

More than two hundred people from two dozen villages were accused of witchcraft during the Salem Witch Hunt. Most were jailed under horrible conditions. While many went unprosecuted, all were in great peril, facing the condemnation of their community and the possibility of execution. Fifty accused witches confessed and testified against other accused witches. None of the confessed witches were executed. Others who refused to confess weren't so fortunate. Twenty-seven were convicted; fourteen women and five men were executed. Contrary to popular myth, the executions weren't done by burning. All but one were hanged upon Salem's Gallows Hill.

The only victim who wasn't hanged was eighty-year-old Giles Corey. A contentious fellow, it was rumored that, sixteen years earlier, he had beaten a hired hand to death. When his wife was accused of witchcraft, he told friends, perhaps sardonically, that he could give testimony that would convict her. In court, he had at first said little in her defense. When it became clear that his wife was in danger of conviction and execution, however, Corey turned to her defense. He denied having spoken against her, but witnesses contradicted him. Perjury was considered a very serious crime in Puritan Massachusetts. Soon, Corey himself was jailed and indicted as a witch.

Under New England law, answering an indictment required the accused to answer two questions. The first asked for a plea. Corey pleaded not guilty. The second question was a bit of legal ritual. The accused was required to announce how he would be tried. To this, the accused was supposed to respond, "By God and this court." This signified that the accused recognized the authority of the court to try him. To this, however, Corey stood mute. A man who stood mute could not be tried until he recognized the court's authority. Torture was prohibited as a means of gathering evidence but was allowed as a means of forcing a defendant to recognize the court. It was ordered that Corey be "pressed" until he complied.

Corey was taken to a spot by the Salem jail, stripped naked, and forced to the ground. A pallet was placed upon his chest and rocks gradually piled upon it, crushing the elderly man. Several of his friends begged him to recognize the court but Corey refused. It is said that he replied only, "More weight." After two days of torment, Corey died. A witness wrote that his tongue had swollen out of his mouth as he was crushed and that the sheriff supervising the torture had casually forced it back in with a poke of his cane.

Some historians believe that Corey refused to be tried, knowing that a guilty verdict was certain and that his family would be left penniless when the state confiscated his property. Others believed Corey refused as a protest against the witch hunt. His gruesome death—it is the only recorded pressing in American history—did shock some, but the witch hunt went on.

Devil Dumplings

One woman was accused of being a witch simply because she had concocted a way of baking apples inside dumplings. This was thought impossible without deviltry. She managed to avoid conviction and death by demonstrating her cooking techniques in court.

The Salem Witch Hunt peaked when the girls accused the wife of Sir William Phipps, the royal governor of Massachusetts. They claimed she had tormented them in spectral form. The governor refused to allow his wife to be labeled a witch and condemned spectral evidence, writing "the devil had taken upon him to assume the shape of several persons who were doubtless innocent and to my certain knowledge of good reputation." Without spectral evidence, convictions became nearly impossible, and the authorities drew back.

Relatives of the accused went further than the governor, claiming that the accusing girls were "distempered persons" viciously attacking innocents. Nearly as quickly as the hysteria had begun, it now turned on its instigators. The accusing girls were seen as heartlessly conniving for public attention at the expense of human lives. The horrific jail conditions that the accused had had to endure and the terrible punishments given the convicted witches were seen as the girls' fault. Those who had joined in the accusations also began to draw blame. It became apparent that they had often been motivated by petty village grudges and fear of appearing insufficiently anti-witch. The ministers who had loftily debated the forms of evidence and the possible guises of the Devil while innocents were abused and hanged were charged with failing to provide timely moral leadership when it was desperately needed. The authorities were seen as abusing their public trust by going along with the popular hysteria.

A wave of revulsion spread through the region. Within just a few years, many of those who had participated in the trials publicly apologized. The people of Salem Village were so ashamed of their popular repute that they changed the name of their town to Danvers. Witches were never again subjected to such persecution or executed in America. The Salem Witch Hunt ultimately helped secure the legal rights that had been so crudely abused. An inscription on the stone marking the grave of Rebecca Nurse, a victim of the hysteria who refused to confess to being a witch in return for being spared execution, neatly encapsulates the remorse and gratitude New Englanders came to feel for the hysteria's victims.

> *O Christian Martyr who for Truth could die*
> *When all about thee owned the hideous lie!*
> *The world, redeemed from superstition's sway,*
> *Is breathing freer for thy sake to-day.*
>
> Inscription upon the grave marker of Rebecca Nurse,
> hanged on July 19, 1692

Curiously, in the 1980s, some nature lovers made a striking discovery near Salem Village. Upon a large boulder, popularly called the Devil's Altar, they found faint, painted markings. Close examination revealed a pentagram and other mysterious drawings. A sample of the paint was analyzed at Harvard University, where it was determined that it dated to the late seventeenth century, the time of the Salem Witch Hunt. The pentagram is used in Satanic rituals and, while the accused witches of Salem were undoubtedly innocent of Devil worship, someone in the community wasn't.

Broomsticks

It was commonly believed that witches flew about their evil work on broomsticks. The first written account of such travel dates back to 1453, when a Frenchman claimed that he had flown upon a broom. The witch-broomstick connection may have come from the dances and ritual jumping done around a fire at witch sabbats. Witches sometimes mounted brooms to simulate riding horses. Ritual jumping was supposed to promote fertility in the witches and in the local crops. The higher the witch could jump, the more effective the ritual. If performed while holding a broom, the witches could vault high into the air and appeared to be trying to fly. Witches themselves commonly believed that after applying an ointment, they could fly using a broom. Anthropologists believe that the ointment contained powerful natural hallucinogens that produced visions of flight while also inducing giddy sensations.

Ordinary folks believed witches could fly and feared this aerial menace. Witch experts believed that if a witch heard a church bell while flying, her flight would be instantly halted, causing her to fall to her death upon the ground below. Consequently, church bells were rung on important occasions to ward off witches. Another anti-flying-witch tactic was similar to the measures taken during World War II to fend off parachute troops—sharpened stakes planted point up to impale landing witches. A less blood-thirsty defense against broom-flying witches was to lay a broom across the doorway; if a witch attempted to enter your house, he or she would grab up the free broom and fly off.

Curiously, some depictions of broomstick-flying witches show them holding the broom bristles forward. This is because straw, the material commonly used in brooms, draws up water through capillary action. This phenomenon was thought to be magnified through witchery so that the broom would draw upon the air itself, pulling the witch through the sky.

The Evil Eye

From Europe to India to South America, sorcerers and witches have been said to be able to blight an enemy with just a look. This is called the "evil eye." Anthropologists believe the legend arises from the way an image of a person is reflected in the pupil of someone staring at the person. Someone with eyes of mismatched color, an unusual color, oddly set, habitually squinted, or visibly injured was often thought to possess the evil eye. Possessors of these traits were often attacked as a precaution or forced to avert their gaze from others. As late as 1883, folklorists Thomas and Katharine Macquoid, in *About Yorkshire,* described a Yorkshireman who believed that he possessed the evil eye but had no control over its power. He spent his life with his eyes downcast, fearing to look at any man, woman, child, or animal, lest he curse them.

There are several ways to protect oneself from the evil eye. The oldest, thought to date back to ancient Egypt, is a necklace of blue beads. The hand gesture known as the "horned hand" or "Devil's horns" was a counticharm. It was formed by folding the two middle fingers and thumb while extending the small finger and the index finger. The gesture is thought to be an imitation of the crescent moon or an invocation of the power of the Horned God, mentioned earlier. An amulet in the form of the horned hand or the crescent moon could deflect the evil eye more constantly than the corresponding hand gesture. Making the sign of the cross and spitting are also countermeasures. Sometimes, a person feeling himself the object of the evil eye might go so far as to spit in the offender's eye.

The evil eye wasn't always fatal. One of the minor injuries inflicted by it was hiccoughing.

Witch Superstitions

- Painting your barn red will protect it and its contents from witches.

- Hanging a bit of mountain ash or rowan wood from the barn door and scattering primroses on the ground will keep witches out.

- Putting tar behind a cow's ears and at the base of her tail will keep witches from stealing her milk.

- Placing a silver coin in a butter churn will prevent witches from spoiling butter making.

- Braiding ribbon into a horse's tail or placing in the stable a stone with a hole through its center will prevent witches from stealing rides at night. These stones were called hag-stones, witch-stones, or fairy-stones. Such stones were sometimes placed upon bedposts to ward off nightmares.

- Salt was anathema to witches and could be used to frighten them away. Newborn children were washed in salt water to prevent witches from injuring them.

- Iron has long been a charm against evil spirits. The Egyptians placed iron objects in tombs to protect their dead. An iron knife or scissors hidden under a doormat will prevent witches from stepping over it into your home. An iron horseshoe over the doorway will also ward off witches. It will bring good luck as well, but only if hung to mimic the letter shape of a U—if it's turned the other way, the good luck will pour out (the U is thought to be an invocation of the power of the Horned God described earlier).

- According to old residents of the Isle of Wight, witches always recognize each other when they pass upon the roadway. They might not exchange a word, a nod, or even a glance, but after they pass by, each will give a soft, small laugh.

MODERN WITCHCRAFT

During the late nineteenth and early twentieth centuries, there was growing interest in supernatural folklore. The spread of spiritualism made it natural for someone attempting to contact the dead to wonder if earlier peoples had methods better than séances and Ouija boards. The disappearance of old folkways as the population moved into industrial towns also fueled interest in what was becoming rare, quaint lore. The new sciences of anthropology and archaeology offered up exciting new theories about foreign cultures and the past. The still newer field of psychology used mythology to explain the human mind. Freud's Oedipus complex is a familiar example. Jung made references to archetypes linked to magic from the human past. Even the settling of the American West and European empire building helped increase interest in the supernatural. Both brought Europeans into contact with previously unknown cultural practices and supernatural stories. When studied, the old ways sometimes seemed more appealing than mainstream beliefs. More and more intellectual and artistic people dabbled in reconstructions of what they called witchcraft.

By the beginning of the twentieth century, books such as Margaret Murray's *The Witch-Cult in Western Europe* and Robert Graves's *The White Goddess* had popularized the notion of a pre-Christian, nature-oriented, fertility religion centered on an ancient Earth Goddess. Scholars immediately poked some large holes in the historical accuracy of these works, but the books remained popular and inspired many to try to follow the faith they described.

WICCA

One such spiritual explorer was Gerald Gardner, a British plantation manager who collected ceremonial items and tales of ritual magic while working in Malaya. In 1954, in *Witchcraft Today,* Gardner claimed that, shortly after retiring to England in 1936, he had met a wealthy woman nicknamed Old Dorothy. She told him she was the leader of a secret coven of witches that had survived from ancient times. In September 1939, while the rest of Europe was lurching into World War II, Gardner became a witch. In his book, he described the activities of his coven as primarily naked fertility dances and feasting conducted in veneration of a goddess and her consort god.

In later writings and many lectures, Gardner elaborated on his coven story. His works became a guide for others anxious to join in a religion they believed dated back to prehistoric times. Gardner popularized the name *Wicca* for this new-old faith. The name was derived from the ancient Indo-European root word *weik,* meaning "wisdom." This root produced the Middle German word *wikken,* "to predict," which led to the Old English *wicca,* meaning "sorcerer" or "witch."

Both male and female Wiccans can be called witches. Wiccans don't like male witches being referred to as warlocks. They note that *warlock* is an old Scots word meaning "oath breaker" or "traitor."

Wiccans believe in an Old Religion that emphasizes the unity of the natural and spiritual world. They hold that all living things have spirits and spiritual power. They view the world as a complex inter-relationship among these spirits and their powers, which produce the natural cycle of life. These forces are personified in the Great Goddess and her male consort.

The Great Goddess has four aspects: maiden, mother, wise woman, and attendant to the dying and dead. Wiccans trace their Great Goddess to earlier Earth Goddess religions going as far back in time as 25,000 B.C. They claim their Goddess manifested herself to prehistoric peoples as a fertility goddess with her consort as the god of the hunt. Later, they say, the Goddess was worshiped as Diana, Isis, Brigid, and in many other guises.

The consort of the Great Goddess has fewer names. The most evoca-tive is Cerne the Hunter. He wore a crown of stag horns and followed a pack of supernatural hounds on a ferocious nighttime hunt. The con-sort has been linked to the Greek god Pan. As described earlier in this chapter, the consort is often referred to as the Goat God, and his wor-ship may have been in rivalry with worship of the Great Goddess. Wiccans believe the consort balances the Goddess, as an equal, opposing, yet complementary force.

During the 1960s, many people sought new forms of and approaches to spirituality. Wicca fit in well with this trend. It was a colorful and romantic religion, with interesting ceremonies that attempted to touch the cosmic in novel ways. Wiccan belief in magic corresponded with a growing interest in the occult. Its concerns with nature coincided with new ecological concerns. It pleased feminists, with its emphasis on sexual equality and what it described as femi-nine mystical forces (some Dianic Wiccan covens go so far as to ban male membership). Women were revered as living vehicles for the Earth Goddess, and the higher priesthood of Wicca is predominantly female. Wiccans were open to casual sexuality, unlike mainstream faiths. Wicca appealed to those who wished to live nontraditionally with the greatest of its injunctions, the Wiccan Rede, which decreed: Do what you wish, so long as you do no harm. Many varieties of Wicca coexist with a reasonable degree of harmony. Such lack of restriction and flexibility made for an attractive alternative to rigid cults and restrictive mainstream religions.

Wiccans wisely disassociated themselves from the unsavory aspects of earlier Earth Goddess religions, which had practiced both animal and human sacrifice. Many Wiccans are vegetarians. The old religions had little problem endorsing warfare. Wiccans, in keeping with 1960s antiwar politics, are pacifists or believe in violence solely in self-defense.

Wiccans also draw a clear distinction between their faith and Satanism. They argue that the Satanic witches described by witch hunters of the past were false representatives of their faith constructed from crazy stories extracted through torture from people who weren't witches, and that any who had actually followed Satanic practices weren't true witches. Wiccans claim that true witches, such as themselves, suffered persecution and murder because of these false confessions and false witches. Wiccans claim not to even have a concept of a Satan-like entity who preys upon human souls.

Despite Wiccan claims, however, there is little reason to believe that their faith is the heir of an unbroken chain of belief dating back thousands of years. Ronald Hutton, in his book *The Triumph of the Moon: A History of Modern Pagan Witchcraft*, closely examined Wiccan claims. Comparisons of Wiccan rituals with ancient European religions led him to conclude that Wicca couldn't be dated any earlier than 1900. He concluded that Wicca is an imperfectly reconstructed faith composed of what its adherents select as the best of ancient beliefs. Many Wiccans readily admit this, referring to the claims of ancient origins as a "foundation myth." These Wiccans see themselves as pioneering a new faith and believe that while ancient roots give a religion a degree of majesty, they aren't required, and Wiccans might be wise to avoid tainting their faith with false claims.

Even with questionable origins, Wicca is growing in adherents. Partly, this is because the faith has assumed political significance.

Feminists embraced it as a marvelous matriarchal faith that had been destroyed by the evil patriarchy. In the 1960s, the Women's International Terrorist Conspiracy from Hell (WITCH) extravagantly exaggerated the Wiccan origin story to claim that the entire populace of pre-Christian Europe had been witches led by "courageous, aggressive, independent, and sexually liberated women." The Christians had destroyed the witch covens as part of "a war against feminism." WITCH claimed that as many as nine million witches had been killed. These claims were ridiculous and offensively twisted Europe's varied religious history.

Wicca has also proven attractive to those active in the environmental protection movement. Wiccans proclaim themselves nature worshipers, revering the forces of the natural world. Environmental defenders have seized upon this as a tool to advance their agenda. It gives a religious veneer to their political-economic beliefs.

Both feminism and environmentalism enjoy favorable repute, and just as they have been eager to benefit from Wicca's religious status, Wiccans have been eager to soak up some of the popularity of the feminist and environmentalist movements. It's understandable that a minority religion would be eager to grab onto any set of coattails waved in its direction in order to increase its numbers. It may be working. According to one of the oldest incorporated Wiccan organizations in America, the Covenant of the Goddess in Berkeley, California, there are about fifty thousand Wiccans in the United States today.

Wicca's growth has provided some odd moments. On March 20, 1999, a group of forty Wiccans celebrated the vernal equinox with the Rite of Spring at Fort Hood, the largest Army base in the United States. All the celebrants were serving members of the U.S. Army. The chaplain at Fort Hood, a Christian, is required by military regulations to facilitate the Wiccans' ceremonies. The base has set aside an area where Wiccans have drawn a sacred circle for worship.

The success of Wicca has encouraged others to reconstruct pagan religions. Asatru, for example, is a revival of pre-Christian Norse beliefs. Versions of ancient Roman, Greek, and Egyptian beliefs are also being revived. These efforts are collectively referred to as Neopagan. Marginalized non-Christian faiths are also seeking to revitalize themselves. Some Pacific Island peoples, for example, are seeking to renew their mythologies, and Native Americans are trying to preserve their religions.

Wiccans have introduced an element of partisanship into how historical witches are viewed. They project their own good intentions backward onto witches of the past. Undoubtedly, there were witches who braved the stake, trying to ease the suffering of those around them using techniques they honestly believed would work. There may also have been genuine believers faithful to their religion who endured persecution. The terrible witch trials and the horrific punishments inflicted upon suspected witches engage the sympathies of any fair-minded, decent person. Nevertheless, we'd be foolish to believe that every single one of the witches who worshiped in the woods was a harmless follower of an Earth Goddess identical to the amiable Wiccans of today. An examination of traditional forms of witchcraft still vibrantly alive in less developed parts of the world today can suggest how some sorcery was once practiced in Europe.

The Blair Witch Profit

When the horror film *The Blair Witch Project* became a hit in 1999, Burkittsville, Maryland—the town where the story was supposed to have occurred—found itself the object of a great deal of unwanted attention. Tourists clogged the narrow roads of the town of two hundred. Vandals stole road signs and defaced tombstones. The most annoying visitors were those who didn't understand that the film was fictional and insisted on asking endless questions or went wandering in the woods, searching for the Blair Witch. So many phone calls were made to the town's office that Mayor Joyce Brown placed a curt message on the official answering machine: "This is the town office, Burkittsville, Maryland. If this is in regards to *The Blair Witch Project,* it is *fiction.*"

Eventually, the town's residents discovered that the tourists had lots of money to spend. Soon, handwritten signs offering WITCH STUFF appeared on telephone poles, and any number of locals would sell you copies of the stick dolls made infamous by the movie. There was even discussion of renovating the two-hundred-year-old farmhouse featured in the film and turning it into a museum or hotel.

WITCHCRAFT IN OTHER CULTURES

Belief in traditional sorcery remains strong throughout Asia, South America, and Africa. Many there blame any misfortune upon evil witchcraft. This gives power to those who claim to be able to inflict or prevent magical harm. The unscrupulous seek out ways to magically harm enemies, while both the unscrupulous and scrupulous seek out magical defenses. A contender for a lover might seek out a hex to injure a rival. Businesses sometimes employ a sorcerer to thwart the evil spells cast upon them by competitors. Sorcerers have even lent their magical powers to football teams, seeking to sharpen skills.

In November 1999, in western Tanzania, in several separate incidents, thirty-four women were killed by villagers who believed them to be witches. Red eyes are traditionally viewed as a sign of being a witch. Unfortunately, ordinary women who spend years standing over cooking fires made with cow dung develop red eyes as they age. The women killed were all older women who had suffered the eye affliction. A government official blamed superstition but also noted that the greedy, hoping to take an older female relative's property, will sometimes claim the woman is a witch so that frightened neighbors will kill her. The official noted that witch killings in the region had increased.

In 1999, a court in Addis Ababa, Ethiopia, sentenced the owner of a flour mill, a sorceress, and her friend to death for the murder of a seven-year-old girl. Abametcha Abageda, the mill owner, believed that evil spirits were sabotaging his mill. He consulted the sorceress, who confirmed his diagnosis. She told him he must sacrifice a small girl, then sprinkle her blood around his mill to cast out the spirits. The mill owner paid the sorceress to take care of the details. She paid four criminals $2.40 each to kidnap a girl. The sorceress, her friend, and the owner then ritually killed the child.

Police discovered the murder and the miller, the sorceress, and her friend received death sentences. The $2.40 kidnappers got life sentences.

Not all witch trouble ends in murder and prison. In December 1999, a high school in Santiago, Chile, expelled five young girls, accusing them of being witches who told fortunes and bathed in blood. A school official claimed that the girls were aggressive and that the school was fearful of what they might do in the pursuit of their interest. Paula Contreras, one of the accused witches, said, "If we had lived in the sixteenth century, we would be dead. They would have hanged us, drowned us, burned us at the stake." Instead of these dreadful fates, the girls weren't permitted to attend the prom.

In December 2000, two women were stripped and beaten by a mob in the middle of a busy Nigerian street. A man had told the mob that the women were witches who had stolen his penis through magical means. In Nigeria, it is commonly believed that witches can steal a man's sexual organs through incantation or even a handshake. By the time the police broke up the mob, the robbed man had disappeared. Police asked the mob if they had actually seen the theft. They said no but claimed that they had believed the man's charge because he "held tightly on to his trousers."

Sorcery can be employed in nonadversarial ways. A potion might ease rheumatism. A blessing might purge evil spirits from a home. A ritual may ensure that a deceased loved one makes it safely into a happy afterlife or encourage bountiful crops. Secret rites might ease childbirth or toothache. Good luck might be encouraged through charms. Many Africans wear small bags prepared by sorcerers slung from string around their necks that are filled with protective objects, such as bits of bone, bark, pebbles, and feathers. Similar packets are part of Voodoo, American Indian magic, and other beliefs.

More Moo Moo Magic

In 1999, following a hearing of Swaziland's National Council, Mgabhi Dlamini, speaker of the House of Assembly, was officially asked to resign his position after he was linked to an unusual crime that threatened King Mswati III, the absolute monarch of Swaziland. The king and other members of his royal family had just attended a traditional ceremony at a royal cattle pen when a man was spotted gathering dung from the pen. When confronted, the man led members of the king's entourage to a nearby waiting limousine. Inside, with more dung, was Speaker Dlamini.

Dlamini claimed that he had had a dream in which spirits warned him that the king was in danger; he had masterminded the dung theft to conduct secret magical rituals to make the king invincible to harm. The authorities didn't accept this explanation. While it is true that, in Swaziland, dung from the royal cattle is believed to have magical powers, they didn't believe Dlamini's professed patriotic motive. They believed he intended to use the dung in black magic, possibly directed against the king.

Slow to Change

The practice of witchcraft was illegal in Britain until 1951.

SATANISM

People have always been attracted to the negative side of whatever constitutes the predominant faith of the moment. In Europe, after the pagans were converted, this was Christianity. It identified Satan as the principal enemy of God. He was inferior in power but still capable of great evil. Godly people feared Satan, but ungodly people saw in him an alternative. Perhaps the Church was lying about God's being superior in power. The world was full of evil, and evildoers certainly seemed to prosper. Individuals hopeful of joining in this prosperity began to investigate Satan worship.

Satanic worship parodied formal Christian worship. Prayers were said backward, crosses displayed upside down, and ritual veneration of Christian symbols reversed to ritual abuse. The epitome of Satanic worship was the Black Mass, a point-by-point desecration of the Catholic Church's Mass. Satanists gathered in groups that mimicked the congregations of the Church and even had their own clerical hierarchy similar to the Church's. Sometimes Satanic priests were actually priests of the Church, who, like Cold War spies, hid inside the organization of the opposition. While not all witches were Satanists, there were certainly many

Satanists in the witch covens, and Satanists established their own covens that had no connection to any pre-Christian traditions.

Satanic cults went through periods of popularity and decline. One peak was in the twelfth century, another occurred during the reign of Louis XIV in France, and still another is occurring now.

Modern Satanism dates to the late nineteenth century. Indeed, the term *Satanism* was unknown until that time. Adherents of the occult attempted to meld black magic lore and anti-Christian sentiments with a hedonistic philosophy that embraced attitudes and activities that Christianity condemns. As with Wicca, Satanists trace their faith to ancient pagan beliefs. These roots are emphasized as proof that their belief is more than just an inversion of Christianity.

Satanic groups claim that their worship doesn't mean they revel in evil or seek to do evil. They claim they are an alternative to restrictive mainstream religions. Satan, or Lucifer, is identified as the Lord of Light, who proclaims as virtues pride, passion, pleasure, love of money, love of power, and the unrestrained enjoyment of earthly pleasures, such as sex. The virtues of the Christian Church are mocked as hypocritical and unnatural. Chastity, in particular, is condemned as a pointless denial of the self. Satanists also believe that instead of turning the other cheek, any injury should be avenged.

By the beginning of the twentieth century, Satanism had become popular with a small group of intellectuals seeking to reject bourgeois conventions. Aleister Crowley (1875–1947), who rejoiced in the nickname the Great Beast and had the reputation of being "the wickedest man in the world," was prominent among them. The son of a preacher, he was educated at Malvern, Tonbridge, and Trinity College, Cambridge. The effect of this education was that, immediately after receiving it, he began a life of drugs, orgies, and occult worship. He eventually established his own coven, with a single rule: "Do what thou wilt shall be the whole of the law." Crowley spent the rest of his life preaching his sexual theories and making scandalous headlines. Crowley's hedonism attracted similarly minded people around the world. California proved particularly fertile ground for Satanism, with one of the most influential and largest congregations, the Church of Satan, established in San Francisco in 1966.

Satanism attracts adherents for a variety of reasons. Some believe that Satan is the true god. Some join to reject Christianity. Some Satanists merely want to shock those around them. Heavy-metal rock-ers and teenagers living the "Goth" life often fit into this last group. Still other Satanists offer a more philosophical explanation for their faith, viewing Satan as a guiding life principle rather than an entity. The last of these Satanists aren't particularly anti-Christian or anti any other religion. They proclaim their beliefs to be: Be kind to those who deserve it, indulge all your lusts and passions, and, when injured, get revenge.

Not all Satanists are hedonistic philosophers. Some have embraced Satan as an excuse to commit terrible crimes. Richard Ramirez is just one of the more infamous killers to have indulged in Satanism. Such evil-minded, psychotic murderers often enjoy associating themselves with the foremost symbol of evil. Formal Satanists reject any such connections, countering that plenty of murderers have justified their killings using Christianity.

Exorcism

In many cultures, evil spirits have been thought capable of taking possession of a person's body. The possessed person is tormented by the spirits into doing irrational and destructive actions. Sorcerers perform a variety of rituals to exorcise these spirits. Herbal potions might force out demons. The smoke of special plants might do the same. Prayers, gestures and dances can be used to force the spirits out.

In the Christian tradition, Satan and his demons are believed to be able to possess hapless persons. In the New Testament, Christ casts out evil demons possessing a tormented man. The demons are transferred into a herd of swine, which madly plunge over a cliff. Christ shared with his apostles the power to cast out demons. While Protestants rejected exorcism during the Reformation, the Catholic Church continues to invoke this power, and there is an official ceremony of exorcism. The Church is reluctant to casually perform the ceremony, reserving it for situations where it feels the rite will be beneficial and not exploited for its sensationalism. In practice, this has meant that the Church most commonly performs exorcisms in cases of purported hauntings. Here the rite is more of a "spiritual intervention" wherein the spirit of a deceased person is confronted with his departed status and coaxed into moving on to his eternal reward, rather than a classic battle with a demon for a human soul.

The film *The Exorcist* is based on a real-life demonic possession of a young boy. The case, while bearing little similarity to the film, is well documented, and participants are still living who corroborate the terrifying events.

MODERN WITCH HYSTERIA

In the 1980s, concern over legitimate child abuse became twisted into hysteria over highly improbable Satanic child abuse. Poorly trained social workers, at the behest of headline-hungry law enforcement officials, coerced children into claiming that their caregivers, teachers, and parents were using the children in bizarre black magic sex rituals, which sometimes included human sacrifice. Satanic hysteria extended to adults. Psychiatrists, using hypnotism, "recovered" repressed memories of Satanic child abuse in adults. The coerced and the recovered memories were used to dispatch the supposed abusers off to prison.

The parallels between this evidence and the spectral evidence used in the Salem witch trials are surprising. Both are subjective and verified only by the witness. In both, the bizarre behavior the witness presents is used as proof that his or her testimony is true. Also in both, anyone challenging the evidence is accused of showing a heartless lack of sympathy for the witness and is subjected to social stigma and suspicion. Even worse, legitimate cases of child abuse were being undermined by the absurd false cases.

The hysteria subsided a bit when the evidence was examined by cooler heads. It was shown that the social workers were often pressuring the children to invent stories. Repressed-memory evidence lost its power under the critical gaze of more scientifically minded psychiatrists who pointed out its flaws. The largest flaw, as victims of terrible events such as war or criminal attack can certify, is that traumatic memories aren't easily forgotten. Indeed, one of the problems these victims must deal with is the inability to forget.

While individuals and small groups claiming Satanic association have committed fiendish crimes and would commit larger crimes if they could, there is little reason to believe that there are grand Satanic criminal conspiracies. Extensive investigation by numerous law enforcement agencies has failed to expose a single one.

Why a Duck?

There have been legal challenges to the repressed memory theory. Patricia Burgus, 42, won $10.6 million in a lawsuit against a psychiatrist and a hospital. She claimed that, when she went to Dr. Bennett Braun in the late 1980s to be treated for depression, he used drugs and repressed memory therapy to persuade her that she had 300 separate personalities. Among these were a cannibal who turned friends into meatloaf, a child molester, and the high priestess of a Satanic cult. After spending two years in a mental hospital, Burgus finally rejected the psychiatrist's diagnosis. She told the Associated Press, "I began to add a few things up and realized there was no way I could come from a little town in Iowa, be eating 2,000 people a year, and nobody said anything about it."

Dr. Braun, who was once considered a leading authority on multiple personality disorders, accepted a two-year suspension and five years' probation in a settlement with the Illinois Department of Professional Regulation.

In an even stranger case, in 1997, Nadean Cool won $2.4 million from her psychotherapist, Dr. Kenneth Olson. He had used repressed memory therapy to convince her that she had 120 personalities, including Satan and a duck. Even more outrageously, Olson had billed Cool's insurance company for "group" therapy because of her many personalities.

6

GHOSTS

She was like the new moon seen through the gathering mist—like a watery beam of feeble light, when the moon rushes sudden from between two clouds, and the midnight shower is on the heath.—Clouds, the robe of ghosts,—rolled their gathered forms on the wind.

James Macpherson (1736–1796), *Ossian,*
an epic poem inspired by old Gaelic poems
gathered in the Highlands

What happens to us when we die? Religion and philosophy offer many answers that are debated every day in churches, universities, coffeehouses, and Woody Allen movies. Meanwhile, folklore and superstition offer one disturbing possibility that literally "haunts" the common consciousness: That some of us, some of the time, under some circumstances, don't entirely leave this world behind. On these occasions, our spirits, as ghosts, linger on earth annoying or comforting the living.

Ghosts are known in all cultures and every era. As we've seen, Halloween evolved from a festival dedicated to the dead. Quite reasonably, ghosts, the spirits of the dead, remain at the center of the holiday. We might call them the "ghosts" of honor.

EARLY GHOST TALES

The dead continue with us in memory's eye and sometimes in our dreams. Why shouldn't their spirits linger if they could? Early cultures commonly explained the workings of nature in terms of spirits. This is called animism. For the believer in animism, the spirit of the bear might be seen as strong and fearsome, the spirit of the rain as soothing and forgiving, and the spirit of fire as cheerful and comforting but dangerously greedy for fuel. If everything in nature has a spirit, surely human beings do, too; when death comes, maybe their spirits are freed from ordinary limitations. Perhaps they can touch the living in ways similar to the other spirits. Good fortune might be a result of their help. Bad fortune, a common state given the dangers, uncertainties, and accidents of life, might be the result of the enmity of the dead. Wasn't it reasonable to suspect that the dead might grow envious of the pleasures of life that they could no longer share? And there was also the character of the dead to consider. Someone evil in life would probably remain evil in death, while someone victimized in life might seek revenge from the grave. As with any danger, once perceived, the prudent take steps to avoid it.

To placate the dead, early peoples offered tributes of flowers, food, and other goods that were buried with the dead or sacrificed in funeral rites. Over time, both tributes and the ceremonies of burial became more elaborate. The Egyptians, probably the most death-oriented culture, carefully embalmed the body, then interred it with sumptuous property. Their kings were shelved away inside gigantic pyramids that will mark their graves for tens of thousands of years to come. In China, one emperor had an army of thousands of life-sized terra-cotta soldiers and bureaucrats buried with him. Norsemen would bury warships with their dead, or in rites that would later become Hollywood favorites, they would load a warship with the body and tribute, and then, at sunset, light the ship ablaze and send it sailing out to sea.

The most dramatic of tributes to the dead were human sacrifices. Many cultures indulged in this horrid practice, from Scandinavian tribesmen who murdered young women to bury with dead chieftains to nineteenth-century India, where women were routinely coerced into throwing themselves upon their dead husbands' funeral pyres to demonstrate their overwhelming love for husbands they more often than not hadn't even chosen. But despite these gestures, the dead don't always lie quiet in the graves.

One of the earliest recorded ghost tales was written by Pliny the Younger (62–113), a Roman writer and politician. He was the nephew and adopted son of the Roman encyclopedist and scientist Pliny the Elder, who was killed while studying the eruption of Mount Vesuvius in A.D. 79. In a letter to his patron, Lucias Sura, the younger Pliny wrote of a ghost story he had heard. His account has many of what have become classic elements of the ghost tale. He wrote that in the

city of Athens, a villa had acquired a reputation for being haunted by the ghost of a ragged, dirty old man burdened with clanking chains. He appeared at night, terrifying the villa's residents by groaning piteously and rattling his chains, as if begging to be released. Eventually, no one would live in the house. When the philosopher Athenodorus (circa 74 B.C.–A.D. 8) found himself looking for a cheap place to live, he thus secured the haunted villa for a very low rent.

It was Athenodorus's habit to write late into the evening. He was at his work on his first night in the villa when the ghost of the old man made his usual, noisy appearance. The philosopher, an imperturbable fellow, impatiently waved the ghost away, indicating that he had work to do and didn't want to be bothered. At this, the ghost grew angry and increased his groaning and rattling. He seemed to want the philosopher to follow him. Finally, spurred by curiosity, Athenodorus rose, took up a lamp, and beckoned to the ghost to lead the way. The ghost conducted him through the house and out to a garden, where he stopped at some shrubbery and abruptly disappeared. Athenodorus marked the location then returned to his work and, later, his bed.

When Athenodorus awoke the next day, he went to the local authorities to tell them what had happened. He suggested that the marked spot should be investigated. They took shovels and dug where he indicated. A human skeleton bound in rusty old chains was just beneath the surface. Someone had murdered a man after keeping him prisoner for an unknown time. The authorities gave the bones a proper burial, then arranged for the villa to be ritually cleansed. Afterward, the ghost never reappeared, and Athenodorus's rent probably went up.

Boo!

The custom of shouting *"Boo!"* to scare the unwary dates to early medieval times. There was a ferocious Gothic captain, reputed to be the son of Odin, named Bo (or Boh, in old Runic). Members of his army were very proud of their captain's fierce reputation and, when charging into battle, yelled his name to

frighten their enemies. Over time, others took up the call, alter-
ing it to "Boo."

Alternative etymologies trace *boo* to the Greek *boa-ein* and
the Latin *bo-are,* both meaning "to cry."

GHOSTS IN CHRISTIAN TIMES

When Christianity became dominant in Europe, it brought a different view of the afterlife. It became both a far more pleasant and a far
more horrid place. The virtuous were promised a wonderful, eternal
reward in Heaven. The sinful were threatened with damnation to Hell,
where demons would inventively torture them forever. The dead were
not supposed to want to leave Heaven nor be able to leave Hell to
become earthly ghosts. Ghosts came to be viewed as souls who had
not been properly dispatched into the afterlife, either through mishan-
dling, demonic influences, the suddenness of the death, or refusal to
accept death. While demonic influences are now dismissed, the other
causes are still presumed by parapsychologists to create ghosts.

TYPES OF GHOSTS

Ghosts can be given some classification by the manner in which they
became ghosts.

THE TOO-SUDDEN DEAD

The most common of the "ghost-creating" situations is a sudden,
violent death. It is theorized that such a death leaves the deceased
bitter at being cheated of a full life, angry at the injuries that caused
death, or unaware that death has occurred because of its quickness.
Battlefields are a classic producer of such ghosts. Murders, such as
the supposed killing of the two young princes by Richard III in the
Tower of London, and fatal accidents, such as train or auto wrecks,
are similar producers of ghostly legends.

THE DEAD UNREADY TO GO

Another situation producing ghosts occurs when someone has an
overly strong connection with the world of the living. Lovers kept
apart sometimes become ghosts because of the connection of their

thwarted romance. Many rivers, lakes, and waterfalls in America are associated with legends of unhappy love affairs between Native American couples from warring tribes on either side of the waters. Kept apart by their families, much like Romeo and Juliet, one or both tried to swim across the water to be with their beloved and drowned in the attempt. Their spirits, still seeking each other, are said to haunt their watery graves and to sometimes be visible in the mists that form over the waters.

THE PUNISHED DEAD

Sometimes a spirit is thought to be punished by being forced to continue as a ghost, barred from the comforts of the afterlife. Jacob Marley's ghost in Charles Dickens's *A Christmas Carol* is a good fictional example of a spirit punished for a bad life with an unending half death as a wandering ghost.

The Green Lady—A Punished Spirit Released

Banffshire, Scotland, is said to have been host to a ghost who proved a "lifesaver" to those she haunted. Many years ago, the wife of the local laird died. One evening six months later, a plowman in the employ of the laird was out riding. He came upon a small stream. A woman dressed in green with her face hidden by a green hood stood by the water. The plowman bid her a polite hello, and the woman asked him for a ride over the stream. The plowman obliged. After dismounting on the other side, the woman thanked him and showed him her face. A sudden chill covered the plowman in a cold sweat. The woman was the laird's dead wife. She told the man that he would see her again. He did. The woman, now called the Green Lady for her clothing, began making regular appearances at her former home.

The Green Lady expressed no interest in her husband, the laird, but did seem greatly concerned with the management of the household. While the laird never saw her, the servants saw her over and over again. She'd ask them about their tasks and about their cares and became so familiar to them that they accepted her as part of the household. She was clearly unhappy, in a ghostly way, but despite this kept up a cheerful front. She even laughed on occasion and would perform minor pranks.

After about a year of this friendly haunting, the Green Lady abruptly appeared to the family nurse in her bedchamber. The ghost insistently warned the nurse that two of the laird's children were in danger. The pair were visiting the seaside and the nurse rushed there, finding them clutching desperately at a rock in the roaring surf, about to be swept away. The children were rescued and returned home with the nurse.

At home, the nurse found the Green Lady in her room sitting by the fireplace. She told the nurse that now that she had done a good deed she would be leaving. She said that she had been forced to remain on earth because of a secret crime. Years earlier, she had heard someone in the laird's orchards. With a servant, she had confronted a wandering peddler there. He had been stealing fruit. At the Green Lady's bidding, the servant struggled with the peddler and killed him. The Green Lady had been about to summon her husband when she saw that the peddler's satchel held a bundle of beautiful green silk. A little more investigation also discovered a purse filled with gold coins. The Green Lady took the money and the silk, telling the servant to secretly bury the corpse. She gave him some of the gold to assure his silence. The green silk had been used to make a dress that, in time, became the garment that the woman was buried in.

The Green Lady had been cursed by the peddler's spirit to remain a ghost until she could make amends. She told the nurse where to find the remaining gold and the peddler's body, then disappeared, never to be seen again. The money and corpse were found where the Green Lady had said. The coins were used to pay for a proper burial for the peddler.

The above classified ghosts by causes. The following classifies them by their actions. These groupings often overlap.

WARNING SPIRITS

Ghosts often seek to warn the living of some specific danger. In legend, disasters such as train wrecks, ship sinkings, and air crashes are often presaged by a warning spirit. Marley's ghost in *A Christmas*

Carol is a warning spirit for a mortal danger. He seeks the reformation of his old business partner, Ebenezer Scrooge. He wants Scrooge to see that he is failing to do good in the world, and that after death, like Marley, he will regret that he can no longer aid the suffering.

The banshee of Ireland and Scotland is a warning spirit. The word is derived from *Bann-sidh,* meaning "woman of the mounds" or "Fairy woman." She appears as an ancient crone or, more attractively, as a pretty girl who wears a red petticoat or a green gown under an enveloping gray, hooded cloak. She approaches the house of a doomed person and wails in a keening, unearthly voice to warn of a coming death. Hearing her means there will be a death in the family; seeing her means you will die. Certain families, such as the O'Brians, the O'Rourkes, the O'Malleys, and the O'Donnals, are noted for having been warned of family deaths by a banshee for generations.

The people of Wales have their own version of the banshee. She was called the *gwrach-y-rhibyn,* meaning "hag of the dribble." She was a morose crone with a screechy voice who made an appearance when death was about to visit a family. Anthropologists trace both spirits to Celtic beliefs.

Animal apparitions have also marked approaching tragedy. Commonly, hounds have been reported to bay after or just before a death. One explanation offered by spiritualists is that a dog's subtle senses can detect the presence of a ghost returning for one last visit home. When predicting death, perhaps the hounds can detect Death approaching and, just as they might for the mailman, they seek to warn their family of a stranger.

The Hapsburg dynasty, masters of the Austro-Hungarian Empire, were warned of danger by a flock of large white birds. They were said to have appeared in 1889, circling and screeching, before Crown Prince Rudolf and his mistress were found dead, mysterious suicides, at Mayerling. The ominous birds were also said to have appeared before the Archduke Franz Ferdinand was murdered in Sarajevo in 1914. That killing touched off the killing of millions during World War I.

COMFORTING AND BENEFICENT SPIRITS

While most ghostly phenomena are frightening, some are quite the opposite. Sometimes ghosts of loved ones will appear to inform those left behind that the departed are happy in their new state. During moments of danger, ghosts sometimes appear to the endangered to reassure them that they will survive. My father-in-law, Harry Powers, had one such encounter while serving with the U.S. Army in France during World War II. During a sticky moment under fire, he was worried that he would acquit himself well and whether he might be killed or wounded. His worried thoughts were suddenly interrupted by the voice of his long-dead brother, who said, "You'll be all right, Harry." The words helped him overcome his fears and carry on. He survived the war with a feeling that someone had been watching out for him.

Some spirits are more materially helpful. On rare occasions, ghosts have been known to point out hidden treasure or to help loved ones find important missing documents. The heiress of an English aristocratic family was unable to find an important paper needed to settle the estate. She decided the paper had been destroyed and had resigned herself to a long, costly legal process to establish her claims when, on a quiet evening, the ghost of a great uncle killed during World War I appeared and held up a paper. It was the missing document. The heiress renewed her search and immediately found the desired paper.

SUPPLICANT SPIRITS

The ghost in the tale of Athenodorus wanted a service—in his case a decent burial—from the living. Ghosts often want the living to take some action that they no longer can perform themselves. Decent burial is a common demand, but other demands can include vengeance against living enemies, justice for an unrighted wrong, the completion of a task that the deceased could not finish, respect for a concern important to the spirit, or action to aid a cause or person important to the ghost.

MENACING GHOSTS

Ghosts that harm the living are rare, but not unknown. In 1777, in England, the Reverend James Crawford and his sister-in-law Miss Hannah Wilson encountered such a spirit while out riding. Wilson sat behind Crawford on his horse. They came upon a small river that Crawford was certain he could safely walk the horse across. Wilson protested that the water was too deep and the current too strong. Crawford answered by pointing to another rider and horse that had entered the stream just ahead of them and were sedately ambling across. Crawford called to the rider, asking if there was any danger. The rider turned to them and they saw a terrifying sight. The rider's face was as white as a fish's belly, his hair hung limp and damp like waterweeds, and his eyes glowed with evil menace. He beckoned them to follow but Wilson, quite reasonably, began screaming. Crawford swung his mount about, and they galloped away from the river as quickly as they could.

When Crawford and Wilson told others of their encounter, they learned that a local legend described the rider. According to this tale, he would make an appearance just before someone was to drown in the river. Crawford was frightened but felt compelled by his religious office to reject such un-Christian superstition. He maintained that he didn't believe in spirits.

On September 27, 1777, Crawford placed his person in consequence of his beliefs. He rode his horse out into the river. Before he could reach the other side, he was swept into the water and drowned.

CRISIS APPARITIONS

Another kind of ghost, often described in folklore, is the crisis apparition. These ghostly manifestations often involve the spirit of a suddenly killed spouse or relative who makes an appearance seemingly to bid good-bye to distant relatives. There are numerous stories of soldiers killed on remote battlefields making such spectral visits to the home front.

One famous crisis apparition story begins on the night of December 29, 1972. Eastern Airlines Flight 401 from New York was approaching the Miami airport. The landing gear of the new Lockheed L-1011 wasn't operating correctly, and its crew members were so distracted by their efforts to fix them that they didn't notice they were flying lower and lower. Abruptly, their distraction ended when they flew straight into the Everglades. One hundred and one passengers and crew died. Fortunately, there were seventy survivors. In the days following the accident, it began to be rumored that something else had survived the crash. Flight crews on Eastern Airlines flights reported that they were seeing the ghosts of Captain Bob Loft, Flight 401's pilot, and Don Repo, the flight engineer. Many of the witnesses were people who knew the men. One flight engineer reported seeing Repo at his seat on the flight deck. He said Repo told him he had already done the preflight check, then disappeared. A flight captain and two attendants saw Captain Loft in the first-class section of their aircraft just before takeoff from New York. They claimed to have spoken with him before he vanished. In this case, the flight was canceled.

Writer John G. Fuller, after hearing these and other stories about Flight 401, wrote a book titled *The Ghost of Flight 401*. It was successful and was made into an eerie TV movie. Fuller suggested that the supposed practice by airline companies of reusing parts salvaged from crashed aircraft may have caused the ghosts to haunt airliners that received these parts. Airlines deny the practice.

The sightings of the Flight 401 crew ended after an exorcism was held on the airliner that had reported the most visitations.

CELEBRITY GHOSTS

To the above ghost classifications, we can add the category of "celebrity ghost." This is the ghost of some famous or infamous dead person whose sole purpose for visiting the living seems to be to perpetuate his or her celebrity—a sort of personal appearance or "photo op" without photography. Anne Boleyn is a good example. Boleyn was King Henry VIII's second wife. He had defied the Pope and created the Church of England so he could divorce his first wife to marry Boleyn. She was quite beautiful, and Henry hoped she would give him a male heir. She gave him a daughter, who would reign famously as Elizabeth I, but Henry wasn't satisfied. He wanted to try a new wife, so he arranged for Boleyn to be convicted on charges of incest and adultery. Since these crimes were committed against the king, they required execution. This would allow Henry to marry again without the embarrassment of a second divorce.

In 1536, Boleyn, just thirty years old, was taken from the Tower of London and conducted to the Tower Green, where she knelt, modestly covering her ankles with her long skirt. An expert executioner, imported from France for his skill with the sword, quickly stepped forward and, with a single sweep of his blade, decapitated the queen. Boleyn's body was placed upon a litter with her severed head tucked under one arm and carried off for a quiet burial. She didn't lie quietly in her grave. Soon, she was spotted in spectral form.

Over the centuries, Anne Boleyn became a regular nighttime wanderer through the corridors of the Tower of London. Sometimes she is reported to walk around carrying her head; sometimes it rests more decorously upon her shoulders. But Boleyn's visits are not limited to the Tower; she has also been reported standing on the bridge over the River Eden at Hever in Kent, near one of her childhood homes. She makes more dramatic visits to another childhood home, Blickling Hall in Norfolk. On the anniversary of her beheading, an elaborate spectral coach pulls up near the hall. Inside, Boleyn sits with her head rocking in her lap. The driver of the coach matches Boleyn's appearance; he, too, is headless.

POLTERGEISTS

One of the most common of ghostly phenomena is the poltergeist. Some spirits seem to have nothing better to do than to torment the living with crude and sometimes dangerous practical jokes. They knock books from shelves, upset milk pitchers, rearrange furniture, rattle the kitchen pots, turn lights on and off, and perform other annoyances. These spirits are called poltergeists, a German word meaning "noisy spirits."

The earliest recorded poltergeist was, aptly, a German ghost. In the ninth century, a German farmer living near Bingen was plagued by a noisy spirit that loudly accused him of sleeping with the daughter of one of his workmen. Wherever the farmer went, the poltergeist followed him, throwing stones, shaking the walls, and setting fires. The hapless farmer was forced to become a recluse when his neighbors naturally grew reluctant to visit him or host his visits.

All the noisy pranks inflicted on the German farmer are typical of later accounts of poltergeists. Also typical was the presence of a young person, often an adolescent girl, in the vicinity of the poltergeist activity. Spiritualists suggest that young people have some sort of special psychic energy that sustains the poltergeist. Skeptics suspect that the stunts are performed surreptitiously by the youths themselves.

In the United States, one poltergeist is said to have committed murder. Between 1817 and 1821, the modest plantation of John Bell in Robertson County, Tennessee, was victimized by a poltergeist. At first, what Bell called the "Family Problem" was just odd noises and knockings. Then Bell saw a strange animal that resembled a large dog by his home. He shot at it, with no effect. He then saw an odd bird, which he also shot at. Again, his bullet seemed to have no effect. After these encounters, the poltergeist grew more and more active. The spirit rapped on the walls of the house. The family heard the sounds of ferocious dogfights but found no sign of dogs. The spirit pelted the family with sticks and stones. The eight Bell children were pinched and slapped by invisible hands. At night, their blankets would be snatched off them. Bell's only daughter Betsy, twelve, became the center of the peculiar attacks. She complained of stomach pains then vomited up pins and needles. When she visited a neighbor, the poltergeist followed her. Eventually, John Bell sought out the help of James Johnson, a neighbor and lay preacher.

Johnson, with a committee of locals, investigated. They could find no signs of a hoax. They decided that the family was being plagued by a witch but were unable to suggest a means to drive the witch away. Curious neighbors dropped by the plantation to witness the activity and to make suggestions. These didn't work either, and the witch seemed to grow more powerful with the more attention it got. It began to whisper to the Bell family. Its voice was at first faint, sounding like soft whistling. This grew in volume until the witch was screaming at the Bells. Some thought young Betsy might be using some form of ventriloquism to create the voice, but even when her mouth was tightly covered, the voice continued to speak. It also began to answer questions addressed to it.

The first thing the Bells sought to discover was the witch's identity. It said, "I am a spirit from everywhere, Heaven, Hell, and the Earth. I'm in the air, in houses, anyplace at any time. I've been created millions of years. That is all I will tell you."

Despite the witch's proclamation of silence, it soon grew chatty and answered more questions. It changed its self-identification, claiming to be the ghost of a person buried in the woods nearby. It said that its grave had been disturbed and one of its teeth stolen. It further said the missing tooth was under the Bell house and that it was looking for the tooth. The Bells searched and dug but could find no tooth. After they gave up, the witch laughingly told them that there was no missing tooth to find. The story had been a trick to set them to fruitless labor.

After the tooth prank, the witch told the Bells that it was the ghost of an early settler who had hidden a fortune near the house before dying. The Bell family renewed their digging but again found nothing. At this, the witch laughed, telling them the treasure story was another trick.

The Bells and their visitors continued to question the spirit. Now it claimed, "I am nothing more nor less than old Kate Batts, witch." This was a strange assertion, as Kate Batts, another Bell neighbor, was alive. She was known to hate John Bell, but she was also known for endlessly quoting the Bible, hardly typical for an evil witch. While some believed Batts was to blame, most thought the witch was just trying to make trouble; it seemed to enjoy spreading malicious gossip. Batts wasn't blamed by the Bells for the poltergeist.

While the witch never made its identity known, it made its feelings plain. It hated John Bell, threatening over and over to destroy him. Bell bore the threats poorly. His health failed. On the morning of December 19, 1820, he fell into a coma. When the doctor arrived, the witch proclaimed that it had substituted poison for Bell's tonic. "It's useless for you to try to revive Old Jack," it gloated. "I've got him this time. He'll never get up from that bed again." Bell did die, and it was discovered that his medicine had been tampered with. During Bell's funeral, the witch could be heard cackling and singing with delight.

After John Bell's death, the witch seemed to lose interest in his family. A few months later, a burst of smoke filled the Bell's living room and the witch declared, "I am going and will be gone for seven years. Good-bye to all!" The witch did vanish for seven years. When it returned, many of the family members, including Betsy, had moved away. The witch snatched bedclothes and made odd noises but it didn't speak; in just two weeks, it left again. One of Bell's sons said he had heard the witch say it would return in 107 years. In 1934, when it was due to reappear, the descendants of the Bell family reported no visitation.

The story of the Bell witch remained just a local legend until the 1840s, when Richard Williams Bell, John's son, who had been six years old during the odd happenings, wrote an account of them. It wasn't meant for publication, but in 1891, Williams's son passed it on to a professional writer, who rewrote and published the account. Dr. Charles Bailey Bell, a great-grandson of John, wrote his own version of the story in 1934. He claimed to have gotten his information directly from Betsy Bell, who lived to eighty-three. The passage of time may have caused the story to be embellished, but it contains many of the classic poltergeist phenomena. Skeptics have suggested that the whole incident was an elaborate ruse to disguise the murder of John Bell. If so, it succeeded, for no one was ever charged with Bell's murder.

One element of the Bell witch legend adds a unique historical twist. According to the story, one day, while driving a wagon to the Bell plantation, a family friend had an odd experience. The wagon suddenly stopped and, despite the straining of its team of horses, it wouldn't budge. The friend exclaimed that a witch must be holding the wagon to the spot. In reply, a voice from the thin air said, "Let the wagon move." With this, the wagon was just as suddenly free to move. The act, while mysterious, wasn't unique. Rooting a wagon to a spot is a common spirit trick in folklore. What was unique was the victim of the act. The family friend was Andrew Jackson, the hero of the Battle of New Orleans, who would later be U.S. president from 1829 to 1837. Tellers of the Bell story claim that he left the Bell cabin halfway through the night of his visit, saying, "I would rather face the whole of the British Army than deal with the wrath of Bell witch."

GHOSTBUSTING TRADITIONS

Ghosts can be annoying. They keep you up at night. They scare your pets. They make your overnight guests flee, screaming. In cases like this, in the words of the famous movie ad campaign, "Who ya gonna call?" For many, it's a Catholic priest to bless the haunted location and send the spirit away through the rite of exorcism.

Mediums also intervene to send ghosts on to the next world. They commonly hold a séance, during which the ghost is advised to move on. Some ghosts are said to be unaware of their death and need to be informed. Others, linked to the Earth by duties or obsessive interests, must be persuaded that they no longer need be concerned with this world.

Funeral rituals commonly incorporate elements meant to keep the dead from returning to plague the living. Nearly every culture has such customs, for prevention is always a prudent way to handle spirit infestation.

Death is a shadowy, unsettled half existence for the Dogon of West Africa. The spirits of the dead are said to be reluctant to leave this world; they wish to remain in their former villages with their still-living relatives. These hauntings aren't fortunate. The dead meddle in the affairs of the living and can bring disease and drought. Dogon funeral rites are meant to encourage the dead to accept death.

At these rites, the young men of the tribe dance in masks representing various parts of life the dead may miss. One might be an animal the dead had owned. Another might be a person the dead had loved. The dance gives the dead a chance to say good-bye to these parts of his old life. It is accompanied by chanting that asks the dead to stay away.

If a dead person is suspected of returning from the grave, his corpse may be given tribute to appease it. If this fails, the tribe may attack the corpse and mutilate it.

The people of the West Indies also believe that the dead return, seeking the things they enjoyed in life. Widows wear red underwear during the time they mourn because ghosts are supposedly repelled by that color.

Many cultures try to confuse the dead as they are taken to the grave so that they can't find the path home. The bearers of the body might take long, circuitous routes to the cemetery. Balinese mourners carry the dead to their funeral pyre in a tower borne upon the mourners' shoulders. Periodically, the bearers stop to bounce and shake the tower to confuse the dead by making them dizzy.

Commonly, the body doesn't even exit through a door. Instead, the bearers take it out through a window. Fijians cut a hole through a wall. The Inuit peoples of the Arctic used to pass the body up through the smoke hole in the top of their igloos.

Mourners returning from the grave commonly try to confuse the dead who might follow them. In Siberia, a century ago, the funeral party would disguise themselves as animals and make bestial noises as they took a jumbled route home. Some link the custom of wearing black clothing at a funeral to such disguises. Others have suggested that dark clothing was meant to show that life wasn't pleasant, and the dead shouldn't envy the living.

Physical restraints were sometimes used to keep the dead in their graves. In Australia, in India, and among the Inuit, corpses often had their toes or thumbs tied together to make it difficult for them to clamber out of the grave. Troublesome spirits were sometimes put to rest by digging up the body and jumbling its bones. The Kwearriburra of Australia carried corpse mutilation to an extreme. They severed the head from the corpse, buried the body, then burned the head atop the grave. Any charred remnant was smashed to flinders. If the ghost of the buried person rose, it would find itself headless.

SPIRITUALISM

The desire to communicate with departed loved ones is powerful. Witchcraft was the predominant means of making contact until it began to fade away at the end of the eighteenth century. A more

rational age sought more "scientific" forms of necromancy. Salt penta-
grams and demonic invocation were replaced by crystal gazing, card
reading, and other rituals with few or no religious associations. By the
beginning of the nineteenth century, necromancy had so far removed
itself from black magic that even religious people felt few qualms about
attempts to speak with the dead. Some even saw verification of Christian beliefs in the messages transmitted from beyond the grave. This
new, cleaner form of necromancy is called spiritualism.

Spiritualists speak to the dead using séances, wherein a circle of
sympathetic people under the direction of a psychically talented "spirit
medium" join together to project an invitation to the dead to visit.
The medium, assisted by the mental energy of the gathering, goes into
a trance within which he or she contacts a friendly, helpful "spirit
guide." The guide, often the spirit of an American Indian, is a
deceased person who helps the medium reach the targeted spirit. The
séance originated in a peculiar set of events in upstate New York in
the middle of the nineteenth century.

In 1848, in the small village of Hydesville, New York, there was a
simple house that had served several families as cheap lodgings. At
this time, John D. Fox, a farmer and blacksmith, lived in it with his
family. Fox was a glum man who had been a heavy drinker before
discovering the sobering effects of Methodism. While religion had
freed him from drink, it hadn't improved his personality. His wife
was a poorly educated woman who had stayed with her husband
through the worst of his drunkenness and the worst of his sobriety.
Their daughters Maggie, fifteen, and Kate, eleven, lived with them.
Two older Fox children, David and Leah, had left home to live on
their own. In March 1848, the dreary cold of late winter was interrupted by strange happenings in the Fox household.

The unusual events began with unexplained noises that couldn't
be traced to any thing or person. The family was frightened and grew
more fearful as the noises continued. Maggie and Kate nicknamed the
maker of the noises Mr. Splitfoot. One night, after a long bout of odd
sounds, the girls begged their parents to let them sleep in the parents'
bedroom. Their parents agreed but were of little comfort. The noises
didn't stop. Finally, Kate snapped her fingers, demanding, "Mr. Splitfoot, do as I do." She then clapped her hands and waited expectantly.
Amazingly, the sound of a knock replied. Maggie clapped four times
and the invisible visitor made four knocking sounds. The girls con-

tinued asking the thin air questions, which were answered with knockings. When they asked how old one of the girls was, the unseen noisemaker tapped out the correct number of knocks. The Fox family called their neighbors to witness the knocking and to themselves ask questions. The invisible visitor responded to them. Soon, people from miles around were calling on the Foxes to ask questions. The spirit answered and its story emerged.

The Hydesville spirit claimed to be the ghost of a man murdered by an earlier resident of the house in a robbery. The ghost said his body had been buried in the house's cellar. Reportedly, digging in the cellar produced human bones and teeth. Others claimed this was untrue. The most vocal of these was John C. Bell, the man the ghost blamed for the murder. Bell, who had moved out of town, quickly returned when he heard about the ghostly accusations. The spirit refused to communicate with him, and Bell insisted the Foxes had made up the entire story. Several of his friends signed a petition identifying him as an upright man. Lucretia Pulver, who had worked as a maid for the Bell family when they lived in the house in 1848, refused to sign. She said that in 1844 a peddler had visited, saying he would return. He never did when she was in the house, but Pulver claimed she saw Bell's wife mending clothing that matched the peddler's outfit. Pulver also claimed she had seen disturbed soil in the cellar. She suggested that this might have been a hastily dug grave.

Surprisingly, when the rapping ghost was asked for details of his murder, he gave few. He said his initials were C. R., that he had lived in Orleans County, New York, and that he had had five children. The authorities could find no account of any such person going missing in 1844. They decided the girls were perpetrating a hoax and refused to charge Bell with murder. Intriguingly, fifty years after the charges of murder and long after the Bells had died, a man's skeleton was found buried near the Fox home along with an empty peddler's trunk.

The case of the Fox girls might have ended as a typical case of poltergeistism but for the mood of the moment. The 1840s were a decade much like the 1960s. All across Europe, revolutions were replacing and reforming governments. In the United States, the populace was surging westward in search of gold and other untapped bounties while bitterly arguing over the issue of slavery. The middle class was growing as science and industry became more and more powerful and productive. Some intellectuals and artists had doubts.

They nostalgically believed that humanity had lost some mystic connection to the earth by substituting reason for faith. This nostalgia
was augmented by the homesickness of thousands of more ordinary
folks, who left their villages and farms behind for the cities and fac-
tories. People both high and low searched for new spiritual beliefs to
replace the older superstitions and legends they had left behind.
Some found themselves enchanted by spiritualism.

Curiously, the questioning, skeptical attitude that came with scientific progress encouraged interest in the supernatural by placing all
things, even sacred things, under scrutiny. People felt free to concoct
their own theories about the workings of the world. Just as tinkerers
had sought to devise productive mechanisms like the steam engine
and the railroad, tinkerers in the metaphysical tried to devise new
explanations for the cosmic. Spiritualism was such a constructed
belief. Unlike earlier attempts to communicate with the dead, it
avoided links to black magic. It managed to secure the endorsement
of many religious leaders who saw it as a confirmation of life after
death and even the existence of God. Many of the messages that spiritualists received were explicit descriptions of Heaven, angels, and
even the face of God. Some thought they were discovering a new
religion that could substitute communication with the dead for faith.

The region that the Fox family lived in was well known as a
hotbed of religious, political, and social theorizing. The abolitionist
movement, the women's suffrage campaign, utopian communes, and
even new religions found the northeastern United States a fertile spot
to grow (Mormonism and Seventh-Day Adventistism, for example,
have roots not far from Hydesville). In these tumultuous times and in
this area, the Fox girls found it easy to gain followers.

The Fox girls soon perfected their performances. They worked out
a code of raps and taps so that more elaborate messages could be
received. The similarity between this "spiritual telegraphy" and the
telegraphy being introduced by Samuel Morse added a veneer of scientific authenticity to the rapping. Interest exploded as the girls began
to receive messages from spirits other than the murdered peddler.
One message—"We are all your dear friends and relatives"—was particularly evocative. It suggested that the Fox girls could provide a
mechanism for communicating with anyone who had entered the
spirit world. They soon had plenty of eager people lining up to contact deceased loved ones.

Maggie and Kate Fox, joined by their sister Leah, began offering private sittings for money. They gave lectures and demonstrations. In a few years, they were appearing before sold-out audiences in New York City. Horace Greeley, the influential editor of the *New York Tribune*, became a true believer in the girls' powers. Several critics, however, claimed they were fakes. One said Leah secretly made the rappings by snapping her knee joints. Despite these attacks, the girls continued to be very successful.

A measure of the Fox sisters' success is that, in 1852, they received an invitation from President Franklin Pierce to conduct a private séance in the White House to help his wife contact their dead son. The boy had died tragically young, and his mother was nearly insane with grief—which the Fox sisters did little to ameliorate. In 1854, Senator James Shields of Illinois presented a fifteen-thousand-signature petition to the U.S. Congress demanding a commission to prove spiritualism was factual. By 1855, there were more than two million spiritualists. Such notables as Frederick Douglass, Harriet Beecher Stowe, and Cornelius Vanderbilt announced that they believed the spiritualists' claims. P. T. Barnum, ever quick to see an exploitable situation, hired the Fox sisters to appear at his American Museum in New York City.

Imitators of the Fox sisters, claiming similar gifts, began appearing. Those who received spoken or written messages from beyond were called mental mediums. Others, who produced more spectacular effects such as jumping tables, floating tambourines and horns, and even ghostly images, were called physical mediums. The séances of Connecticut-born Daniel Douglas Hume, a highly adept physical medium, featured disembodied hands, mysterious music, and even his levitating. He had numerous wealthy clients for his psychic services. Séances were soon being performed all around the world. Spiritualists proclaimed a new science-religion they named theosophy.

Spiritualism received a powerful boost when Sir Arthur Conan Doyle, the creator of Sherlock Holmes, became a fervent advocate. He traveled the world giving lectures describing the wonders of the spirit world. An appearance at New York's Carnegie Hall so enthralled one listener with the beauties of the spirit world that she went home and committed suicide, using her gas stove.

In 1888, the followers of spiritualism received a nasty shock when Maggie and Kate Fox, who had been reduced to poverty by alcoholism, announced that they had faked the Hydesville phenomena. They said that they had just wanted to frighten their mother with mysterious, faked noises they made by pulling a string tied to a dried apple and by cracking their big toes. When outsiders began to marvel at their trickery, they were delighted and extended their efforts. Leah, whom they told of the prank, suggested that they try to make money out of all the excitement. Once started on this path, the girls said they couldn't recant without embarrassment and charges of fraud. Devout spiritualists refused to accept the Fox girls' new story. When both sisters later recanted their recantation, the spiritualists triumphantly claimed vindication.

Spiritualism was plagued with con artists who heartlessly exploited the gullible and never recanted. The magician Harry Houdini did much to expose the techniques these crooks used. An example of the kind of people who perpetrated such frauds was Kate Bender of Kansas. During the early 1870s, Kate, with her father, mother, and brother, ran a frontier inn in Cherryvale, Kansas. Kate staged séances, gave psychic readings, and lectured on spiritualism to her neighbors. These enterprises weren't lucrative enough for the Benders, who devised a nasty way to increase their income. They ran a canvas wall across one room of their inn, where they served meals. The dinner table and a chair were positioned so that its occupant had his back to the canvas. If the guest was traveling alone, the Benders would companionably ask where he was bound, whether anyone was expecting him, and whether he had any family. If the guest wouldn't be missed and seemed well heeled, one of the Benders would go behind the canvas wall, take up a sledgehammer, and smash the guest's skull through the canvas. The Benders looted their victims, then secretly buried them.

In 1873, a sheriff in nearby Lawrence, Kansas, grew suspicious of the number of people reported missing near the Benders' inn and decided to raid the place. Fortunately for the Benders, Kate was rather attractive. While she had been plying her spiritualist trade in neighboring towns, she had acquired a loyal boyfriend, who, when he heard of the sheriff's plans, warned her. By the time the sheriff arrived, the family had disappeared. The sheriff and his men discovered fourteen bodies buried in and around the inn. No one knows how many other bodies may have gone undiscovered. The Benders were never tracked down. In an ironic twist, Kate's warning boyfriend had more than his girl to miss: Before running away, Kate pinched his wallet.

Frauds?

Magician James Randi is a skeptic when it comes to spiritualism and mediums. He routinely demonstrates that the results mediums produce can be reproduced using the techniques of stage and carnival mind readers. The phony psychic begins with general observations that can be used as questions to elicit answers from the client, which the psychic can then use to devise more specific observations/questions. For a client who is unsmiling, he might begin with a question such as, "You experienced a loss recently?" If the client answers positively, the psychic twists what had been a question into an observation. He might say, "I saw darkness around you," then continue with another observation/question, such as, "It was someone close to you?" If the answer is negative, the psychic immediately retreats or twists the answer into something positive—"No, it's you I see in darkness. Danger is causing the darkness. You face a risky situation that could go against you, unless you are careful." Since we are all facing some sort of risk, the prediction seems true.

Randi gave an example to *Time* magazine of how psychics can conceal errors: "If a woman says her husband recently died, the medium will say, 'Did he die suddenly?' If the wife says, 'No, he lingered for a while,' the medium then says, 'Oh, because he's saying to me, 'I wish I had died quickly.'" Too often, the psychic can count on the client to help accentuate correct guesses and minimize errors.

Some psychics do a little research to produce accurate observations. Carnival mind readers sometimes employ pickpockets to go through the purses and pockets of members of their audience to gather information. The pickpockets return the filched items before they're noticed missing.

A far more reputable effort in spiritualism was announced in *Scientific American* in October 1920, by Thomas Alva Edison, inventor of thousands of devices, including the lightbulb, the phonograph, and a movie camera. He said he had begun work on a device with which he hoped to speak to the dead. He didn't admit to believing in the spirit world, but said that, if it existed, it would probably be characterized by some electromagnetic phenomena. Edison hoped that a sensitive device might be able to detect efforts by the dead to manipulate it. Such a machine would give the dead "a better opportunity to express themselves than the tilting tables and raps and Ouija boards and mediums and the other crude methods now purported to be the only means of communication." Edison worked on the problem for the next decade but died without having created a successful machine.

The spiritualist movement faded during the first half of the twentieth century, only to be revived during the 1960s, when there was a renewal of interest in all things occult. Serious scientists joined in this interest. The result was a separation of extrasensory phenomena (ESP)—psychic powers such as clairvoyance and telekinesis—from traditional spiritualism. Scientists managed to produce some curious results and interesting theories, but have yet to show that anyone has reliable supernormal powers. Despite this, traditional spiritualist efforts to contact the dead benefited by association from these scientific studies. Psychics and mediums returned as popular celebrities.

By the 1980s, the New Age movement had incorporated many spiritualist elements. New Age mediums, called channelers, attracted large followings that included Hollywood celebrities. They collected fortunes for their services. Non-celebrities could find psychic advice at the end of a pay-per-minute telephone call. Successful movies such as *Ghost* (1990) and *The Sixth Sense* (1999) reflect the speculative yearnings of the public, which is more and more willing to believe in spirits. A survey conducted by the University of Chicago National Opinion Research Council in 1990 reported that 42 percent of Americans believe they have experienced some sort of spirit contact with someone dead. A survey in Britain in 2000 produced identical results. It reported that 42 percent of the British public had seen or felt the presence of a ghost.

Saying Hello

The search for proof of life after death has taken on a scientific cast at the University of Arizona, where Dr. Gary Schwartz, a professor of psychology and medicine, and his wife, Dr. Linda

Russek, have instituted the Susy Smith Project. The project, named for a medium, seeks to prove that there is life after death by receiving a verified message from the dead. The project signs up volunteers, who select a secret phrase that is encrypted by a computer and stored at a Web site. No one has access to the stored phrases. When the volunteer dies, he is supposed to try to communicate his secret phrase to a living person. That person logs on to the Web site and enters the phrase. If the phrase matches the recorded, encrypted phrase, the project will have proof that there is an afterlife.

There are weaknesses in the Susy Smith Project. As computer scientists know, information in a computer is never entirely secure. A talented programmer or a persistent hacker can crack encryption schemes. There are also simpler mechanical means of intercepting information before it is encrypted. A nefarious programmer could set up a site mimicking the Susy Smith Project site. A deceived volunteer might give the fake site his secret phrase. The fakers then use the phrase to register with the official site. Later, if the volunteer dies, the fakers can claim they received the phrase from the spirit world.

So far, the Susy Smith Project has borne no results. None of the volunteers who recorded secret phrases has died.

If you'd like to participate, the experiment's Web site is afterlifecodes.com. Or you can write: Human Energy Systems Laboratory, Department of Psychology, University of Arizona, P.O. Box 210068, Tucson, AZ 85721-0068.

HAUNTED PLACES AND HAUNTED HOUSES

Ghosts are often associated with a specific site or building that was significant in their life or death. Battlefields, for example, are often said to be haunted by the ghosts of the soldiers who fought and died there. The battlefield of Gettysburg is now a national park, and a park ranger working there once claimed to have encountered a group of Confederates preparing for a charge. He had thought them to be a group of Civil War buffs costumed for a battle reenactment and had passed them by without much notice, then realized that they were in an area reenactors were barred from using. He turned to move them along and discovered no one and no sign of anyone's having been there.

Harry Martindale, a plumber in York, England, had a similar experience with veterans of a far older campaign. He had gone down in a cellar to repair some pipes when he heard a harsh trumpet blast. He turned to see a column of men dressed as Roman soldiers silently marching by him. They had the tired, gritty appearance of combat veterans returning from battle. The legs of the soldiers were calf-deep in the floor. The plumber later learned that an ancient Roman road had run through that spot, with its surface just calf-deep under the floor of his cellar. The centuries had buried the road, but it still seemed to be carrying traffic. Martindale's story was commonly dismissed until two archaeologists, seven years later, saw the same ghostly troops. The archaeologists identified the soldiers as belonging to the fourth century.

England has many other haunted buildings. One spot, notable for the kind of haunting done there, is Glamis Castle in Scotland. Shakespeare mentions the castle in his play *Macbeth*. Visitors to the castle are often told that Macbeth murdered King Duncan there. There is good reason to believe that this wasn't the case, but several other murders did occur in the castle, and a number of ghosts are said to haunt it. The most notable supernatural fixture of the castle isn't a ghost, however. It's a sealed room hidden within the structure said to contain ghosts.

According to one legend, in the fifteenth century, the second lord of Glamis, nicknamed the Wicked Lord for his decadent habits and also Earl Beardie for his luxuriant beard, became very drunk one Sabbath. Earl Beardie drank heavily every day of the week and saw no reason to abstain on Sunday. He also loved to gamble and, on this Sabbath, wanted to play cards, another activity generally considered unsuitable for the day. When no one would oblige him, he grew vexed. Finally, he swore that he'd gamble with the Devil himself. With this, there came a loud knock at the castle's door. It was a tall, somber man dressed in black. The drunken earl invited the visitor to a game of cards. The earl's servants saw the pair go into a room and close the door. Fearfully, the servants pressed their ears to the door. They heard the sounds of cards being shuffled and dealt. Soon the earl could be heard swearing and complaining about his losses. He finally was heard to shout that he had nothing left to wager. There was a murmur from the visitor then a loud, snarl of assent from the earl. The game resumed, then abruptly ended with a still-louder snarl.

One servant peeked through the door's keyhole. Before he could make out anything in the gloomy chamber, a great blast of searing light hit his eye. He stumbled back. The earl, hearing this, kicked open the door and swore at his servants, calling them spies. He turned back to the visitor but the visitor was gone. On the table, left behind, were the stakes the earl had lost. The servants knew, however, that one of the wagered items had gone with its winner: The visitor had been the Devil, and the last wager had been for Earl Beardie's soul. The flash of light had been produced by its being pulled from its owner to disappear with the Devil.

For a few more years, Earl Beardie continued his drinking and gambling, then died in a pool of his own retch. The night he was buried, the servants of the house heard the sounds of carousing from the room where he had gambled with the Devil. They fearfully edged the door open and peeked within, where they saw the pair at cards again. The door was quickly shut and locked. The castle's new owners had the room bricked shut and sealed with plaster. Despite this, sounds of the infernal card game can still be heard if one listens quietly on a still Sunday night.

The legend of Glamis Castle's secret room has other variants. According to one, Janet Douglas, wife of James, the sixth lord of Glamis, poisoned her husband and got away with it, only to be charged some years later with witchcraft. Some say she was tried and executed in Edinburgh in 1537, but others claim her punishment was to be walled up in one of the castle's rooms, where she died of starvation.

Another version claims that the occupant of the sealed room is actually a servant girl who was a vampire. She was caught drinking the blood of a member of the household and sealed in the room as punishment. Since this isn't one of the traditional methods of destroying vampires, some believe she remains alive—or at least as alive as the undead can be—in the sealed room, waiting for some future home renovator to set her free.

Still another variant of the story of Glamis Castle's secret room is more poignant. By the nineteenth century, Glamis Castle had been inherited by the earls of Strathmore. In 1821, the earl of Strathmore of the moment supposedly used the secret room as a nursery for his deformed child. The child was the eldest son but so monstrous in appearance that his parents claimed he had been born dead, and the estate was later passed on to his younger brother. It was thought that the unfortunate child would soon die; instead, he grew to adulthood and continued living, for decade after decade, hidden away from the critical eyes of the world in the care of the castle's steward and the Strathmore earls, each of whom was told the secret upon his twenty-first birthday. Each earl was said to undergo a dramatic change in personality, becoming morose and haunted, upon learning the secret. In 1876, the then-earl's transformation was so shocking that his son refused to be told the secret when it came his turn. The monster presumably fell to the care of the steward and his heirs, for it was reported that the poor wretch lived in seclusion until 1941.

In 1880, the legend of the secret room gained some substance when a Scottish newspaper reported that a workman had accidentally smashed his way into a secret passage in the castle that led to a locked door. After telling the steward of the door, the workman disappeared. It was rumored that he had been given a large sum of cash and a boat ticket to Australia in return for promising never to tell anyone of the door's location.

Glamis Castle has a connection with the current Royal Family of Britain. It is the family home of the Queen Mother's family. She was born there.

Web Ghosts

In 1937, in the Willard Library in Evansville, Indiana, a janitor was on his way to stoke the furnace in the cellar when he came face to face with a veiled, spectral woman dressed all in gray. The janitor ran, and since then, the lady has been seen by dozens of library staff members. In 1999, the *Evansville Courier and Press* decided to attempt an unusual kind of ghost hunt in the library. The newspaper set up a Web cam in the stacks and displayed its images on its home page, www.Courierpress.com. Patrons were invited to watch and report any images that they thought contained ghosts.

Two mysterious images were recorded. One seems to show a shadowy woman's head behind a computer. The other seems to show the wispy form of a woman returning a book to a shelf. The site drew more than 173,000 hits in one day and is expected to be widely imitated with Web cams at other haunted sites.

The most famous house in America is also purported to be haunted. The White House has at least one presidential spirit that seems to refuse to leave office. The ghost of Abraham Lincoln, assassinated in 1865, is said to have made several appearances. During the Benjamin Harrison administration (1889–1893), a member of Harrison's personal staff was so frightened by his many encounters with Lincoln's spirit that he went to a medium to arrange a séance in which he could politely ask the ex-president to leave him alone to attend to his duties undistracted. His entreaty was apparently persuasive, because it wasn't until the administration of Theodore Roosevelt (1901–1909) that Lincoln reappeared. This time it was to the president himself.

Teddy claimed to have seen Lincoln in several different rooms of the White House and described him as "shambling, homely, with his sad, strong, deeply furrowed face." During the Coolidge administration (1923–1929), First Lady Grace Coolidge saw Lincoln "dressed in black with a stole draped over his shoulders to ward off the draughts and chills." Lincoln reappeared in 1934. A staff member reported seeing him sitting on the bed in the Rose Room, pulling on a pair of boots. That room is also called the Lincoln Bedroom because of its Lincoln-related contents, which include Lincoln's bed. Lincoln used the room as an office and signed the Emancipation Proclamation in it.

During World War II, Queen Wilhelmina of the Netherlands, who had fled her Nazi-occupied nation, stayed in the Rose Room. She claimed that one night she heard a knock at the room's door. When she opened the door, the ghost of Lincoln, complete with stovepipe hat, was standing in front of her. She promptly fainted, spending much of the night on the floor. At breakfast the next morning, she reported her encounter to President Franklin Roosevelt. Roosevelt was unsurprised and told her that Lincoln often made appearances.

British prime minister Winston Churchill was later lodged in the Rose Room during an official visit. He also claimed to sense Lincoln's presence and requested a different room to sleep in. Margaret Truman, Harry Truman's daughter, often reported the sound of knocking upon her bedroom door late at night. There was never anyone at her door when she opened it. President Eisenhower never saw Lincoln's ghost during his administration (1953–1961), but did say that he felt his predecessor's presence on more than one occasion.

Abraham Lincoln had his own psychic experiences. While he loved jokes and was a gregarious, companionable man, he also had a melancholy side, which seems appropriate, given the thousands of deaths and maimings produced by the Civil War. Lincoln often had dreams that he interpreted as foretelling a sad ending to his life. He told his law partner William Herndon, "I am sure I shall meet with some terrible end." Just days before his assassination, Lincoln had a particularly disturbing dream, which he was persuaded to describe over the dinner table in the White House. The retelling was witnessed by several of Lincoln's associates and recorded by his friend and social secretary Ward Hill Lamon.

Lincoln said that, ten nights earlier, he had gone to sleep late, after staying up to receive some war dispatches. His sleep had been interrupted by the sounds of sobbing in an otherwise "death-like stillness." Lincoln said he had risen from his bed and gone downstairs to discover the source of the crying. According to Lamon's account, Lincoln said, "I went from room to room; no living person was in sight, but the same mournful sounds of distress met me as I passed along. It was light in all the rooms; every object was familiar to me; but where were all the people who were grieving as if their hearts would break?"

Lincoln continued searching till he came to the East Room. "There I met with a sickening surprise. Before me was a catafalque, on which rested a corpse wrapped in funeral vestments. Around it were stationed soldiers who were acting as guards; and there was a throng of people, some gazing mournfully upon the corpse, whose face was covered, others weeping pitifully. 'Who is dead in the White House?' I demanded of one of the soldiers. 'The President,' was his answer; 'he was killed by an assassin!' Then there came a loud burst of grief from the crowd, which awoke me from my dream. I slept no more that night."

The dream must have been quite shocking, but Lincoln passed it off as meaningless when his friends urged him to take extra care. He had a fatalistic streak that let him set aside an omen that would have terrified others into elaborate safeguards.

On the night of April 12, 1865, Lincoln had another strange dream, which he told his friends about. He dreamed he was a passenger on a great ship rapidly moving toward an undefined shore. Lincoln had had the same dream preceding the battles of Bull Run, Antietam, Gettysburg, Stone River, Vicksburg, and Wilmington. The president chose to interpret the dream as foretelling another important event in the Civil War. Lincoln hoped it would be General Sherman's reporting an end to all hostilities. On the fourteenth, however, Lincoln was mortally wounded at Ford's Theater. He died in the early hours of the fifteenth. For several days before being sent by train to Springfield, Illinois, Lincoln's body lay in state upon a catafalque in the East Room under a military honor guard, just as his first dream had foretold.

Ironically, General Ulysses S. Grant and his wife were supposed to attend the theater with Lincoln, but Grant's wife had had her own dream premonition of danger. She insisted that they stay home. They did, and Grant avoided assassination.

A Premonition That Went Off with a Bang

Robert Morris, thirty-nine, was a successful merchant in Oxford, Maryland; his son would later sign the Declaration of Independence. One day in 1750, he awoke from a bad dream and knew that if he went outside his house that day, he would be shot and killed. However, one of his ships was in port, and it was customary for the owner to visit the ship for dinner with the captain. Morris explained his premonition to the captain, but the captain insisted. Morris gave in. He took a small boat to the merchant ship and was heartily entertained. As Morris was returning to shore, the crew fired a loyal salute, which accidentally blew his skiff out of the water.

THE AMITYVILLE HAUNTING

In 1975, George and Kathleen Lutz purchased a large house at 112 Ocean Avenue in Amityville, a middle-class suburb on Long Island,

New York, for eighty thousand dollars. The price was high for the 1970s but lower than that of comparable surrounding homes. The real estate agent had told them the house had been the scene of a murder, but the family members weren't superstitious. The Lutzes soon had reason to become so. Odd noises woke them in the middle of the night. Windows opened and shut by themselves. Something invisible pulled the front door out of its frame. One night, they saw glowing red eyes at their window. In the morning, they found cloven hoofprints in the snow where the eyes had been seen. A room became infested with flies. Finally, George discovered Kathleen floating above their bed. When he pulled her down, she seemed to take on the appearance of a withered hag. Her appearance returned to normal but, when this incident was followed by the appearance of green slime oozing out of the walls, the family gave up. On January 14, 1976, after living in the house for just four weeks, they fled, leaving nearly all their possessions behind. The family turned the house over to the bank holding the mortgage. The Lutzes blamed the haunting on the house's murderous history.

In November 1974, the DeFeo family—father, mother, two brothers, and two sisters—had been shot to death in the house by Ronald "Butch" DeFeo, the elder son of the family. After suggesting that the murders were linked to the Mafia, DeFeo had pled insanity, claiming voices had ordered him to murder his family. A court decided that the young man, who had led a dissolute life that included drug abuse, had murdered his family to benefit from their life insurance and not at demonic command. He was sentenced to six consecutive life terms.

The DeFeo murders had been a major news story in the area and, when word of a haunting connected to it spread, there was much interest. A New York television news team assembling a story on haunted houses interviewed the Lutz family. Their story suggested that the police had confirmed parts of the Lutz account. They hinted that the Catholic Church and prominent parapsychologists were interested in the bedeviled house. The reporters also claimed that the house had a history of supernatural happenings, and that it had been built on a haunted spot. They claimed that local legend said the house had been built on a site that local Montaukett Indians had believed to be cursed and where they buried enemies and dead thought to have been involved with demons. The lawyer for Ronald

DeFeo brought further media attention when he made a dramatic public statement claiming the haunting proved his client innocent and that he should be released. He wasn't, but the Amityville haunting became national news.

The Lutz family contracted with writer Jay Anson to put their story in book form. The book, *The Amityville Horror*, published in 1977, stated that, during the late 1600s, John Ketcham, a Satan worshiper driven out of Massachusetts, had taken up residence on the spot where the Lutz house had later been built. There he had continued his black practices; when he died, he had been buried on the property. Anson's book went on to vividly describe all of the Lutzes' misadventures in such compelling prose that the book became a bestseller. In 1978, it was turned into a feature film starring Rod Steiger. The enormous success of the book and movie brought the attention of skeptics.

The Lutzes had known about the DeFeo murders before buying the house. Skeptics theorized that the family hadn't been able to keep up mortgage payments on the home and had concocted the haunting story to explain their leaving. They claimed that when the family's story drew public interest, they had embellished it, then cashed in by publishing it.

Investigators discovered that the television news report had been concocted out of rumors and supposition. The police didn't support the Lutz account, the Catholic Church hadn't been interested in them, and parapsychologists became interested only after the story went national. A historical review of the house site revealed no earlier accounts of ghostly happenings. No linkage to a John Ketcham could be proved. Descendants of the Montauketts said there was no curse upon the spot or Indian graves there. Jay Anson admitted that he had based his book completely on the Lutzes' account and had not challenged their veracity. None of the incidents in the haunting could be independently confirmed. The people who have lived in the house since the Lutzes have reported no paranormal phenomena. It was also evident to both believers and disbelievers—and even the Lutz family—that Hollywood had greatly exaggerated the story for dramatic effect. In the end, while the story was widely accepted by the public as true, not even the most ardent believer in the supernatural felt comfortable defending it. Ironically, the most popular story of a haunted house is one of the least credible.

Hauntings as Business Opportunities

In the past, a building with a reputation for being haunted would be shunned. Today curiosity seekers so eagerly seek out ghost-frequented abodes that a good ghost story can do more for a hotel than an expensive ad campaign. The Logan Inn in New Hope, Pennsylvania, for example, entertains its guests with ghosts from the American Revolution. Maggie Smith, the inn's manager, told ABC News, "Washington's troops used the basement as a morgue. A few folks say they've seen a headless soldier. They're not scared, they're fascinated." She added that fear has caused only one couple to check out in the last decade.

The Fall River, Massachusetts, house where Lizzie Borden was charged with hacking up her stepmother and father has become an inn. Despite stories of lights being switched on and off by invisible hands and eerie presences, every room in the place is reserved a year in advance at two hundred dollars a night.

Ghost stories are so valuable to the tourist trade that some cities promote themselves as haunted. The most notable of these is New Orleans, which features haunted house tours and cemeteries crowded with tourists.

Houses are not the only structures that can be haunted. London has the world's oldest subway system. Called the Underground, some of the millions of passengers who have used it have reported strange goings-on. Passengers at the Liverpool Street Station have complained of bad odors. The station is thought to have been built upon a pit into which victims of the plague were thrown centuries ago.

When workmen did some digging on a line near the Bank of England's gardens in the nineteenth century, they discovered a long-forgotten graveyard. Soon afterward, the ghostly figure of a nun appeared at Bank Station. It was thought she might be the ghost of Sarah Whitehead, a nun whose brother had been hanged in 1811 for forging checks drawn on the bank. After his death, Whitehead had protested his fate by silently standing outside the bank dressed in black. She had done this for forty years, before dying and being buried in the disturbed cemetery.

Covent Garden Station is supposedly haunted by the ghost of William Terriss, an actor stabbed to death in 1897 near the Adelphi Theatre, which is close to the station. Terriss, dapperly dressed in frock coat, pale gloves, and hat, is said to walk the tunnels and the station's staff room.

Lest you think you can escape spectral copassengers by choosing a bus over an underground train, there are also reports in London of a phantom bus. It is said to carry the number 7 and to frequent the Ladbroke Grove area. Motorists have been startled into swerving, because it moves with no regard for other vehicles. One driver is said to have been killed after crashing while trying to avoid the bus.

ANIMAL GHOSTS

Ghostly animals have often been reported. Scott S. Smith, in his 1999 book *The Soul of Your Pet*, documents 125 accounts of animal ghosts. One story tells of a woman who absently petted her dog, which had settled down by her chair as she was watching television one evening. Some minutes after lifting her hand from her dog, the woman abruptly remembered that she had taken her dog to the vet earlier that day. She looked down, and her pet had vanished. The next day she called the vet to check on the dog's condition, only to discover that it had died the night before.

Not all ghostly animals are so benign. Demons and evil spirits commonly took animal form. Among the most noteworthy of such manifestations were large, spectral black dogs in Britain. These dogs, sometimes called nightwalkers, were spotted roaming nocturnal roadways. They were much larger than natural hounds and had glowing red eyes. Seeing one was bad luck, because they were believed to be an omen of death. East Anglia's spectral hound was called Black Shuck. In Yorkshire, it was Padfoot. In Lancashire, it had two names: Shriker and Trash-hound. Arthur Conan Doyle, in *The Hound of the Baskervilles*, used a legend of a ghostly black dog as the basis for a murder mystery solved by Sherlock Holmes.

The spectral dog legends may have originated in Greco-Roman stories of Cerberus, the three-headed hound that guarded Hades, or of Hecate's two hounds, which loped after her as she went strolling in graveyards. Another source may be the accounts given during witch trials by confessed witches, who described sabbats in which the Devil appeared in the form of a large black dog with burning eyes. One other possible source might be the old English folk belief that the ghost of whoever is buried last in a cemetery must stand nightly guard over it until relieved of duty by the next person to die. It was said that this rule had resulted in unseemly rushing when two people happened to die at the same time. Funeral trains might wind up racing to the cemetery so that their dead relative would be spared a turn at guard duty that might never end if no one else was buried in the cemetery. Supposedly, this fear faded after a witch suggested that a human guardian wasn't required. She proposed that a dog be sacrificed so that it could stand guard. It wasn't long before the ghosts of such guard dogs were reported lurking in the roadways by the cemeteries, looking for someone about to die—after all, everyone knows how much dogs like to bury bones.

THE LATEST THEORY

Recently, Vic Tandy, an engineer and an expert in computer-assisted learning at Coventry University in Britain, made an interesting ghostly observation. One night, he had been working late in a campus laboratory rumored to be haunted. A fencer, Tandy had placed one of his fencing foils in a vise to adjust it. He left the foil to do some writing. As he wrote, he began to feel nervous. The *London Sunday Telegraph* quoted him as saying, "I was sweating but cold and the feeling of depression was noticeable—but there was also something else. It was as though something was in the room with me. Then I became aware that I was being watched, and a figure slowly emerged to my left. It was indistinct and on the periphery of my vision, but it moved just as I would expect a person to. It was gray, and made no sound. The hair was standing up on the back of my neck—I was terrified. I decided I must be cracking up and went home."

The next day, Tandy returned to the lab. He went to remove his foil from the vise and was surprised to find it vibrating. Tandy wondered if the blade might be reacting to very-low-frequency sound waves. Human beings can't hear these sounds. He obtained sensitive sound-detection equipment and discovered a "standing wave" trapped in the lab. Sound waves bounce off objects and can become concentrated in a particular area. The sound was at its strongest right by Tandy's desk.

Tandy traced the source of the wave to a recently installed extraction fan meant to clear the lab's air. It produced an extremely low, nineteen-cycle-per-second vibration that formed the standing wave. When the fan's mounting was altered, the wave disappeared. Curious as to the health effects of what he had been sitting in the middle of, Tandy contacted Dr. Tony Lawrence of the university's health school. Together, they made a rather startling discovery: Low-frequency sound can create ghostly phenomena.

In 1998, Tandy and Lawrence published their findings in the *Journal of the Society for Psychical Research*. They related that acoustic scientists had long known that "infra-sound"—low-frequency sound at about nineteen cycles per second—can cause many physiological effects, including sensations of fear, breathlessness, and shivering. They also noted that the National Aeronautics and Space Administration had discovered that sound at eighteen cycles per second could cause the human eye to vibrate in sympathy, distorting and smearing vision. An ordinary object could seem strange and out of place. Before Tandy and Lawrence, no one had linked these physiological effects to ghosts. They theorized that some ghostly encounters, such as that experienced by Tandy in the laboratory, might actually be encounters with infra-sound.

Tandy has linked infra-sound to other hauntings. One occurred in a laboratory while a wind tunnel was in operation. Tandy has noted that machinery isn't necessary for the generation of infra-sound. Wind blowing through a long corridor and past a window can generate low-frequency vibrations. In such a case, there would be no visible mechanism that might be linked to the haunting.

DO GHOSTS EXIST?

We must recognize ourselves for what we are—the priests of a not very popular religion.

Sir Fred Hoyle, (1915-), English astronomer
and supporter of the scientific method

To answer the question "Do ghosts exist?" we must first make a few observations:

- Ghosts are the most widely reported unauthenticated phenomenon in history. Despite thousands of years of sightings, no one has ever been able to prove that they saw what they reported.

- There are psychological mechanisms—still poorly understood—that offer explanations of ghostly phenomena. For example, there are near-sleep states wherein the human mind is very susceptible to illusions that seem vividly real.

- There are physical mechanisms, such as infra-sound, that produce ghostly phenomena. These phenomena are not readily detected without specialized equipment. There may be other physical mechanisms that are yet to be discovered.

- Psychological reasons exist for unconsciously embellishing memories or incorporating the accounts of others into our own memories. Studies have shown that children can be easily manipulated into believing a falsehood when that falsehood has an authoritative person insisting that it is true. This is called the false-memory syndrome. It has figured in the reversal of several convictions for child sexual abuse, where social workers had convinced unabused children that they had been abused. Recent studies of adults show that they, too, can be manipulated into believing falsehoods. College students, for example, were told that they had experienced a concocted event as a child and were urged to remember it. Leading questions were asked and details suggested. Quite often, the college students came to believe the concocted event had actually occurred. This process is sometimes called confabulation.

- There are natural explanations for otherwise mysterious phenomena. The simple expansion and contraction of a house cooling at nightfall can produce odd creakings, groans, and pops. Acoustic peculiarities can turn wind brushing a window into a sinister whisper. Tricks of lighting aren't limited to desert mirages. An unexpected, odd shadow can look like a phantom. A mysteriously cold corner of a room may simply be the most poorly insulated corner of the room.

- Myriad human emotions fuel supernatural observations. These include: wishful thinking, grief, the excitement of participating in an unusual event, a desire to feel special, a need to believe in something grander than the ordinary, an urge to be the center of attention, reluctance to be the only dissenter in a group of believers, and, not the least, fear. We may fear that we will be completely extinguished by death and wish to prove to ourselves through a ghost sighting that the soul endures. More simply, we may allow ourselves to be spooked by a place. A walk by an abandoned house on a moonless night can put us in the mood to see a torn, old window curtain as a beckoning, spectral being.

- Finally, there a reward for false memories and concocted memories of ghosts. The sighter gets a good, attention-grabbing story to tell. He or she might even manage to sell the story. There are myriad cases of nefarious persons exploiting the supernatural to make money. The supernatural can also be a lot of fun, as anyone who's misused a Ouija board to terrify a kid sister can attest.

Given the logical explanations, should we believe that ghosts exist? As Dr. Samuel Johnson (1709–1784), the great lexicographer, observed of ghosts, "All argument is against it, but all belief is for it." Ghosts make good stories, and it is simply fun to believe. Until the day when some gregarious ghost makes an appearance on live television and answers all our questions while scientists measure its every parameter, we will remain fascinated by the possibility of ghosts. And things that go bump in the night will make us shiver and wonder, "Is there anyone there?"

7

CREATURES
OF THE NIGHT~
ICONS OF HALLOWEEN

BATS

It's easy to see why bats are viewed with dread. They are ugly and hunt by night, moving nearly invisibly with hackle-raising, flittery flutter. Their appearance was once an omen of death. Protective charms were commonly uttered when a bat was spotted. A bat discovered inside a home was chased out with ferocity because it was feared bats could be witches in disguise trying to do evil. Witches didn't treat bats well, either, using bat blood in an ointment meant to give the power to fly, and bat wings and bat entrails in their brews. Despite their unpleasant repute, bats are extraordinary animals.

Bats are found all around the world, being most plentiful in tropic regions. They are the only mammals capable of true flight. Bat wingspans vary from 6 inches for the hognose bat, to over five feet, for the flying fox known as the *Pteropus vampyrus*. The bumblebee bat of Thailand is the smallest mammal, weighing less than a penny.

Like birds, bats have a light skeletal structure. The delicacy of their bones requires them to carefully drag themselves about by their forelimbs when they aren't flying. If they attempted to walk upright, their own weight could break their bones. This fragility is one reason bats hang upside down. The position places the burden of the bat's weight upon its tendons and muscles instead of its bones.

Bats are commonly believed to have bad eyesight. Actually, they

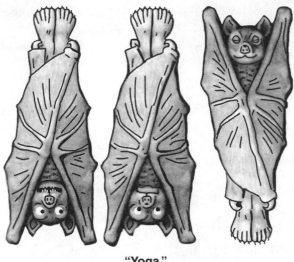

"Yoga."

see quite well, but, being nocturnal hunters, have developed a better mechanism for detecting obstacles and prey in the dark. They use echolocation, emitting high-pitched squeals that bounce off surrounding objects.

The majority of nine hundred bat species use echolocation to capture insects. Most of the remainder eat fruit or nectar. In South America and Mexico, there are two species of blood-drinking bats belonging to the genera *Desmodus* and *Diphylla*. These have sharp incisors with which they puncture the flesh of horses, cattle, and other large mammals, including human beings, while asleep. The bats then drink the blood released. So delicate is their approach, that their victims seldom are wakened by the bite.

Officials in northern Mexico routinely issue alerts warning of attacks by vampire bats. The blood-sucking committed by the bats isn't the concern causing the alerts; it is fear of rabies that might be transmitted to bat victims, both animal and human. A six-year-old child died earlier in 1999 in the Mexican border state of Chihuahua of bat-borne rabies.

Bats have few natural predators. Their roosting sites are difficult for other species to reach. Bats usually die as a result of disease, famine, accident, shifts of climate, or age. Some species live as long as thirty years.

For most species of bats, the female produces a single offspring per year. The baby bat weighs about a third of the mother's weight. Bat young are born with very little or no fur. Commonly, like kittens, bats are blind at birth and open their eyes after a few days. Bat infants can fly at three weeks of age.

Bats usually swarm to hunt. Some swarms in the southwestern United States have been recorded as flying as high as 10,000 feet in flocks that can spread out for ten miles in width. U.S. Air Force air traffic controllers routinely monitor bat flocks on their radars, diverting aircraft from flying through them. Jet engines don't digest bats easily.

Hair Raising Experiments

In 1959, in Britain, the Earl of Cranbrook tested the legend that if a bat becomes entangled in a woman's hair it will become so ensnared that the hair must be cut to free it. Three female volunteers allowed the Earl to thrust bats into their hair. He experimented with four different breeds of bats. Fortunately, each time the bat could easily extricate itself.

Bats are useful animals. Insect-eating bats can greatly improve the livability of areas plagued by mosquitoes. A single bat can eat 600 mosquitoes in a single night. The bats that surround the city of San Antonio, Texas, alone have been estimated as eating one million pounds of insects every night. Nectar-eating bats help plants pollinate. As with bees, pollen clings to the bats when they collect nectar, and they spread it to the next plant they visit.

Bat Superstitions

- Carrying a bat bone will protect the carrier from witches in bat form.
- A home can be protected from witches in bat form by catching a bat, carrying it around the house three times, then killing the bat and nailing its carcass by a window or on the home's outhouse door.

A Simple Bat House

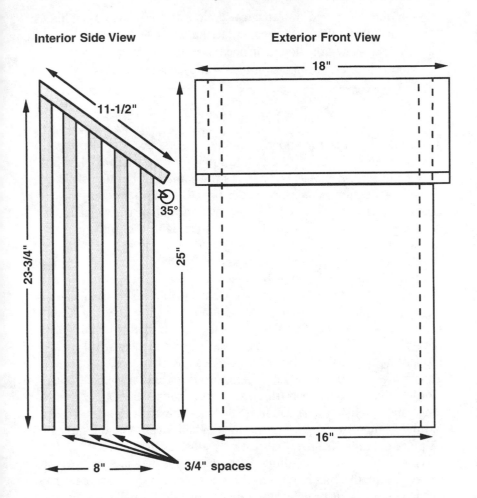

Interior Side View

11-1/2"

23-3/4"

25"

35°

8"

3/4" spaces

Exterior Front View

18"

16"

Interior surfaces are roughened to make it easier for bats to attach themselves. Plastic mesh can be stapled inside for the same purpose. The plywood should be caulked and painted.

This bat box is made using 1" exterior grade plywood. Interior panels are 14" wide. 6" wide side panels (not shown) close the sides. The box can be mounted on a pole or on the side of a building or tree.

- Washing your face in bat blood will give you the power to see in the dark.

- Adding bat blood to a magical potion increases its strength. This superstition was so popular that, as late as 1962, officials in New York found it necessary to ban the use of bat blood in magical mixtures as a health hazard.

BLACK CATS

The domestic cat is a member of the family *Felidae*, order *Carnivora*. There are an estimated five hundred million cats on Earth. They are the smallest of the felines but possess the same deft hunting skills as their larger cousins, albeit for smaller prey. Cats have several remarkable traits. They have large brains in relation to their body size. They walk upon their toes in a "digitigrade" style, with the fore and back leg on each side moving forward together—only camels and giraffes move in the same manner. The vertebrae of the cat's spinal column are bound together by muscles instead of ligaments. This lets cat spines stretch, contract, arch and even bend into an "S"-shape. Cat claws are retractable, allowing them to move quickly, then slash and grab. Cats can see six times better than human beings in the dark, have a fine sense of smell, and excellent hearing. A cat's whiskers are thought to help it find its way in darkness and in closed spaces. Scientists are not sure of what other purposes they serve, but a cat whose whiskers have been trimmed short becomes clumsy. The cat's long, supple tail acts as a counter-balance, allowing it to move across narrow beams like a tight-rope walker. When a cat falls, the tail can help the cat right itself so that it nearly always lands upon its feet.

The Egyptians are credited with the domestication of the cat between four thousand and five thousand years ago. These cats are believed to be African wildcats, a desert-dwelling, small cat that still lives in the wilder regions of North Africa. The Egyptian government, embodied in their living god, Pharaoh, recognized the importance of cats in preserving harvests. To protect cats, Pharaoh declared them demi-gods. Only a god could own a demi-god, so all Egyptian cats became the property of Pharaoh. He allowed their owners to retain their pets, but decreed that the owners had to bring the cats to Pharaoh's granaries every evening so the cats could go on anti-vermin patrol. In the morning, the owner could retrieve his pet. To sweeten the deal, Pharaoh gave a tax credit to the cat's owner.

As Pharaoh's property, it became a capital offense to kill or injure a cat, even accidentally. When a house caught fire, the household cats were the first to be rescued, as there was little point in surviving a blaze just to have Pharaoh's officials execute you for leaving Felix or Fluffy behind. When a cat died a natural death, cautious Egyptians went into ritual mourning, exhibiting all the grief that they would demonstrate for any member of their family. One common sign of mourning for a cat was to shave one's eyebrows.

After death, cats were presented to the local priests so that they could declare the death natural. It would then be mummified and bound in linen. Archaeologists have discovered thousands of cat mummies in Egypt. Over three hundred thousand were uncovered at a single site in Beni-Hassan. Mouse mummies have been found with cat mummies—to give the cats something to chase in the afterlife.

The goddess Bast, the goddess of femininity, fertility, family, and joy, was depicted as a woman with a cat's head. Bast traditionally held in her left hand an amulet representing the all-seeing sacred eye. The amulet was called an utchat and often took the form of a cat's eye. Its image was commonly used as a protective decoration. A door might bear an utchat to ward off thieves. An utchat hung from the neck guarded against violence and disease. An utchat surrounded by images of kittens was sometimes given as a wedding present to promote fertility.

The ancient Egyptian word for cats was "mau," in imitation of the cat's meow. In later-day Egypt, utchat became synonymous with cat. Across Europe, in different cultures, utchat mutated into chat, cattus, gatus, gato, cat, katt, katte, kitty, and kitten. Also, in later-day Egypt, the cat-goddess Bast became Pasht. Pasht also became a word for cat, and, as it moved across Europe, it mutated into past, pushed, pusst, puss, and pussy.

The first domestic cats were probably tawny brown, with darker brown stripes. Their owners soon noticed that selective breeding could eventually produce different colors and patterns. The all-black cat seems to have been first bred by the ancient Phoenicians who had obtained cats, perhaps through theft, from Egypt. The Phoenicians, a seafaring, merchant people, traded all around the Mediterranean and as far north as Britain. The value of the creatures as rat-catchers must have made them attractive products. The Phoenicians must have resorted to a great deal of closed breeding to produce more. Many oddities would have been created. One of these may have been the all-black cat.

Cats, both black and otherwise, spread through Europe, the Near East, and North Africa. From these regions they traveled along the caravan routes to India and China, where they also were called "mau" after their meow. Explorers, traders, and settlers brought cats to the New World and spread them across the South Pacific to Australia. By the eighteenth century, cats had figuratively conquered the world.

In Europe, cats at first enjoyed some of the ritual respect they had enjoyed in Egypt. The Norse goddess Freya, who was worshiped on "Freya's Day" or Friday, rode a chariot pulled by two giant cats and surrounded herself with lesser cats. Rituals devoted to Freya included cats. Unfortunately for catkind, as cats became commonplace, people forgot their value as rat killers. The traits that had seemed magical became suspect. The Druids feared cats, believing that they were once human beings transformed into animals by supernatural powers. They began to offer them as sacrifices, along with horses and prisoners, during Samhain fire rituals to ward off evil. When Christian missionaries turned Freya into a demon, the cats that had been linked with her were given demonic properties.

Cats have always struck some as sinister. They are comfortable in darkness that is full of mysteries to less capable human eyes. Their aloof air can irritate those who prefer a more fawning pet. Cats can be easily provoked into a fierce defense, with razory teeth and nasty claws. They also prey upon song birds and small animals commonly thought cute. Yet another negative factor was the fact that dogs, the most-favored of humanity's pets, don't like cats. Consequently, they became a scapegoat when something seemingly supernatural happened. In the superstitious Dark Ages, cats, especially black ones, became associated with the Devil and witches.

Solitary old women were particular targets for witch-hunters. Cats were popular as companions with these women. As pet lovers have always done, they treated their cats as if they were human, speaking to them and offering them treats and comforts. This served as evidence to witch hunters that the cats were demonic familiars that helped the supposed witch in her nefarious plans. A typical incident occurred in 1619 when Joan Flower, one of the Earl of Rutland's household servants at Belvoir Castle, was accused of using her well-favored, black cat Rutterkin to murder two of the earl's sons. She died in custody before she could be put on trial, and the authorities had to settle for hanging her two daughters.

It became commonplace during the Dark Ages for superstitious people to torment and kill cats. Cats were so fiercely hunted that, by 1400, they were approaching extinction in Europe. Fortunately, their numbers recovered as the Renaissance dispelled cat superstitions. A sad comment on the progress of mankind, however, is that even today, in supposedly enlightened countries, animal shelters refuse to release black cats for adoption near Halloween-time. Would-be Satanists sometimes use them in sacrificial rituals.

Cats figure in many folk tales and legends. One story told in the Far East, relates the origin of cats. Supposedly, Noah had problems with the pair of monkeys he brought aboard the ark. The male was too randy, disturbing the other animals with his romantic hooting and exhausting his mate. Noah removed him from her cage to spare her health. He moved the male monkey to the cage containing the giraffes, but the amorous monkey began wooing the she-giraffe. Noah moved the frisky monkey to the elephants' pen, but the monkey tried to seduce that gigantic critter. Finally, Noah decided to put the monkey in with an animal that would frighten him into good behavior. He chose the cage holding the two lions. At first the monkey was afraid, but then he saw that the lions were being tormented by lice. He offered his services as nit-picker. He began with the he-lion because, he respectfully observed, the male was the king of the jungle. The monkey quickly got all of the bugs off the lion. This so soothed the beast that he fell asleep. The monkey then turned his attention to the lioness. Some months later, the lioness bore two kittens unlike any lion kittens ever seen before. They were smaller, cleverer, far more curious, and apishly agile.

Superstitions Associated With Cats:

- In England and Scotland, a black cat crossing one's path is thought good luck. In America, Ireland and parts of Europe, the reverse is thought true. In some spots, the bad luck can be reversed only by stopping and waiting till the black cat crosses back across your path.

- English sailors bought black cats for their wives. As long as the cat was happy, the sailor would enjoy good weather. A cat aboard a ship protects the ship from danger. Chinese sailors liked to have a black cat aboard ship to attract favoring winds.

- In Scotland, a black cat in the home meant the daughters of the house would enjoy many suitors.

- Sleeping with a cat is good luck.

- If a cat rubs you, he is trying to give you good fortune.

- If a cat yawns, an opportunity is coming your way.

- Demons, witches and even Satan sometimes take the form of a cat. If such a cat jumps over a corpse, the corpse will become a vampire. One should never discuss secrets in front of a cat because it might be a witch in disguise.

- Washing a cat will bring rainy weather.

- If your cat meows as you leave on a trip, you will encounter bad fortune.

- Kick a cat, and you will suffer from rheumatism.

- When a cat licks its tail, a storm is coming. When it washes its face, good weather is coming. When it washes its face in a doorway, a clergyman is coming for a visit.

- A cat that claws furniture or drapes is thought to be raising a wind.

- A cat that suddenly starts has seen a ghost.

- A cat sitting with its back to the fire means a frost or a storm is coming.

- If a cat singes its whiskers upon the hearth fire, it will never leave home.

- A boughten cat will be a poor mouser.

The Cat Came Back

The *New York Times* reported that Henri Villette, an elderly gentleman of Alençon, France, decided to rid himself of his cat by hurling it into the river Sarthe. Villette stumbled while heaving the sack into the water, fell in, and drowned. The cat escaped the sack and swam to shore.

SKELETONS

The dead have traditionally been depicted as skeletons, and Death itself is nearly always a skeleton in a hooded robe. But skeletons also have a cheerful side. This may be because, having no lips to hide their teeth, they seem to be smiling. The rattling bones of a skeleton have a merry sound that suggests playful capering. They even look like marionettes and, as any medical student can testify, are often set in playful poses. Even the traditional storage place of skeletons—a closet—suggests a game of hide and seek.

Of the bones of the skeleton, the skull is the most evocative. A rib, a tibia, or a humerus might belong to any animal, but the human skull is distinctive. Consequently, it features in many horrific tales. The most well documented stories are of "screaming" skulls.

In England, there are several legends of skulls that don't like being disturbed. One story is associated with the Pinney family of Bettiscombe in Dorset. A member of the family had traveled to the island of Nevis in the West Indies in search of his fortune. He found it and, in 1740, his son and heir John Frederick Pinney, returned home to enjoy it. Pinney brought a black West Indian slave with him as a servant. When the slave became ill, he begged Pinney to return his body to Nevis if he should die. Pinney, seeking to ease the servant's mind, agreed, but, after the slave died, he dispatched the body to the nearest churchyard. Soon, the dead servant began to indicate unhappiness with this burial.

Screams came from the slave's grave, and the Pinney home was plagued by strange thumps and rattles. Finally, Pinney dug up the corpse and brought it back to his house. The screaming and noises stopped. Thinking this might be the end of the racket, he had the body reburied. The horrid sounds returned. The body was quickly dug up again, and, again, the noises ended. A third burial attempt had the same results, and Pinney decided to keep the body, now reduced to just a skeleton, in the farmhouse where it seemed to want to be. Over the years, the bones of the skeleton were misplaced, and eventually all that remained of it was the skull. Once, the skull was tossed into a pond. The splash of its impact was instantly followed with a clap of thunder and more screaming. It was quickly fished from the water and restored to the house. On another occasion, it is said that the skull was buried in the Pinney garden. During the following three days, the skull supposedly dug itself out of the ground with its teeth. Stunned family members brought it back into the house, where it remains to this day, stored in a cardboard box with a Bible.

Buy Some Bones

Cordell's Anatomical Chart Co. in Skokie, Illinois sells human skeletons. Marshall Cordell, the company owner, ships fifty thousand parcels of real and imitation bones each year. A human skeleton with spring-held jaw and dust covers costs $2,600. A plastic imitation skeleton runs $800, and Cordell's offers a "Budget Bucky" model for just $225. Customers range from medical schools to television shows such as *Buffy, The Vampire Slayer.*

American laws severely restrict the sale of human skeletons. The skeletons of organ donors, for example, don't wind up hanging in lecture halls. India once provided most medical skeletons, but religious objections have caused the practice to be banned. Today, Cordell reports, most real skeletons come from French sources.

SPIDERS

Spiders are arachnids of the order Araneae (scorpions, mites and ticks are other members of this order). The name of the order comes from Roman mythology. Arachne was a peasant girl who had great skill at weaving. When the goddess Minerva, weaver to the gods of Mount Olympus, heard of Arachne's skill, she challenged Arachne to a contest. Arachne's work equaled Minerva's, which angered the goddess. She tore up Arachne's cloth and beat her. Humiliated, Arachne tied a rope to a tree limb and hanged herself. When Minerva heard what her jealousy had caused, she grew remorseful. She sprinkled a magic potion upon Arachne's corpse, transforming her into a spider. As such, she continues to spin and weave.

There are thirty-four thousand kinds of spiders, varying in size from a speck to a pie plate. Every continent except Antarctica supports them. It has been reported that an acre of grass can serve as a home for two million spiders.

Spider bodies are divided into the cephalothorax, the "head" part, and the abdomen, joined by a narrow stalk. The cephalo-thorax sports eight legs, eight beady eyes, and two venomous fangs. The abdomen bears several spinnerets that produce the silk the spider uses to construct webs, cocoons, and nest sacs. Spider silk is stronger than steel thread of the same diameter.

Spiders spin more than one kind of silk. While the silk used for an insect-catching web is sticky, the silk used to wrap a catch isn't. The silk used to descend or climb is stretchier. That used to weave a home

is more durable. Some baby spiders spin a small sail when they are old enough to leave their nest. They catch the wind in it and sail into the sky in search of new habitat. These little hang-gliding arachnids have been tracked soaring along for hundreds of miles. Spiders don't stick to their own webs because they have an oily coating on their bodies.

Most spiders subsist on insects they snare in their nests. The spider paralyzes the insect with its venom, then encloses the prey in a cocoon that holds the insect securely in the web, while the venom causes the insect's interior to liquefy. Once liquefied, the spider can ingest the prey's innards.

Not all spiders use webs. The trap-door spider builds a small den with a lid that can snap open. It hides inside and leaps out to snatch passing prey. The largest spider, the bird-eating spider of South America, hunts its prey by skulking through the tropical treetops. The diving spider uses its silk to create an underwater chamber to store air. Fine hairs on its body trap bubbles of air that it uses like scuba equipment. It brings bubbles of air down to the chamber, which allows it to extend its time underwater where it hunts the insects that hatch there.

Female spiders are usually larger than male spiders. The female black widow spider uses her greater size to kill and eat her mate after mating. She identifies the male spider as food and views mating as a form of hunting, not romance. By hanging around to be eaten, the male satisfies the female's hunger. This forestalls her from mating/hunting again, which lessens the chance of her eggs being fertilized by another male. Consequently, males who provide a good dinner to the female are more likely to pass on their genes.

While spider bites are usually not lethal to human beings, there are a few, terrible exceptions. The black widow spider and the brown recluse spider are very dangerous spiders that are resident to most of North America (ironically, the venom of the fearsome-looking tarantulas of South America is far less poisonous). Care should be taken around dark, enclosed places that have access to nature. Even when the venom isn't harmful, a spider bite can produce an allergic reaction or host a serious bacterial infection.

Witches used spiders in their poisonous brews. Spiders also were said to serve as familiars. According to witch hunters, a spider could find a comfy home in a crone's clothing or hair, where it could mutter gossip it had gathered by crawling through neighbors' homes.

Cobweb derives from the Anglo-Saxon word for spider, "attercoppes," which means "poison head." This was shortened to "cop" and eventually to "cob," hence cobweb.

Spider Superstitions

- Dreaming of a spider means someone will betray you.
- If a spider is spotted at a wedding, the marriage will be unhappy.
- In Switzerland, during the Black Death, spiders were thought to carry the disease from house to house at the secret behest of witches.
- Seeing a spider in the morning is bad luck.
- Seeing a spider in the evening is good luck.
- Eat a live spider in a lump of butter to cure jaundice.
- Eat a spider in jam to cure a fever.
- Cure warts by rubbing the wart with spider web then burning the web.
- Killing a spider will cause rain.
- Run into a spider web and you'll soon see a friend.
- A spider crawling on your clothing means you'll soon receive money. This connection between spiders and wealth dates to the ancient Egyptians, who wore spider charms to attract wealth.
- During the ravages of the Black Death, a spider placed in a walnut shell and hung from the neck with a ribbon was thought to protect the wearer from the disease.
- Cobwebs in the kitchen mean no love in the house.

VAMPIRES

In every culture around the world there are stories of supernatural creatures who drink blood. The region with the most elaborate legends is the Balkans, a cultural crossroads between Europe, Asia, and the Middle East. Centuries of bloody war between Christians and

Muslims during the Middle Ages and the presence of Gypsies, who had migrated over generations from India to the Balkans, created a rich blend of supernatural lore.

The word vampire is derived from the Slavic word *obyri* or *obiri*, which became *vampir* in Bulgarian. The word *nosferatu*, a synonym for vampire, is derived from the Greek *nosophoros*, meaning "plague-carrier." It became *nosufur-atu* in Old Slavonic. The vampire was a dead human being who, through the drinking of blood, lived on in an "undead" state. The preferred means used by the vampire to consume blood was to bite his victim in the neck and drink the blood that flowed out. The vampire's overlarge upper canine teeth left a distinctive pair of holes. A hungry vampire was pale, emaciated, and nervous. A vampire full of blood was ruddy, bloated and relaxed.

Vampires could be created through improper burial, violent death, birth under ill omen, suicide, sorcery, or curse. Misers, murderers, people born with extra-long teeth or pointy tongues, infants who died unbaptized, and even redheads were apt to become vampires upon death. A vampire usually killed its prey but, if he wished, he could drain his victim slowly over a period of time, then transfer some of his own blood to his victim in a final exchange that imbued the victim with the vampiric condition just as he died.

Vampires had many special abilities. They could transform themselves into bats, wolves, and other animals or dissolve themselves into a mist that could pass through the narrowest of openings. Sometimes, vampires were said to be able to fly and even become invisible. They were nearly always described as possessing powerful senses and enormous strength. They also were said to be able to beguile their victims with hypnotic powers. Vampires could command rats and wolves and even the elements to produce storms.

There were restrictions upon vampires. A vampire could be destroyed by sunlight. He could roam by night, but had to return to his coffin before dawn and remain there, dormant, till sunset. The coffin must contain soil from the vampire's homeland. The vampire couldn't pass over running water, tolerate the odor of garlic, enter a dwelling uninvited, or endure sacred objects, such as holy water or a crucifix. A vampire made no reflection in a mirror and cast no shadow. Vampires also have an obsessive-compulsive urge to undo knots and count things. A fistful of knotted twine could cause a vampire to spend hours untying each knot. A bag of spilled seed could make a vampire in full pursuit of a victim stop to count every single seed, even though it might mean being caught out of his coffin at sunrise. Iron was also a bane of vampires. To protect a cradle, iron shavings might be placed in its bottom. An iron nail hung on a string could protect a neck from vampire bite. Wrapping a vampire's coffin in iron chains would confine him.

A vampire could be killed by driving a wooden stake, preferably hawthorn or mountain ash, through his heart. Cremation, sunlight, beheading, or shooting with a blessed silver bullet could also kill a vampire. The best way to attack one was to discover where he hid his coffin, wait till daytime, then apply one of the methods of destruction. A thorough vampire kill required a stake through the heart, the head severed, the mouth filled with garlic, and the head and body, with the vampire's coffin, burned to ashes.

Some anthropologists explain the belief in vampires as arising from contagious wasting diseases. One death would be followed by another within a family or within a circle of acquaintances. The bereaved might confuse dreams of the departed with actual visitations, then, after telling others of the visit, die of the disease. It would appear the dead were preying upon the living. These beliefs were sometimes given substance when the dead were exhumed for investigation and they appeared undecayed. Dead bodies, in the open air, quickly decompose into a pile of bones. The decaying process in human bodies that have been buried, however, is different.

A body may remain unspoiled and lifelike for days or weeks. What spoilage does occur may seem unnatural. The skin may slough away, revealing what appears to be healthy skin. Shrinkage through desiccation can cause a corpse to appear emaciated, with long claw-like fingernails. The gums can retract, causing the teeth to appear to be fangs. Blood and the fluids produced by putrefaction may remain uncongealed. When a stake is driven into the chest or the chest is cut open to examine the heart, this fluid can appear to be fresh blood. Driving a stake into a corpse's heart may even cause air or putrefactive gases to be forced out through the throat with such force that they cause the corpse's larynx to make a horrid groan. All these phenomena could convince the corpse's examiners that the person was a vampire.

Vampires were just obscure folklore until the nineteenth century, when a series of English writers introduced the creature to modern literature. The novels *Carmilla,* by J. Sheridan Le Fanu, *Varney the Vampire,* by James Malcolm Rymer, and *The Vampire; a Tale,* by

John Polidori created a vampire craze. In 1897, with the publication of *Dracula,* Bram Stoker established the vampire as a favorite monster of Gothic horror stories. It became one of the best-selling books of all time and has been translated into nearly every language.

Bram Stoker based his fictional Dracula on Vlad III, the 15th-century ruler of Walachia, part of Romania (not Transylvania). Vlad's father was called "Dracul," meaning "Dragon," after a dragon upon his coat of arms. Vlad was, in turn, called "Dracula," meaning son of the Dragon. It also meant son of the Devil and Vlad seemed to do his best to live up to his moniker.

Vlad's reign was marked by terrible tortures. Unchaste women, for example, were skinned alive. On one notable occasion, Vlad gathered all the beggars and cripples in his kingdom for a feast, after which he asked them if they wished to be freed from lives of suffering. They agreed, and he promptly locked them in a hall, which he then set afire. By the end of his reign, Vlad had murdered one-fifth of his subjects, some one hundred thousand people.

Vlad's favorite form of execution was impalement. The victim would be stuck atop a sharpened post and left to slowly die, a process that could take days. So horrific was this torment that an advancing army of Turks bent on conquering Vlad's domain turned back in horror when they were confronted by the sight of twenty thousand impaled Walachians.

Vlad was eventually forced from power by the Turks and assassinated in 1476. Curiously, his tomb, opened over four hundred years later, was empty.

A Modern Vampire Casualty

In 1973, in Stoke-on-Trent, England, a Polish immigrant, terrified that he might be attacked by a vampire, took elaborate steps to protect himself. Each night, before going to sleep, he placed bags of salt between his legs and by his head. He also placed a clove of garlic in his mouth. Unfortunately for him, when he fell asleep, he aspirated the clove and choked to death.

WEREWOLVES

In psychology, the belief that one can become a wolf is called lycanthropy. The word comes from the Greek words *lykos*, meaning wolf, and *anthropos*, meaning man. In folklore, such wolfmen are called werewolves. As depicted in films, the werewolf is a hapless individual who, bitten by another werewolf, is cursed to change into a savage combination of wolf and human being whenever the moon is full. He then runs wild, attacking and killing. Only a silver bullet can end his curse, by killing the werewolf. Most of this is pure Hollywood invention.

In legend, werewolves weren't created by being bitten by another werewolf and were as vulnerable to bullets—silver or otherwise—as any other creature. They also weren't the unwilling objects of a curse. They were evil men and women who chose to become werewolves through sorcery so that they might indulge in murder and cannibalism.

Stories of werewolves are very old. The ancient Greeks believed that the region of their homeland called Arcadia was particularly cursed with the creatures. A cult linking Zeus with wolves was active there. Priests of this cult held a yearly feast during which animal flesh mixed with human flesh was eaten. Whoever ate the human meat became a werewolf and would remain one until he abstained from human flesh for nine years. The cult was linked to the myth of Lycaos, a king of Arcadia. When Zeus paid a visit in his palace, Lycaos attempted to curry the favor of Zeus by offering him the flesh

of a child. Zeus was furious and punished Lycaos by transforming him into a wolf.

As Europe became Christian, Satan became the maker of werewolves. Those unfortunates identified as werewolves were usually burned at the stake. By 1270, one could be burned for simply not believing in werewolves. It took over three centuries before werewolves began to be dismissed as superstition.

A Werewolf at Work

In 1603, in a small village in the southwest of France, children were disappearing. Some went missing while playing. Others vanished while on errands. One infant was even stolen from his cradle. No one knew what could be happening till a thirteen-year-old girl tending cows was attacked by a mysterious creature resembling a large reddish dog. The snarling creature snapped at the girl and tore her clothing. She gamely fended off the monster with the iron-tipped cattle prod. When she reported the incident, the villagers knew what was preying on their children: a werewolf.

After the cowherd told her tale, Jean Grenier, a boy of the same age, boasted to a girlfriend that he was the werewolf. He claimed he had a magical wolf pelt that, with an exotic ointment, allowed him to become a wolf. A mysterious tall, dark man in the woods that he identified as the Lord of the Forest had given him these items in return for his swearing eternal service. Grenier said that he and some fellow werewolves spent their nights hunting and eating human children. Overheard at his boasting, Grenier was arrested.

Instead of protesting his innocence, Grenier proudly gave details that proved his involvement in the murders. A court ruled Grenier insane and confined him in a Franciscan monastery in Bordeaux. The monks noted that he had a demonic appearance with a thin frame and black eyes set deep in a feral face. He loved hearing stories about wolves, often went about on all fours, and kept his fingernails sharp as claws. After eight years of confinement, the confessed child murderer died peacefully.

PART II

Celebrating Halloween

8

HALLOWEEN COSTUMES

I bet living in a nudist colony takes all the fun out of Halloween.

Thirteen-year-old contestant in a contest to write a "Deep Thought" in the manner of *Saturday Night Live*'s Jack Handey

According to the National Retail Federation, as mentioned earlier, about $1.5 billion is spent each year in America for Halloween costumes. Countless commercially prepared costumes are available, but a lot of fun can be found in creating your own. The back of your closet, the attic, the local thrift shop, and art supply stores can all provide materials. The following are a few simple outfits that can be quickly put together. They are divided into children's and adult costumes, but the categories aren't exclusive. A child's costume can be adapted for an adult, and vice versa.

CHILDREN'S COSTUMES

Children love to wear costumes. Fortunately, a wide variety of outfits can be made using simple techniques and inexpensive materials. Many of these costumes involve modifying ordinary clothing, especially sweatshirts, which can be unmodified for après-Halloween use. Here are a few costume ideas.

Wings and Antennae

Wings can be made by cutting two large ovals from white posterboard or craft foam. Stitch the wings to the back of the child's costume. You may be tempted to use ribbon or string to tie the wings around the child's neck, but this creates a risk of strangling.

More elaborate wings can be made by stretching white pantyhose over coat hangers bent into wing shapes. The ends of the hose can unravel if cut, so roll them up and secure them with fabric tape. Be sure to cover any protruding ends of the coat hanger with tape to prevent injury.

Antennae can be purchased at novelty stores or made using pipe cleaners, small Styrofoam spheres, and an elastic headband. Paint the spheres to match the costume, then push the pipe cleaners through the spheres. Secure the spheres by bending the pipe cleaner around and twisting it on itself. Twist the other ends of the pipe cleaners around the headband.

BAT

A child's bat outfit can be made using a gray or black hooded sweatshirt and two yards of cheap black cloth. Fold the cloth once to form a one-yard by one-yard square. Cut a curve beginning at the crease and running to the opposite diagonal corner, with the curve bulging away from the crease. Cut scallops into the curve to simulate a bat wing. Stitch the bat wings to the back of the sweatshirt across the shoulders and along the back of the sleeves. Cut two large, pointed bat ears from black cardboard and stitch them to the hood of the sweatshirt. A more realistic costume can be made by stitching gray fake fur to the front of the sweatshirt. The fur should run from the shoulders down past the edge of the sweatshirt.

Use a stick of black greasepaint to draw arched eyebrows and to blacken the tip of the nose. Finish the costume with a black eye mask.

BEE

Buy a roll of yellow duct tape and a black, hooded sweatshirt. Run the tape horizontally around the sweatshirt, leaving bands of black of equal width. This may be easier if the sweatshirt is on the wearer. Fashion wings for the costume. Put the hood of the sweatshirt up,

Template for a Child's Mask

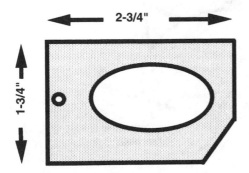

Fold a 1-3/4" by 5-1/2" piece of thin cardboard in half. The oval for eye is centered 1-1/2" from left side. The nose opening is cut approximately 2-1/4" from left at the bottom and 1-1/8" from the top on the right. Make a small hole on the side. Unfold the cardboard.

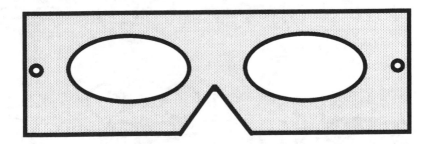

The mask's dimensions can be altered for smaller or larger children. Test for size by placing the template on the child's face. Once a fit has been found, you can use the template to design more elaborate masks.

Using the Template

Lay the template upon a sheet of thin cardboard. Trace the eyes and nose then mark where the holes for the elastic should be cut. Next, draw the mask. Crayons or markers can be used to color it appropriately. Here, the mask is a cat. Below are a few other Halloween masks.

tighten its strings, and tie them. Add black antennae and a simple black eye mask.

For a novel touch, try changing the bee costume into a killer bee costume, such as were featured in the 1970s on *Saturday Night Live.* A comically large sombrero, a pair of six-shooters with a gun belt, one or two bandoleers, and a false handlebar mustache make the costume.

BUNCH OF GRAPES

A purple leotard, a few dozen purple balloons, and a hat made of green construction-paper leaves make this costume. This is a cute outfit for a female but a potential risk for males (Richard Simmons got his show-biz start in a similar outfit doing underwear commercials). Also be warned: Popping the balloons is always some idiot's idea of high wit.

BUTTERFLY

Little girls love butterflies. Paint a pair of wings to mimic a butterfly. Add antennae. The girl can wear a frilly, go-to-church dress or a leotard that matches the colors used on the wing.

CAT

Little girls also love cats, and a cat costume can be easily improvised. A black leotard with a black rope for a tail and a black hair band with two black triangle ears attached with fabric tape make the costume. Cat whiskers can be drawn on the face with an eyebrow pencil. The tip of the nose can also be darkened to increase the cat-like appearance.

An alternate cat outfit for colder weather can be made with a hooded sweatshirt of a cat-appropriate color and a length of rope dyed to match. Attach the tail to the back of the sweatshirt. Cut two triangles for ears from cardboard, paint them, and attach them to the hood, bending them into a catlike position. Apply cat makeup as above.

CAVEMAN OR CAVEWOMAN

A caveman costume (see Figure on page 167) can be made using fake fur from a fabric store. Take a piece of string and hang it from your shoulder until it reaches to your knee. Mark off the length on the fake fur. Cut a slit wide enough to pass your head through across the fake fur at this point. Mark off the string's length again from this point. Cut across the fake fur at the second spot. Fold the fake fur at the neck opening and stitch up the edges to about a foot from the fold to make a simple tunic. The costume's appearance is helped if you use brown yarn and very large, crude stitching. You may need to make adjustments. Cut a strip of the fake fur and use it for a belt. Wear sandals. Some accoutrements can improve the costume. Start with a bone necklace made by cutting bone shapes from white cardboard and stringing them together. A club can be made using a cardboard tube. Wrap it in newspapers to form a club shape, securing them with carton tape. Spray-paint it brown to simulate wood. The caveman can appear more fearsome by smudging his cheeks with charcoal.

A cavewoman costume can be made in the same way. Modesty, or lack of modesty, can require adjustments. A cardboard bone in the hair is a nice touch.

CLOWN

Go to a thrift shop and purchase the loudest, most colorful shirt, tie, and pants you can. Pajamas are often very clownlike in appearance. You can make a garish outfit by painting large dots of red, green, blue, and so on, upon a white shirt and a pair of white pants with fabric paint. Using greasepaint, whiten the wearer's face, redden his nose, arch his eyebrows, and draw a wide smiling mouth. A colored clown wig can be bought at a novelty store. A bulb bicycle horn makes a nice accoutrement.

COWBOY OR COWGIRL

Blue jeans, a cowboy shirt, a red bandanna, cowboy boots, and a cowboy hat are all you need for this costume. A six-shooter with gun belt makes a nice accessory. The bandanna can be tied across the face to become a bandit. A cowgirl can wear a denim skirt.

DEVIL

A devil costume can be made with a pair of red sweatpants, a red hooded sweatshirt, and a bit of matching red cloth. Make a devil tail by painting a length of rope red. Cut a three-inch triangle from cardboard and paint it red. Attach it to the end of the rope and stitch the other end inside the bottom back of the sweatshirt. Make horns for

Caveman Tunic

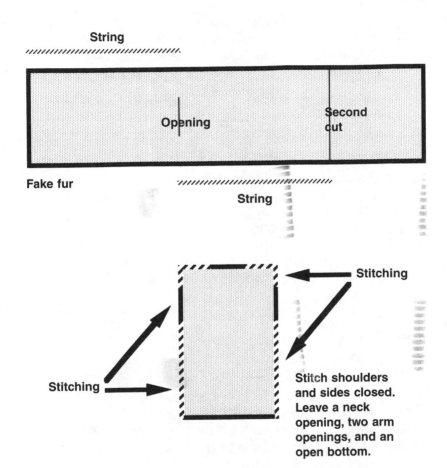

String

Opening

Second cut

Fake fur

String

Stitching

Stitching

Stitch shoulders and sides closed. Leave a neck opening, two arm openings, and an open bottom.

the devil using red construction paper rolled into small cones. Use glue to hold them together. Attach to the hood of the sweatshirt with a few stitches of red thread.

DINOSAUR

This costume can be constructed using a green, hooded sweatshirt. Add a short triangular tail using a piece of matching cloth. Use two long sheets of craft foam to make pointy spine plates. Spray paint them green and attach them with safety pins.

Felt for Costuming

Felt is a good material for costume making. It's inexpensive, can be easily cut, doesn't fray, and doesn't need to be hemmed. Felt also comes in many colors. Some newer brands have sparkly bits worked into the material. This can make for interesting wizard robes. Larger, more visible patterns of sparkles can be made with glue and glitter. Cutouts of stars, comets, and planets can be cut from a contrasting color of felt and glued onto a felt costume.

FAIRY GODMOTHER OR PRINCESS

These make good costumes for females and males who don't mind a lot of teasing. For adults, find the gaudiest old prom dress or bridesmaid's gown in the thrift store. It should preferably reach the floor and have a full skirt. A child can wear a pink leotard with a skirt of multicolored netting to become a fairy or a cut down, satiny adult dress to be a princess. A fairy godmother can wear a cardboard tiara painted silver with glued-on glitter or antennae tipped with glitter-covered stars. A princess can wear a tiara, a crown, or a tall cone made from stiff paper. Glue one end of a silky piece of fabric to the top of the cone and let the other end drape around the shoulders. Attach an elastic chin strap to the cone to keep it secure. White gloves make good accessories.

The fairy godmother should have a wand. A stick with a cardboard star attached to one end then painted silver will suffice. Toy stores sometimes have wands with tips that light up when a switch is pressed.

Fairy godmothers also need wings. Decorate them with lots of sparkles.

GHOST

This is the classic do-it-yourself costume—just an old sheet with eyeholes cut into it. It is common, however, to have problems seeing from inside the sheet. This can be dangerous for small children, who tend to charge about with little thought of risk. There are a few tricks that can be used to make a safer ghost costume. Have the wearer dress in the sweater or coat that he will wear under the sheet. Put the sheet over this before cutting the holes. Have the wearer extend his arms. Using diaper safety pins, attach the sheet to the wearer's cuffs and to his coat behind his head. The wearer should then be able to move his arms freely. Use colored chalk to mark where the eyes are under the sheet (be careful not to poke the wearer in the eye). Also mark where the wearer's hands will protrude from the sheet, and trace a hemline that clears the ground by at least one foot so that the wearer won't trip on the sheet. Remove the pins and take off the sheet. Cut the eyeholes, the hand holes, and the hem. Brush glue along the cut edges to prevent fraying. Ordinary white glue can be used (laying the cloth out on waxed paper for the gluing may help prevent unwanted attachments).

A ghost who is a good roller skater can add an eerie touch to her costume by wearing skates. It will make the ghost seem to float and swoop along.

HIPPIE

This costume is guaranteed to put a shiver of disquiet into aging Boomers. Some thrift shops have corners where tie-dyed or paisley shirts, fuzzy vests, bell-bottoms, miniskirts, and even peace symbol necklaces can still be found. An old pair of small-lensed, wire-rimmed, reading spectacles can be turned into granny glasses (just remove the lenses). A bit of tinted cellophane can give them a "trippy" appearance. A wig with long, straight hair is required for both males and females. A bandanna or flowery scarf folded into a band can be worn as a headband. Sandals and beads are good accessories. A bag of oregano makes another fun accessory and gives you an excuse to act extra stupid—but look out for narcs, man.

LADYBUG

A ladybug costume can be made using a black sweatshirt and felt. Cut a circle of yellow felt that will cover most of the sweatshirt's back. Stitch it into place. Cut six three-inch-wide circles out of black felt. Using a glue gun, hot-glue these circles around the larger circle like the numbers on the face of a clock. Cut a one-inch strip of black felt long enough to reach across the large yellow circle. Glue this vertically across the circle. Add a hat—a little bowler, a flat cap, or even a straw hat—to the outfit. Attach antennae to the hat. Finish the outfit with a black or yellow eye mask.

MUMMY

A mummy costume can be fashioned using cheesecloth, white adhesive tape, a white hooded sweatshirt, and sweatpants. Cut the cheesecloth into three-inch-wide strips. You will need at least fifty

feet for a preteen. Have the child put on the pants. Wind cheesecloth around the pants, using adhesive tape to secure it. Wind loosely so that the pants can be slid off if needed. Next, have the child put on the sweatshirt. Wrap it with cheesecloth strips. Don't cover the hands or face, and wind the strips loosely so the sweatshirt can be slipped off over the head. Cover the child's face with white greasepaint. Darken his eye sockets and draw lines on the cheeks to simulate gauntness. The child's hands can be covered with white gloves. To avoid tripping, the child's feet should be left uncovered except by ordinary footwear—a pair of white sneakers makes a good choice.

The mummy costume can be very warm. This makes it wonderful for trick-or-treating in a cold climate but can make it a sauna in warm weather or indoors.

PIRATE

Take an inexpensive felt cowboy hat and bend up its brim on three sides, creating a tricorner hat. Secure the brim in place with staples or hot glue applied with a glue gun. Obtain a loose white shirt. Make a vest to wear over the shirt by cutting the sleeves off a solid-colored shirt. A red shirt makes a good choice. Obtain a solid-colored pair of pants. Leggings can be fashioned by wearing white, knee-high stockings. Tuck the pants into these. Wear black shoes or tall black rubber boots. Wind a scarf around the waist. An eyepatch can be made with a large rubber band and a bit of black paper. An eyebrow pencil can be used to draw a scar upon one cheek. A gold, clip-on loop earring and a cardboard sword tucked through the scarf complete the costume. A nice accessory is a toy parrot attached to the shoulder. The pirate can provide a voice for the bird and demand, "Polly wants a treat."

A simpler pirate's hat can be made with black craft foam. Cut two sixteen-inch-wide by six-inch-high pieces of the foam. Place the two pieces one atop the other. Using chalk, draw a curve rising from two inches above the bottom of the hat to the top at the center of the foam then back down to 2 inches above the bottom of the hat. Then cut along the chalk line. The hat will resemble what Napoleon wore. Rub off the chalk and glue the far edges of the cut foam together. Place the hat upon the child's head. You may have to shrink the head opening by gluing more of the hat together. Affix a paper skull and crossbones to the center of the front of the hat.

SKELETON

To create this outfit, purchase a hooded black sweatshirt, white gloves, and a roll of white duct tape. Put the sweatshirt on the costume wearer. Cut the tape into bone shapes. Place the tape on the sweatshirt in the pattern of the body's bones. Don't worry about anatomical accuracy. Whiten the wearer's face with powder and darken the eye sockets and tip of the nose. Draw black lines across the lips to simulate teeth.

ROBOT

A robot can be produced using a cardboard box over the body and a box over the head. Begin with a gray sweatshirt and sweatpants. Cut the bottom out of the box that will be used over the torso. Cut armholes and a neck hole. Cut out the bottom and the face of the head box. Detergent bottle caps and other odds and ends of plastic can be glued to the boxes to simulate robotic controls. Don't use anything sharp or pointed. Add antennae to the head box. Rolling the antennae into coils can be effective. Spray-paint the boxes gray. Battery-powered lights can be added.

You may be tempted to cut just eyeholes in the head box, but this will severely limit the wearer's vision. For young children, it's wise not to wear the head box. Use a hooded sweatshirt and attach the antennae to the hood.

With a little alteration, the robot can become a spaceman or a knight in armor.

UNIFORMS

Attics often contain old uniforms. Military uniforms can be soldier costumes. An old nurse's hat can be matched with a white dress to make a nurse costume. An old football helmet and uniform can be used to become a football hero. The folks at the Goodwill store recommend using foam rubber to pad out too-large helmets so they'll fit and not obstruct vision.

WIZARD

An old graduation gown can be turned into a wizard's costume. Make a pointed wizard hat out of posterboard. Decorate it with stars and crescent moons cut from felt. A white or gray wig and a matching beard improve the disguise. A wizard's wand is a good accessory.

The PC Police Are Watching

When choosing a costume for a child, parents must consider the political beliefs of those who might take offense at the outfit. Schools, in particular, have established policies about what kinds of costumes can be worn at school Halloween parties. Costumes that might offend an ethnic group are commonly banned. The great majority of families wouldn't consider such a costume. A second category of banned costumes is far more problematic, however. These are costumes that school officials deem too violent or that include "weapons."

In 1998, Jordan Locke, age five, was suspended from kindergarten at Curtisville Elementary School in Pennsylvania for wearing a firefighter's costume that sported a five-inch plastic fire ax. The toy ax violated the school's zero-tolerance weapon policy.

ADULT COSTUMES

LAUREN BACALL

This costume can be made with a wig that can be styled into a 1940s do, a knee-length dress with puffy shoulders, a necklace of large beads, and clunky-heeled shoes. A slinky evening dress, faux pearls, and a faux-fur wrap produce a more glamorous look. Wear light, pinkish makeup and bright red lipstick. Dark eyebrows can give you a Joan Crawford look. Use a washable marker to draw a line up the back of your pantyhose. When you're done, ask your boyfriend if he knows how to whistle. Or if you want to return to the Crawford look, exaggerate the red lips and padded shoulders, get a few wire hangers, and go out as a true nightmare monster, "Mommie Dearest."

HUMPHREY BOGART

Buy a fedora, a 1940s-style suit with broad lapels and baggy pants, an old trenchcoat, and a wide, sober tie from a thrift shop. Squint, work the lips, Bogart-style with an unlit cigarette, and do your best "Play-it-again-Sam" impersonation of the guy who didn't get the girl in *Casablanca*. Nice accoutrements include a Zippo, a pistol, wing tips, and a plastic toy bird that can be painted black to serve as a Maltese Falcon.

CARMEN MIRANDA

A brightly colored turban, a flowery, also brightly colored dress, a pair of wedge sandals, and a small basket filled with various plastic fruits are needed for this costume. Attach the basket to the top of the turban. Wear 1940s-style makeup, with bright red lipstick and bright red nails. A necklace of plastic bananas makes a nice touch. Cultivate a South American spitfire attitude and accent.

COWBOY OR COWGIRL

A comic version of the cowboy outfit described earlier for children can be made by wearing a huge cowboy hat, high-heeled boots, and an overly embroidered cowboy shirt with pearl buttons. An extra-large pistol and a gun belt with lots of faux silver help. A pair of chaps made from shaggy, white fake fur can be very amusing. Add a large tinfoil sheriff's star and cardboard, tinfoil-covered spurs. Affect an exaggerated Texican accent, pardner. If you can twirl a lasso, you'll be the life of the party.

DILBERT

Dilbert is the downtrodden engineer in the comic strip of the same name created by Scott Adams. A short-sleeved white shirt, a red-and-black-striped tie, black plastic eyeglasses (remove lenses), and black dress slacks make this costume. The tie can be given the upward curve sported by Dilbert by gluing pipe cleaners inside and bending them. For cold weather, you can add a white lab coat.

DOCTOR OR MAD SCIENTIST

A white lab coat can be matched with a black tie and a pair of spectacles (remove lenses) to make a doctor's costume. Thrift stores often carry hospital scrubs. Match with a shower cap and a face-mask, and you can be a surgeon. Get a generic bill pad from an office supply store and spend a few minutes making out "bills" for brain adjustments, nose jobs, buttocks realignment, et cetera, with huge fees. Pass these out to your friends and demand payment. Alternatively, you can use a notepad to make out prescriptions for a large bottle of IQ pills, a brain replacement, two gallons of whiskey a day until problems disappear, and so forth. You might carry a large plastic bottle with a label PLACEBOS filled with candy-coated chocolates to offer "patients." Toy stores can provide you with a stethoscope, tongue depressors, and other medical tools.

A false goatee or odd mustache, madly tousled hair, and a jug filled with green soda can turn the doctor costume into a mad scientist costume. For a mad surgeon, add a white apron and heavy rubber gloves from the hardware store. Copiously smear your outfit with washable red paint. Purchase a severed hand from a novelty store and stick it, fingers out, in a pocket. A child's plastic set of toys can provide mad implements such as a screwdriver, monkey wrench, pliers, and a plastic saw. These will be easier to carry and safer than the real things. The instruments can be touched up with red paint for added horror. Mutter and repeat: "Mad, they said! Mad? I'll show them mad!"

DOROTHY

America's favorite Kansas farm girl can be an easy and effective costume. A white, short-sleeved blouse, a bibbed, blue gingham dress, and a pair of low-heeled shoes covered in red glitter are the basics. Put your hair in pigtails with ribbons. A basket with a toy black terrier dog is a necessary prop.

Fake Blood

Mix 1 cup creamy peanut butter with 1 quart corn syrup, ½ cup powdered dish detergent, and 2 ounces vodka. The vodka helps prevent the mixture from hardening when splattered. Use 1 ounce of red food color and 12 to 18 drops blue food color to give the blood its crimson hue. To make thinner blood, use less peanut butter or more vodka. If it becomes too thin, add flour to rethicken it.

The peanut butter is meant to hold the food coloring and helps prevent it from staining fabric. Despite this, it can still stain. Don't get it on anything expensive to replace. Spilled mix should be cleaned up quickly using ordinary soap. The blood can spoil or grow moldy. It should be kept refrigerated (shake well before using) and thrown out after a couple of days.

The mixture is nontoxic but should not be consumed.

DRAG

A quick costume can be made for a male by finding an old prom dress or bridesmaid's gown of suitable size. Some garish makeup and a cheap wig complete the outfit. A big vinyl purse makes a nice accessory. The larger the guy, the more humorous the effect. A five o'clock shadow makes a nice touch.

ELVIS

The later, plumper Elvis makes a good character to impersonate for Halloween. Get a pair of white bell-bottoms and a white shirt. Glue cardboard inside the shirt collar and the front of the neck opening to make it stand up stiff. Glue sequins all over the shirt and pants. Wear a white scarf around your neck and a big-buckled belt. A pompadour and sideburns are necessities. The former can be gotten using hair gel; the latter can be made with fake hair. Carry a microphone, strike a kung fu pose, and when people give you candy, thank them, thank them very much.

FIFTIES GAL

Put your hair in a ponytail. Purchase from the thrift shop a white, Peter Pan–collar blouse, a wide black belt, and a solid-color skirt that goes down well below the knee. Tie a bow around the ponytail with a scarf of the same color as the skirt. Wear a pair of white tennis shoes with white ankle socks. Limit your makeup to pink lipstick. Harlequin glasses (remove the lenses) and a poodle appliqué on the skirt make nice touches.

FIFTIES GUY

This is a simple costume. Wear a plain white T-shirt, blue jeans with cuffs, and pointy-toed black shoes or biker boots. Using hair gel, slick your hair back in a pompadour. A package of cigarettes rolled in your T-shirt sleeve makes a nice touch. A leather jacket can be worn for a "bad" boy look or a letter jacket for a "good" guy look. James Dean wore a red cloth jacket.

MARDI GRAS MASKS

Ornately decorated masks are a Mardi Gras tradition. Simple masks bought at a novelty store can be decorated in the same manner. Trace spirals of glue, then sprinkle glitter on them. Using a hot-glue gun, attach exaggerated feather "eyebrows" to the mask, or multicolored sequins. Ribbons, beads, or loops of gold-colored chain can also be attached. The masks are a nice way to costume yourself for a formal Halloween party where you're required to wear a tuxedo or gown.

GRIM REAPER

Add a cowl to an old black graduation gown to create this outfit. Use stage makeup to whiten the face, then darken the eye sockets to give a skull-like look. Draw vertical lines across the lips and darken the tip of the nose to heighten the skull effect. A scythe can be improvised by attaching a cardboard blade to an old broom handle. Be sure to attach it securely, because it's apt to be flailed around a great deal. Also, be sure that the point of the blade is blunt to avoid injuring others.

GYPSY FORTUNE-TELLER

Cover your hair with a brightly colored scarf. Wear a puffy white blouse and a long floral-patterned skirt. A second scarf can be tied around the waist. Several strings of beads and some gold loop earrings are good accessories. You can have fun by "reading" palms or by placing elaborate curses on your associates.

HAWAIIAN MAIDEN

A grass skirt can be fashioned using a length of green felt. Cut slits from one edge to within about three inches of the other edge. A safety pin secures the skirt. Wear it over a leotard. Top the outfit with a Hawaiian shirt tied at the tails in front and leis made with artificial flowers. Bobby-pin an artificial orchid behind your ear.

LAWYER

This costume is far more frightening than any vampire—after all, a vampire can be staked and buried at a crossroads. Lawyers can't be so easily defeated, and even if one may fall, a hundred others spring up in his place.

To dress as a lawyer, get a sober gray or blue suit and a briefcase. Wear glasses. Label a stack of papers with legalese: WRIT, SUBPOENA, COURT ORDER, and so on. Glue these into the case in such a way that the labeled parts protrude. Carry a big fist full of similarly prepared papers. More papers can be protruding from your pockets and attached to your suit. Shout legal battle cries such as, "I'll sue!" or, "If it doesn't fit you must acquit!" or, "I object!" Using large wads of play money, stuff your pockets.

MAN IN BLACK

All that's needed for this costume is a black suit and tie with black sunglasses. A pocket flashlight to wipe memories makes a good accessory. A toy store can provide a ray gun, or a large squirt gun can be spray-painted silver to look like an alien vaporizer. A rubber squid can be turned into an alien by spray-painting it neon green. The alien can be stuffed in a pocket with its tentacles dangling free.

NERD OR NERDETTE

A pair of dark or plaid "high-water" slacks, white socks, a white shirt, a pair of thick-rimmed glasses, and a pocket protector stuffed with pens make this costume. Penny loafers or a too-small cardigan are nice touches. Slick your hair down or give it a nerdish cowlick with hair gel. Girls can substitute a plaid skirt for the slacks. A belt that is several inches too long can increase nerdity, especially if the slacks or skirt are worn high on the waist.

PUNK GAL

Wear a black, torn T-shirt, a leather or rubber skirt, fishnet stockings with many torn spots, and hiking boots. Draw crude fake tattoos on yourself with washable markers. Wear black lipstick, nail polish, and lots of dark eye makeup. Spike your hair with hair spray and gel. If you have pierced ears, wear large safety pins through them. You can also put a few safety pins through your shirt. Close some of the holes you tore in it with them. Novelty stores sell colored hair spray that you can use to give your hair a blue or green tint. Snap on a wide dog collar. You can add a punkish slogan to your shirt. Don't worry about neat lettering or spelling or even if the letters are made correctly.

PUNK GUY

This is the same as the punk gal, but substitute torn jeans for the skirt.

SCARECROW

A pair of bib overalls, a flannel shirt, a bandanna, and a straw hat make this costume. Bits of straw taped inside the shirt cuffs, pant cuffs, and shirt collar suggest straw stuffing.

SIXTIES GAL

A flouncy blouse, a miniskirt, a wig with long, straight hair and bangs, and fishnet stockings make this outfit. Wear a very pale color of lipstick and heavy eye makeup. Solid stockings with 1960s-style patterns are an alternative to fishnets. Tall disco boots and lots of long beads make good additions.

SIXTIES GUY

Think Austin Powers. A Beatles wig, bell-bottoms, a velvet jacket, and a flouncy shirt with a frilly collar are needed for this outfit. A thrift store may even provide you with Nehru jacket.

TWENTIES GAL

Wear a black wig cut in a bob style. Apply a coat of talcum to your face to give it a pale Theda Bara look, and use bright red lipstick to draw Cupid's-bow lips. Get a knee-length sleeveless dress that has no waist or a very low waist. A silky material looks good. The best dress—but one that's hard to find—is one covered in fringe. Wear a sparkly headband with a small plume above your forehead. Secure the plume by pinning it to the headband with bobby pins. Wear low-heeled patent-leather shoes. An extra-long strand or two of fake pearls is a must. Wear pale hose and a second sparkly headband as a garter. A fake cigarette holder can be made with a thin dowel painted black with three inches of white paint simulating the cigarette. A feather boa looks good with this costume. Think flapper and learn the Charleston.

TWENTIES GUY

Baggy pants, a white shirt, suspenders, a loud and large bow tie, a V-neck or high school letter sweater, and a straw hat with the brim folded up make this outfit. Slick down your hair with hair gel like Rudolf Valentino, or part it in the middle like Alfalfa. Thick-rimmed, round black glasses (remove lenses) suit this costume. An old full-length fake fur coat can stand in for a raccoon coat. A hip flask, a megaphone, and a varsity pennant on a cane make nice accessories. Think twenty-three skidoo and learn the Charleston.

VAMPIRE

For males, an old tuxedo with a red scarf to serve as a cummerbund make this outfit. A cape can be fashioned from a few yards of black cloth (a red lining makes a nice vampire look). A black skirt can be quickly turned into a cape by cutting it vertically at the point where the dress snaps, then hemming it along the cut or by using black fabric tape to cover the cut edges.

Female vampires can wear a black, low-cut dress, a cape, fishnet stockings, and black high heels.

Plastic vampire fangs can be easily purchased, along with white makeup to give the face a deceased look. The hair can be slicked back Bela Lugosi–style with hair gel. Homemade fangs can be made using a strip of plastic cut from a washed, plastic milk jug. Cut a thick strip, then cut a W from the strip, leaving the fangs now attached to a narrower strip. Tuck the fang strip into the upper mouth. Talcum powder can substitute for makeup to give a nice undead pallor to the face. Bright red lipstick for both male and female vampires suggest they have been sipping their beverage of choice.

WITCH

There are two types of witch: the hag and the sex bomb. Both need pointy hats. These are readily available at novelty stores. You can make your own with black posterboard and tape, but the store-bought hats are cheap, save time, and look better. If the point droops too much for your taste, stuff the hat with a little twisted tissue paper.

The hag wears a ratty black dress and clunky shoes. Top this off with a shawl, cardigan, or cape. They should be black or dirty gray and decrepit. Dye can be used to achieve a morbid black or gloomy gray. A ratty old baby afghan, for example, can become a black shawl. If you use dye in your washing machine, be sure to run the washer through a few complete cycles with no load, then do dark loads before light or white loads. As with the vampire outfit above, a black skirt can be turned into a cape. A thrift store can supply one, and a bit of tearing will make it look hag-suitable.

A novelty or costume store can provide makeup for a witchy look. The hag can streak her hair with white or green temporary hair spray and, using spirit gum, attach a large, well-warted rubber nose. Add a hairy wart on the chin and blacken out a few teeth with wax. Use green powder to give a reptilian "blush." Darken the eye sockets with black powder. Draw age lines and darken the hollows of the cheeks. A nice touch is to glue long black, clawlike nails to the fingers using washable white school glue. The nails can be cut from construction paper.

Hag witches scuttle and caper about bent over. Remember to cackle a lot, threaten to eat children, and carry a broom.

The sex bomb witch wears more elegant clothing: a slinky black dress, a silky black wrap, black high heels, and black net hose. The emphasis is on glamour. A novelty store can provide a wig with long, straight black hair. Rub white talcum powder onto the arms, face, and other exposed areas. Be careful applying it; too much can mess up a dark outfit. Wear heavy eye makeup and bright red lipstick. Sex-bomb witches slink and flirt. Remember to growl like Mae West (use some of her lines: "I used to be Snow White, but I drifted") and carry a broom.

A nice addition to both hag and sex bomb is a large realistic rubber frog pinned to the shoulder or peeping from a pocket. The hag can also accessorize with rubber snakes, bats, or rats.

ZOMBIE

While the true zombie is a resident of the Caribbean, movies such as *Night of the Living Dead* have given Americans their own variety of zombie. These are flesh-eating dead people brought back to inarticulate, shambling life. Go to a thrift shop for the costume components. What you're putting together is essentially a burial outfit. For a male, get a dark suit, tie, and white shirt. Rip a few seams in the suit coat, tear a few holes in the pants, and smudge the shirt with a rag dipped in black dye, then green dye. For a female, get a "Sunday-go-to-church" outfit. Rip, tear, and smudge. Use hair spray and teasing to set the hair in an insane rumple. Whiten the hands and face with talcum powder or stage makeup. Use black or deep purple makeup around the eyes, at the temples, on the sides of the nose, and at centers of the cheeks to give a sunken, dead look. Liberally dust your costume with talcum powder to simulate grave dust. Red paint, splattered on the costume, can simulate the blood of the zombie's victims. Smear a little red makeup at the corner of the mouth. When moving, do it stiffly with arms extended and with a lot of groans and growls.

An effective zombie accessory is a limb that the zombie tore off a victim. The easiest limb to make is a man's leg from the calf down. Cut a sixteen-inch piece and a six-inch piece from a two-by-two. Nail the shorter piece to the end of the longer piece to form an L. Wrap the wood in crumpled newspaper to give it the crude shape of a leg. Use tape to secure the paper. Dip the severed end in red paint. The frayed paper will look like chewed flesh. Let the paint dry, then put an old sock and shoe over the foot. Cut the leg from an old pair of pants and put the severed leg in it. Glue or stitch the sock, shoe, and pant leg securely to the "limb."

If you want the leg snack to be even more revolting, you can buy some large red rubber bands from an office supply store to simulate veins. Snip a few of them then attach the strips securely with staples to the severed end of the leg before wrapping it in newspaper.

A final gruesome possibility is to get a squirt bulb with a length of hose. Fill the bulb with ketchup and secrete the bulb in the pant leg. To horrify your friends, make blood spurt out of the leg. Since it's ketchup, you can even taste it and groan "Goooood!" then grab a floppy vein in your teeth and pull on it, with rubbery result. Red string licorice can be tucked into the leg, then pulled out and eaten.

Costumes that might seem bland can be made more horrific by converting them into zombiefied versions. A cowboy can become a zombie cowboy by sprinkling with talcum powder "grave dust" and wearing zombie facial makeup. A football player can become an undead footballer in the same way. Undead lawyers, clowns, hippies, and tourists are all fun possibilities.

Costumes for the Physically Challenged

There's no reason a person with a physical disability can't participate in Halloween costume fun. Nearly all of the costumes described above can be worn, but there are also outfits that lend themselves to particular disabilities. Kathy Troquille, a counselor for the handicapped and a family friend who is herself paralyzed, dressed as a Volkswagen Beetle for a costume party. Another family friend, Dr. Terry G. Harris, a professor of English at Louisiana State University in Shreveport, who was born missing part of his right arm, attended a costume party dressed as a "one-armed bandit."

Using cardboard and poster paint, wheelchairs can be disguised as race cars, pickup trucks, fire engines, airplanes, tanks, or other vehicles. Other objects can also provide ideas. Try dressing the chair as a washing machine with the occupant's head popping out of the hatch.

The sitting posture can be incorporated into the costume. A wheelchair can be disguised as a throne and the occupant dressed as a king or queen. An old-fashioned dress and a bun hairdo can become a Whistler's Mother costume.

There are precautions to observe in costumes for the disabled, in addition to the standard precautions listed in this chapter. Long flowing costumes can become entangled in the spokes of a wheelchair. Precarious headgear is also inadvisable.

Costumes that need constant manipulation or adjustment can become tiresome.

GROUP COSTUMES

It can be fun for a group of friends to get together and costume themselves as a group. A *Wizard of Oz* group can feature Dorothy, her three chums, a wizard, good witches, bad witches, Munchkins, and lots of flying monkeys. Some old band uniforms can be torn up and smudged with talcum powder to transform a few musicians into an all-zombie marching band. A group can dress as cheerleaders and deliver Halloween cheers. This can be particularly amusing with a group of bearded, chunky guys. A group willing to take a PC risk can dress as hooded monks and go as the penitents from *Monty Python and the Holy Grail* (1975). They can chant and smack themselves with slap boards. Hinge a padded board to a second, larger board. Use a bit of string to keep them from swinging more than an inch apart. The victim smacks himself with the padded side. A loud slap is produced without harm to the slapee. Group costumes are particularly effective in Halloween parades.

COSTUME CONTESTS

Costume contests are becoming more and more common. Fast-food restaurants and malls often sponsor contests for children with nominal prizes. Cuteness is key to winning. Bars commonly sponsor contests for adults with cash prizes. The adult contests tend to reward costumes that are clever or, for women, sexy. One fellow won three thousand dollars for dressing as Bill Clinton, with a life-sized Monica Lewinsky doll attached to his outfit. A woman won a contest dressed as Tippi Hedren from *The Birds*. She wore a 1960s-style dress with dozens of toy birds stuck to it. Another woman won a contest dressed in a revealing brick-red bikini and body paint that formed a brick pattern. On her chest was painted a black crescent moon. The costume played on the old descriptive simile that an attractive woman is built like a brick outhouse.

LARGE COSTUMES FOR HALLOWEEN PARADES

Halloween parades are becoming a more common feature of the holiday. This chapter contains two designs for costumes suitable for parades. Both are constructed using poles and fabric. The poles can be wood or—a better, lighter choice—plastic pipe. The first is a witch outfit with a balloon head (see Figure below). The balloon is filled with confetti. A wire is run through a screw eye (a knot around it can prevent it from falling out) so that the wearer can pop the balloon for best effect. This can be very effective when the witch is made to bow down toward a bystander. The pop will always elicit a flinch. Extra "heads" can be carried under the witch's gown to replace popped ones.

The second street costume is more elaborate. It is for a seven-foot-tall ghost (see Figures on pages 185 and 186). Using plastic pipe, lay out a T for the body and an H for a base. The base will allow the wearer to set the outfit down to rest or to manipulate its arms. The shoulders and head of the ghost are created using crumpled paper and duct tape. A sufficient lump is made by balling up the paper; use tape to hold it in place. The arms of the ghost are created using two four-foot sections of pipe. Holes are drilled through their ends and through the central pole (alternatively, pipe fittings could be employed instead of drilling). Rope is run through the holes, joining the arms to the central pole. After the arms are attached, holes are drilled about two feet along the

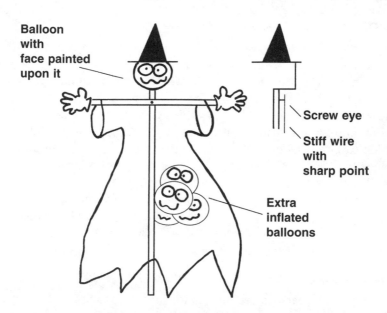

Balloon with face painted upon it

Screw eye

Stiff wire with sharp point

Extra inflated balloons

Pole witch with exploding balloon head

arms. Run a rope through the holes with enough slack so that it can be used to hold the arms upright when passed through hooks on the crosspiece. Tying loops in the rope will make this easier. It will take some trial-and-error measurement to get the length of the rope adjusted so that the wearer of the costume can manipulate it realistically.

Once the arms are attached, they can be covered with fabric. A fire-resistant fabric should be used. A piece roughly four feet by four feet can be folded lengthwise and stitched together. One end is stitched shut. The tube formed is turned inside out and fingers made from strips of cloth stitched onto the closed end. It can then be slid over the arm. It should be securely attached to the arm. Drilling holes through the arm near the central pole and running stitches through the tube and the arm pole should be enough.

The body of the ghost costume is formed in a similar way. Slits must be left in the sides of the body so that the arms can be lifted and lowered freely. A hole should be cut in the front of it so the wearer can see out. The head of the ghost is formed to hang down over the vision hole. The head can be plumped out by paper taped into balls and stitched or taped in place. The interior of the head should be painted black; stitch a piece of black hose in place across the opening to conceal the wearer's face.

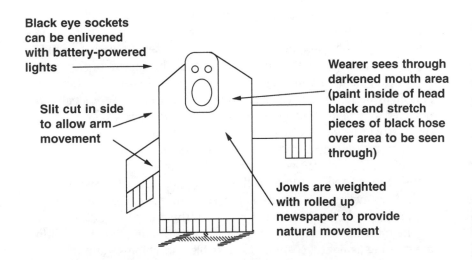

Black eye sockets can be enlivened with battery-powered lights

Slit cut in side to allow arm movement

Wearer sees through darkened mouth area (paint inside of head black and stretch pieces of black hose over area to be seen through)

Jowls are weighted with rolled up newspaper to provide natural movement

Street Ghost Costume

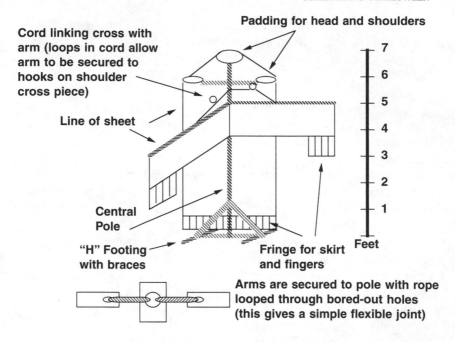

Padding for head and shoulders

Cord linking cross with arm (loops in cord allow arm to be secured to hooks on shoulder cross piece)

Line of sheet

7

6

5

4

3

2

1

Central Pole

"H" Footing with braces

Fringe for skirt and fingers Feet

Arms are secured to pole with rope looped through bored-out holes (this gives a simple flexible joint)

Inner Workings of Ghost Costume

The jowls of the head should be weighed with more paper and tape balls so that the ghost's face can be shaken from side to side without flopping over the ghost's shoulder. The fingers of the arms can be weighted by stitching a washer to their tips so that they can appear to be gesturing when the arms are moved. A set of battery-powered red lights can give the ghost a nice glare. A small tape recorder can be carried by the wearer to play spooky howls.

When moving the costume, one arm is secured by looping it to the crosspiece. The wearer can manipulate the other arm with one hand while carrying the costume by the central pole. He may also secure both arms, when two hands are needed to carry the outfit. If he wishes to use both arms, the H will keep the outfit upright.

The most important considerations in constructing the ghost outfit are creating as light a costume as possible and being certain that the wearer can see clearly from inside the outfit.

MUSICAL ACCESORIZING

Your costume can be given a little embellishment with your own personal theme music. Use a small cassette player, with tapes of music, that matches your costume. Twangy cowboy tunes go well with a cowboy costume. Sixties flower rock improves a hippie outfit. Classic organ music makes a vampire costume more effective.

COSTUME CAUTIONS

- Care should be taken to avoid using flammable materials. Some Halloweeners make outfits using plastic garbage bags or dry-cleaner bags. This is bit like wrapping yourself in kerosene-soaked rags. One dangerous costume described on a teachers' Web site actually suggested that a child wear an orange trash bag stuffed with newspaper as the basis of a jack-o'-lantern costume. If you have doubts about whether a material should be used or not, place a bit of it in a grill outdoors. Touch a match to it. If it burns easily, don't use it. It should be very slow to ignite, very slow to burn, and extinguish quickly. Don't wear baggy sleeves or billowing skirts that might touch a jack-o'-lantern flame. Jack-o'-lanterns should not be placed where trick-or-treaters are apt to brush against them. It's tempting to put them by your door to catch the eye of visitors, but unless they're lit electrically, this should never be done.

- Costumes should be easily removable. This is especially important for costumes that might burn or become entangled in fences, railings, and the like. It also helps if the wearer needs to use a rest room.

- Trim long costumes so that they won't trip the wearer. Remember that an outfit that won't trip trick-or-treaters on even ground may cause them to tumble while climbing stairs.

- Boxes are often suggested as parts of costumes. (The robot described above uses boxes, for instance.) While boxes are useful, care should be taken to avoid obscuring the wearer's vision. They can also be cumbersome and, if not cut to allow free movement, can cause falls.

- Paper bags are also often suggested as the basis for costumes. They can obscure vision if worn over the head, and they are flammable. They may be appropriate for a school costume party where teachers monitor the children and there are few dangers, but they make poor trick-or-treating outfits.

- Masks can limit vision and should be avoided. Substitute makeup or a mask mounted on a handle that can be held against the face on doorsteps and carried away from the face while walking. If masks are worn, be sure eyeholes and breathing holes are adequate. Cut them larger if needed. The child should remove the mask when going from house to house, then put it on at the door.

  Recently, the 3M Company has begun selling masks made with medical adhesive that stick to the face. Called Magic Masks, they don't shift and block vision. They come in a variety of styles, including a cat, an alien, and a witch. The masks are sold in major department stores.

- Avoid dark costumes for trick-or-treating. Drivers may not be able to see them in the gloom. Use light colors, reflective tape, or fluorescent clothing to ensure that children will be visible to motorists.

- Don't use sharp objects as props or as parts of a costume.

- Wigs or false beards should be purchased from a costume store and should be labeled "flame resistant." Home-crafted wigs and beards can be dangerously flammable. Use stage adhesives to secure false hair. Other glues can be hard to remove.

- Children shouldn't carry props that hinder movement or invite misuse. A broom can become too heavy for a small child to carry all evening. A toy sword will always produce a sword fight.

- Dress for the weather.

- Wear sensible footwear. While high heels may make a gown more glamorous or combat boots might make a uniform more combat-ready, they can make feet very sore, very quickly.

- When planning to wear makeup or stage adhesives, apply a bit to your arm the day before to test for any allergic reaction. If a rash appears, don't use the product. Never apply makeup or adhesives over wounds or rashes. Be careful applying makeup around the eyes.

Too Terrific Isn't Terrific

In 1981, Ernest A. Pecek, twenty-three, of Parma, Ohio, wanted a terrific costume for a Halloween party. He decided to be a vampire and thought a large knife protruding from his chest with suitable false blood splashed on his shirt front would be just the thing. He went down into his basement to prepare his getup. He strapped a pine board to his chest over his heart and then stuck a sharp, double-edged dagger into the board. Pecek either hammered it in too far or he slipped and fell, driving the blade too deep. Either way, the knife pierced the board and Pecek's chest, killing him.

PET COSTUMES

Fido can join in the Halloween fun. There are sites on the World Wide Web offering costumes that let your pet accompany you partying or trick-or-treating. One company offered an Elvis "Hound Dog" costume with a small guitar and a cat angel outfit that included wings and a halo. Halloween pet treats such as catnip snakes and squeaky chew spiders can also be purchased online.

PET COSTUME CAUTIONS

Costumes for pets should be made with all the precautions recommended for human costumes, such as fire resistance and nighttime visibility. Additionally, animals can become frantic if they feel trapped in a costume. Limit costuming to light head gear and shirts that cover only the fore-torso.

Post-Halloween Costume Cleanup

The Whirlpool Institute of Fabric Science in Benton Harbor, Michigan, has devoted considerable thought to cleaning up after Halloweeners. Some of its recommendations for specific costume stains are:

- Pumpkin guts are acidic and loaded with fruit sugar. If not quickly removed, pumpkin innards splattered upon clothing will turn brown. Scrape off the pumpkin then run the cloth under cold water. Launder the clothing in the warmest water it can take (check the care tag).

- Oil- or wax-based makeup should be scraped off with a smooth-edged scraper. A plastic spoon works well. The remaining stain must be melted to free it from the fibers of the costume. Again, launder in the warmest water it can take (check the tag).

- Most Halloween treats are composed primarily of fat and sugar. Chocolate and caramel are such treats. To remove these stains, rub a little detergent on the stain, then wash with color-safe bleach. Chlorine bleach can be used on white fabric. Either kind of bleach should be added to the wash during the rinse cycle after the detergent has done its work.

9

TRICK-OR-TREATING

Halloween isn't a date on the calendar. It is in your heart. Every time a little kid cries in fear, that's Halloween. Every time something repulsive ends up in a mailbox, that's Halloween. As long as you carry the spirit of destruction and vandalism in your hearts, every day is Halloween.

Christopher Masterson, as Francis, in *Malcolm in the Middle*

Never try to put on a pullover while eating a candy apple.

Anonymous sticky kid

Trick-or-treating is the classic Halloween activity. After choosing a costume, the next step is selecting a treat bag. A pillowcase is the traditional choice, but making a more elaborate bag can be a fun pre-Halloween activity.

TREAT BAGS

Using some poster paint, a grocery bag can be easily jazzed up for Halloween. Paint it orange, then paint a jack-o'-lantern face on it. When the paint is dry, outline the eyes, nose, and mouth with a black marker. Add a few curved lines to simulate the roundness of the pumpkin.

A Frankenstein monster can be made by painting the bag light green. Paint two glassy eyes. When the paint is dry, draw the monster's face with a marker. Outline the eyes. Give the monster a big nose

191

and a wide mouth. Using black, give the monster some straggly hair. Add some scars with stitches, and don't forget Frankie's neck bolts.

A tombstone design can be made by painting the bag dark gray. Brush a small amount of white paint onto a rough-surfaced sponge. Dab it sparingly on the bag to make it look like stone. A ball of crushed tissue paper can be substituted for the sponge. When the paint is dry, cut a semicircle at the top of the bag's front and back to give it a rounded tombstone look. Trim the sides so they match the low point of the semicircle. Using a black marker, trace a line a half inch from the semicircle and the side edges. This helps give the design a three-dimensional feel. At the top of the bag, inside the semicircle, draw some ornamental swirls or, if you're ambitious, a skull with wings—a traditional tombstone design. Now you can inscribe an epitaph. Don't use a real person's name; try something humorous, such as FRED DEADMAN or G. REAPER. You might write TRICK OR TREAT on one side and THANK YOU on the other.

A mummy design can be made by drawing a set of glaring eyes on the face of a grocery bag. Cut sections of white crepe paper and glue them to the bag. They'll be the mummy's bandages. Leave the eyes visible. Tear through a few pieces, and let the ends dangle to suggest decrepitude. Repeat on the other face of the bag.

Your treat bag will need a handle that can stand up to a—hopefully— heavy load of treats. Use belt webbing from a fabric store and a heavy-duty stapler. Run the webbing deep inside the bag so that you can drive several staples through it and the bag. Be sure the staples are secure and won't detach and get mixed in with the treats.

Since the bag is made of paper, warn its carrier to avoid setting it in puddles or on damp grass; it may break apart. As a safety measure, you might want to staple a plastic trash bag inside the paper bag. A better preventive measure is to use a blank fabric shopping bag. These can be purchased at a fabric or craft store, along with fabric paints that won't wash out. A permanent laundry marker can be used for details. This kind of bag can be cleaned and reused Halloween after Halloween.

TRICK-OR-TREATING CAUTIONS

Children all across North America still go trick-or-treating, despite fears of tainted treats. To make the fun safer, it's wise to take some simple precautions:

- Costumes shouldn't inhibit movement or vision and should be visible in the dark (see chapter 8 for a more detailed list of costume cautions).

- The younger the children, the earlier they should go trick-or-treating and the earlier they should return home. A four-year-old, for example, can have a good time trick-or-treating in the late afternoon before twilight has even begun.

- Younger children should be accompanied by an adult. Older children should travel in groups.

- Parents should help their children plan a route to follow. They should know where their children are going and set a curfew.

- Children should visit only the homes of people they know and should stay away from unfamiliar parts of town.

- Children should avoid dark streets and never ring the bell of a house that doesn't have its porch light on.

- Children should cross streets at corners, looking both ways first, and use sidewalks instead of walking in the roadway. Where there are no sidewalks, children should walk facing oncoming traffic. Tell your children that they should never assume a driver can see them and will avoid them.

- Children should carry flashlights (check that they have fresh batteries), light sticks, or electrically lit jack-o'-lanterns to help drivers spot and avoid them. Torches, candles, or candlelit jack-o'-lanterns should never be carried.

- Children shouldn't eat their treats till they get home, and then only after examination by an adult. Some hospitals will X-ray treats. X-raying candy will detect only metal contaminants. Plastic or wood contaminants or chemical adulteration won't be eliminated. Unwrapped candy or candy that looks like it may have been tampered with should be thrown out.

- Some homes give out small toys as treats. Parents should check that these are not choking hazards.

- Parents should warn their children that tricking can invite angry retaliation from some. Prank playing can also escalate into vandalism, and parents should make it clear that the holiday will not excuse their children from responsibility for their actions.

- Children should be told to report any suspicious behavior they witness to their parents.

- Delivery services should be asked to limit deliveries during trick-or-treating hours. A grocery delivery service, for example, halted deliveries to avoid creating more traffic that might endanger children.

- If you don't want your children trick-or-treating, consider taking them to an alternative party. Parents sometimes stage parties in their homes. Community organizations, municipal recreation centers, and shopping malls often stage carnival-like Halloween parties.

PET CAUTIONS FOR TRICK-OR-TREATING

- Chocolate is toxic to pets. To limit your pet's hunger for treats, feed it ample portions of his regular food before exposing it to temptation. A dog may eat a bit of chocolate without your knowledge. If your dog has diarrhea, vomits, or acts excessively nervous, take it to your veterinarian.

- If a pet is taken trick-or-treating, be sure it's on a secure leash, and limit its exposure to children. It may become overly excited or frightened by strangers, especially when they are oddly costumed and cavorting.

- Pets should wear ID tags. They may escape through doors opened for trick-or-treaters.

- Owners should remember that a dog that is cuddly with them may attack those it finds threatening—and it's difficult to predict what it is that animals will find threatening. Children will try to pet any dog they encounter, and a dog can misinterpret their interest. Repeated visitors can aggravate a dog's fears. Prank players sometimes make animals targets for their tricks, harming them or causing them to attack. Securing pets in a safe area, such as a back room or an enclosed garage, can be wise for their safety and the safety of trick-or-treaters. A radio or television may soothe your pet by hiding the sounds of visitors. For dogs that bark at visitors, securing them away from the door can prevent annoyance.

- Candy wrappers can become choking hazard for pets. Pick up discarded wrappers.

Trick-or-Treating Alternatives

Growing parental concerns over the risks of trick-or-treating and the increasing absence of parents to dispense treats has encouraged the staging of alternatives to traditional trick-or-treating. Some shopping malls, for example, stage parties during which children go from store to store gathering treats. Musicians, mimes, clowns, and magicians perform. Costume contests are held. Halloween games are played. Halloween-themed movies are sometimes shown.

Public schools frequently stage Halloween parties that allow children to enjoy a carefully supervised holiday. The YMCA, the largest community service organization in America, stages Halloween parties in more than seven hundred towns and cities. Aided by sponsors such as Pepsi-Cola and Frito-Lay, the Ys provide family-oriented fun in a safe atmosphere.

TREATS

Halloween treats are one of the principal pleasures of the holiday. In the past, treats were commonly concocted at home. Candy apples, popcorn balls, and cookies were popular choices. While many families still enjoy preparing treats, recipients—and their parents—tend to suspect the homemade goodies. In addition to the fear of poisoning or tampering, there are doubts about the wholesomeness of the treats. They may contain ingredients that can produce allergic reactions, for example, or be prepared in unsanitary kitchens. Consequently, homemade treats are often thrown out uneaten. To avoid this waste and the possibility of disappointing trick-or-treaters, treat givers should use commercially prepared treats. Commercial candy offers plenty of variety and is inexpensive. The candy industry offers many Halloween-themed items manufactured especially for the holiday. Still, despite this, candy isn't a favored treat for all.

Dr. Charles J. Garzik, a Massachusetts dentist specializing in restorative dentistry, considers candy so unhealthy that he stages a candy buyback at his offices after Halloween, paying a dollar a pound for up to five pounds.

"There are alternatives," Garzik says. "You could just be a little bit more creative about what you give them. . . . Just plain chocolate would be better than something that is chewy or takes longer to eat, like a lollipop, because they actually stick to the teeth and hold the sugar right next to the tooth."

Chant of the Candy Extorters

Trick-or-treat!
Smell my feet.
Give me something good to eat.

Lizard scales,
Monkey tails,
Candy-coated slugs and snails,

French-fried owl,
Werewolf chow.
Whatever you've got,
I want it now!

The "Candy Man"

Much of the concern about tainted Halloween candy can be traced to a single evil man and his murderous plan. On Halloween 1974, in a Houston, Texas, suburb, Timothy Marc O'Bryan, age eight, ate some candy from a Giant Pixy Stix package. His father, optician Ronald Clark O'Bryan, told police the boy complained that the candy tasted bitter. O'Bryan said he gave his son some Kool-Aid to clear away the bitter taste and sent him to bed. Soon, however, the boy became seriously ill, complaining of terrible stomach pain and vomiting twice. The boy died as his father took him to a local hospital.

At the hospital, doctors discovered that the candy had been laced with cyanide. Police also learned that, in addition to his son, O'Bryan had given sticks of candy from the package to three other children. Police cars raced to the different households to retrieve the poisoned treats before they could be eaten. Two were quickly confiscated uneaten. At the home of Whitney Parker, a young neighbor of the O'Bryans, the candy couldn't be found. The boys' parents were terrified that their son had eaten it. They ran to Whitney's room to find him in his bed motionless, asleep with the candy in his hand, unopened. The poisoner had resealed the package with a staple, and the young boy hadn't been strong enough to tear it back open.

After retrieving the poisoned treats, the authorities cast a suspicious eye on O'Bryan. It was found that he held a twenty-thousand-dollar life insurance policy on his son. They believed that he had distributed the poisoned candy to other children to divert attention from his motive. A jury convicted him of murder, and he was executed on March 31, 1984.

TRICKS

Playing pranks, as mentioned earlier, was once one of the primary amusements of the Halloween season. Tricks can still be fun, but they've all but disappeared. Only crude vandalism seems to have survived. Perhaps this is because tricking taxes the intellect, and a good prank can take a lot of time. Modern kids would rather collect candy, and, in some ways, tricking has taken on an insensitive repute. No one in our overly sensitized era wants to seem the least bit gleeful at making someone else feel foolish—unless, of course, the fool is one of the approved social villains.

There are new dangers associated with playing pranks. In some situations, a playful trick is seen as an insult demanding lethal retaliation. In other situations, pranking has escalated into criminal destruction verging on rioting. The authorities rightly do what they can to contain this, and lesser pranksters face the possibility of being grouped with criminals.

There is also a very modern fear of legal ramifications to prankery. A flaming sack of dog doo left on a doorstep might cause the person stamping it out to slip and sue. This is unfortunate, because pranks that aren't hostile or destructive or dangerous can be good fun. Despite this, in keeping with our litigious age, we'll fearfully leave the concoction of tomfoolery to other, braver souls who have platoons of lawyers.

Frying an Egg the Hard Way

On Halloween 1994, in Franklin, Pennsylvania, a fifteen-year-old boy tossed an egg at an electrical substation. The egg caused an arc between two thirty-four-thousand-watt transformers, which in turn caused a large fireball that led to a blackout, leaving eight thousand people in darkness.

10

SETTING THE SCENE FOR HALLOWEEN

What a dump!
Bette Davis (1908–1989),
in *Beyond the Forest* (1949)

Halloween can be made even more enjoyable by decorating your home. Although each year more and more commercially made decorations are available, making your own decorations can be a lot of fun—especially when the family does it together. The following are a few easy, inexpensive projects you can make (carving jack-o'-lanterns is described in chapter 4).

DO-IT-YOURSELF DECORATIONS

PAPER SHAPES

In elementary school, we all learned to cut jack-o'-lanterns out of folded orange paper and bats out of black paper. These still make nice decorations and can be a fun family project. Use a little poster putty to stick the bats to the wall. Bats can also be hung from the ceiling with thread. Strings of paper cutouts can be made by joining several sheets of paper together with tape. As shown in the illustrations on page 201, these strips can be folded accordion style and cut to make chains of bats or skulls.

Leaves cut from red, yellow, and orange paper and strung together make a nice seasonal garland. Individual cutout creatures can also be strung together, alternating forms to make a garland.

Paper cutout creatures, such as bats, can be given a little extra menace using red, yellow, or orange cellophane. Cut eyeholes for the creature and tape the cellophane behind them. When light shines through, the eyes will seem to glow fiendishly.

BALLOONS

Black and orange balloons are a quick decoration. Jack-o'-lantern faces can be drawn on the orange balloons with a marker.

COBWEBS

A quick way to make cobwebs is to buy some flimsy cheesecloth and tear it into ratty streamers. A box knife can prove useful. Hang the streamers from the ceiling or anywhere they will dangle drearily. Be careful to keep them away from flames.

PUNCH AND SERVING BOWLS

A witch's cauldron is the most common Halloween punch or serving bowl. Novelty stores often carry plastic cauldrons. A plastic jack-o'-lantern can also serve. A real pumpkin can be turned into a punch or serving bowl by inserting a smaller bowl inside it.

A large, well-cleaned fake spider, rat, or eyeball can be put in the punch bowl to add a horrific touch. Small items shouldn't be put in drinks, because they can be a choking hazard.

JACK-O'-LANTERN CUPS

Simple clear plastic cups can be jazzed up by drawing the eyes, nose, and mouth of a jack-o'-lantern upon their outside surface using a waterproof laundry marker. Serve orange punch.

In addition to jack-o'-lanterns, you can draw slogans like BOO! or HAPPY HALLOWEEN!, the faces of cats, monsters, or vampires, tombstones, haunted houses, spiders, a skull and crossbones, or any other Halloween icon.

COFFIN SERVING-TABLE
AND HALLOWEEN TABLECLOTHS

Cut a piece of plywood in the shape of a coffin lid. Set it atop an old table and drill holes through both. Insert bolts and tighten them. Drape the table in black cloth. White netting can be added to simu-

Silhouette Chains

Fold black or orange construction paper as shown. Cut on folds.

Bat Pattern

Skull Pattern

**Build Your Own
Hearse**

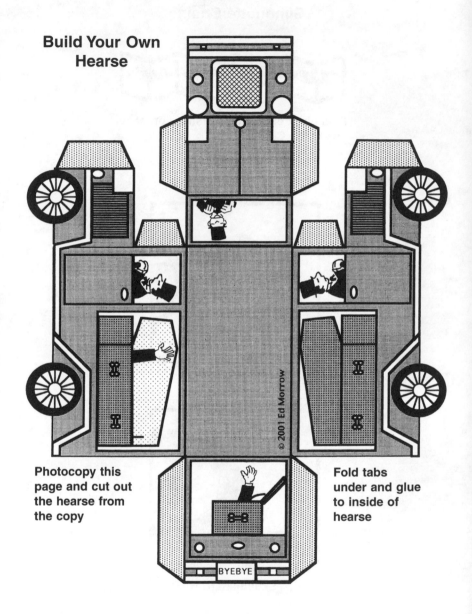

© 2001 Ed Morrow

**Photocopy this
page and cut out
the hearse from
the copy**

**Fold tabs
under and glue
to inside of
hearse**

late a spiderweb. Before using the table, test its balance. Too large a top on too small a table invites tipping.

A more elaborate tablecloth can be made by cutting skulls and crossed bones from felt. Using a glue gun, hot-glue the felt cutouts around the border of the tablecloth. Jack-o'-lanterns, crescent moons, and ghosts also make good cutouts. An orange tablecloth can be decorated with silhouettes of black cats or of multicolored fall leaves.

TOMBSTONES

Gravestones can be made from cardboard painted gray. Make a base for the stone with a smaller square of cardboard and triangular cardboard braces. A more realistic stone can be made using two-inch-thick Styrofoam. Cut it to shape with a jigsaw. It can be glued to a base cut from a board or from another piece of Styrofoam. Paint it gray. You can give it a sponging with white paint to make it appear even more real. There are spray paints that simulate stone, but these can be expensive.

Decorate the stone with amusing epitaphs painted with flat black paint. I'LL BE BACK, YOU'RE NEXT, OR I TOLD YOU I WAS SICK are possible inscriptions. The names of infamous killers, such as Lizzie Borden, Jack the Ripper, or Ma Barker, can be used on the stones. Avoid using the names of anyone likely to see the stones. Some may find it disturbing.

HALLOWEEN TREES

In a sort of reverse Christmas gesture, Halloween trees decorated with eerie ornaments are becoming common. A small, leafless bush or a branch with lots of offshoots makes a good choice. Spray-paint the tree flat black or dead white. Plastic rats, skulls, ghosts, and other Halloween icons are available, but preparing your own decorations is far more fun. Black and orange construction paper can be cut in strips, turned into chains, and wound around the tree. Silhouettes of witches, skulls, bats, and crescent moons can also be cut from paper and hung on the tree. Instead of tinsel, use dried moss, fake cobwebs, or spiderwebs made from white netting. Florist shops, craft stores, and novelty stores are good sources for materials.

Small ghosts can be made using facial tissue, black ribbon, a black marker, and fishing line. Tightly ball up a tissue, then set it in the middle of another tissue. The ball is the ghost's head. Pull the other tissue down to form the ghost's body. Tie a small bit of the ribbon around the ghost's neck to secure the head inside. Tie a loop of fishing line through the ribbon loop so the ghost can be suspended from the tree. Draw two eyes and a screaming mouth on the ghost's face.

Eye masks make excellent decorations for a Halloween tree. Cut the masks from colored paper. A spray of rays on one corner gives a glamorous touch, or the mask can be given harlequin wings. Glitter can be sprinkled on the masks, or designs drawn upon them with markers. Thread ribbon through the edges as tie-ons. The ties can be used to suspend the masks from the tree, or several masks can be linked together into a garland.

Christmas ornaments can be altered for Halloween. A simple string of Christmas lights with all-white bulbs is an effective decoration. Plain white or clear Christmas bulbs can have Halloween designs painted upon them. A skull face—two eye sockets, a nose triangle, a slash for a mouth with short vertical lines to suggest teeth, and two inward-curved lines to suggest gaunt cheeks—painted in black upon a white bulb is effective. A Christmas bulb can also be painted orange, then given a jack-o'-lantern face. A bulb can also be decorated with Halloween stickers.

To set up the Halloween tree, set its base in a bucket of sand or nail a wooden cross to its stub. Unlike a Christmas tree, it won't need watering, but like a Christmas tree, it can be a fire risk. Take care to keep open flames away from the tree.

HALLOWEEN WREATH

Another Christmas decoration adapted for Halloween is the wreath. Florists stock grapevine wreaths that are used for the base of floral wreaths. Spray-paint one flat black and decorate it with Halloween icons. Use a wide purple ribbon to tie a bow on the wreath. A diagonal sash of ribbon with R.I.P. written upon it gives the wreath a nice horrid touch.

GHOST BALLOONS

Floating ghost decorations for indoor use can be made using white, helium-filled balloons and white trash bags. Smear a goodly amount of white glue on the top of an inflated balloon. Pull the trash bag over it so that the balloon forms the head of the ghost. After the glue dries, use a black marker to draw eyes and a howling mouth. The ghost can be secured to tables or other objects by string. A small oscillating fan set up a few yards from the ghost can make it sway and bob.

Larger ghosts can be made by taping several balloons into a crude head-and-shoulders shape, then covering it with a larger white trash bag. If a large-enough bag can't be found, cheesecloth or tissue paper can be used to make the flowing body of the ghost.

These floating ghosts should be kept away from lighted candles and hot electrical bulbs.

RAVENS

A particularly effective decoration can be made using fake birds. Craft stores often have artificial songbirds that are used in flower arrangements. These can be turned into small ravens by spray-painting them with flat black paint. Black, bead-headed pins can be used to give the ravens a malevolent glare. The ravens can be perched all around a room.

GHOST SHAPES

More substantial ghosts can be made using white fabric and fabric stiffener, available at craft stores. Using cardboard and Styrofoam, construct a crude figure of a human being with arms outstretched. Stand the figure on waxed paper. Cut a piece of fabric large enough to cover the figure. Stuff the fabric in a plastic bag with the stiffener. Seal the bag and knead it till the stiffener completely soaks the fabric. Remove it and drape it over the figure. Be sure to form a base at the bottom of the figure to support the ghost. Adjust the fabric to appear as ghostly as possible. After the stiffener has dried, remove the figure and paint eyes and a moaning mouth on the ghost. The mouth can be cut out of the fabric, leaving a hollow maw.

The figure can be reused to make more ghosts.

MOOD LIGHTING

An ominous mood can be created using colored lights. Ghastly green, pumpkin orange, and blood red are good colors. Christmas lights with all-white bulbs can also appear eerie.

BACKGROUND SOUNDS

A tape of scary sounds can be softly played to help create a spooky atmosphere. You can have fun recording your own tape with your family and friends. Subtlety helps. Play the tape at a low volume so that it blends into the background. The tape makes a nice accompaniment for a Halloween party. Keep the tape running even when you are playing music.

Typical sounds include:

- Wolves howling
- Moans
- Sighing wind
- Rattling chains
- Creaking doors
- Footsteps (sometimes with a dragging step)
- Heartbeats
- Witches cackling
- Insane laughter
- Owls hooting
- Sqeaking, fluttering bats

FOG MACHINES

Fog machines make a great addition to any Halloween decor. Using dry ice and gentle blowers, they can fill a room with spooky streamers. Good machines are a bit pricey, starting at two hundred to three hundred dollars and rising to thousands of dollars. If you can't afford this, placing dry ice in a bucket of warm water will produce a similar but much lesser effect (some decorators suggest using a Crock-Pot to keep the water warm). The water-to-dry-ice ratio should be about two to one. It will produce steam for about five minutes. Dry ice will last as long as eight hours in a freezer. Care should be taken when handling dry ice. Do not put it in anything that is to be eaten, and never touch it with bare hands.

FANS

Small oscillating fans that generate very gentle breezes are a simple device to increase spookiness. They can make suspended bats flutter, sway spiderwebs, and send shivery air onto unwary guests. Care should be taken to keep them away from areas where dangling costumes might be caught up in their blades.

SIMPLE SPIDERS

Decorative spiders can be made in many ways. An old egg carton can be used to make a light spider that can safely be hung from the ceiling. Remove the top from the carton. Paint the bottom half with black poster paint. When it's dry, cut out the individual egg cups. Paint the cut edges with the black paint. When the cups are dry, push eight pipe-cleaner legs into each cup. Bend the inside ends so that the pipe cleaners won't fall out of the cup. Glue on eyes, and hang the spiders using white string to simulate a spiderweb.

Larger spiders can be made using the Styrofoam boxes fast-food restaurants serve hamburgers in. Wash them thoroughly, then paint them. Legs can be made using black construction paper that has been folded lengthwise several times. The larger surface of the hamburger box permits the attachment of "google eyes," obtained from a hobby store, which give the spider a more monstrous but humorous appearance.

HALLOWEEN BOUQUETS

A visit to an overgrown lot can provide you with a bunch of dead, withered foliage and twigs. Gather a bouquet and place it in a vase. Tie a black ribbon around the vase. A more bizarre look can be achieved by placing the bouquet in a coffee can set upon some newspapers, then spray-painting them flat white. When dry, place them in a vase with a black ribbon. Alternatively, you can paint the bouquet black and use a white ribbon.

MAKE A SHRUNKEN HEAD IN YOUR KITCHEN

First, you don't need to kill someone. You can make your own phony shrunken head with a large apple and avoid prison. While it won't fool any anthropologists, it can make a nifty Halloween decorator item. The apple is peeled, turned upside down, and carved into the form of a head. The eyes and nostrils should be just slits; the mouth should be wide and full. A smile would be an unlikely expression. All the features should be a bit oversized. As the apple dries, they will shrink. Avoid deep cuts, which may be exaggerated by shrinkage.

Once the head is carved, use black thread to stitch the eyes, nostrils and mouth shut. Don't worry about fine stitching; crude craftsmanship looks more realistic. Shrinkage will alter the appearance of the stitching. It may tighten it or loosen it. If it loosens, gently tighten the thread. The apple's flesh is quite delicate and you may pull the thread through the features if you're not careful.

After stitching the features, make very large loops through the "scalp" of the apple head to create hair. After making enough passes to give the head a healthy crop of hair, cut through the thread loops so that the "hairs" are a variety of lengths. This increases realism.

The Jivaro tribesmen of the Amazon basin, who originated the custom of head shrinking, often had tattoos on their faces. You can decorate your apple head with swirling tattoos, tracing the shapes of the face with a blue or black fiber-tipped pen. Draw some of your lines by using dots. This is also in keeping with Amazonian tattooing.

Once the apple head has been carved and threaded, it needs to be soaked in a strong saltwater solution for a day. Use half a cup of salt to four cups of water. After soaking, hang the apple head by its hair in a cool, dry place for two weeks. Keep checking on the apple head; it may dry quicker or slower. As it dries, it will take on a realistic, ruddy color with numerous ugly wrinkles. Once the apple head has a suitably gruesome appearance, it can be preserved by dipping it in satin water-based acrylic varnish. Water-based acrylics give off no noxious fumes and, while wet, clean up with soapy water. Take care not to get sloppy with the varnish and the thread hair. The varnish can cause the hair to snarl and tangle.

Real Shrunken Heads

The Jivaro of the South American rain forest developed the process of shrinking heads to preserve trophies of the enemies they killed in battle. They believed keeping these heads, called *tsantsas,* trapped the souls of their enemies, giving some of the enemy's spiritual power to the keeper.

The process of creating a shrunken head begins, of course, with killing an enemy. The head is then severed at the collarbone. A vine is threaded through the head to form a sling with which it is carried away from the field of battle. The skin is then removed from the skull, which is thrown into a river as an offering to the anaconda god.

The skin of the head is boiled, then left to dry. This reduces it in size by about half. It is turned inside out, and any flesh left is scraped out. Turned right-side out, the lips and eyes are stitched shut. The head is then filled with hot rocks. When these cool, they're replaced with smaller hot rocks. The heat further shrinks the head. Eventually, the head gets too small for stones, and hot sand is used. During the drying, ash is rubbed into the head. This darkening is thought to prevent the spirit of the head's former owner from being able to see out of the head and avenge his head taking. When the head will shrink no more, it is about the size of a fist. A cord is run through the top of the *tsantsa* so that it can be hung over a fire and smoked to preserve it. The cord also allows the owner to hang the head from his costume.

Once the victorious headhunter returns to his village, there is much feasting to celebrate his success. The shrunken head may be tidied up a bit and decorated with toucan feathers. The Jivaro so highly valued their shrunken heads that they often had them buried with them when they died.

When Europeans discovered the Jivaro and their head collections, they were shocked at the custom. This shock didn't prevent a market for souvenir shrunken heads from developing. Museums also collected the heads to exhibit. The Jivaro were reluctant to sell their trophies and, as their customs changed, fewer were gathered. This increased the value of those heads that did reach the market. Fake *tsantsas* made from animal hides soon began to appear. They were sometimes so realistic that they fooled experts, and more than a few museum cases around the world contain phony shrunken heads. One sure way to recognize a faked head is the absence of nose hairs. Real shrunken heads always possess nose hairs.

DECORATING CAUTIONS

- Take great care with open flames. Candles and candlelit jack-o'-lanterns may look great, but they often cause fires. Substitute electric lights—but be careful not to overload circuits or extension cords. Test lighting arrangements before using them, and discard anything that's damaged or that you suspect is dangerous. It is far cheaper to replace suspect lights than rebuild a house.

Halogen lamps, in particular, generate dangerous amounts of heat. Any decoration—indeed, any drapery or wallpaper—near one is apt to catch fire.

- A popular novelty aerosol product that squirts a string of sticky goo is often used at Halloween for pranks and for creating spiderwebs. This product can be very dangerous. The string is often highly flammable and, when squirted near candles, can ignite. Much like napalm, it sticks to surfaces, intensifying the damage it does. Recent versions of the product are said to be less flammable, but the danger far outweighs the enjoyment produced.

- Avoid using highly flammable decorations, especially where they may be near flames. Even where candles are kept safely away, remember that cigarette smokers may light up or discard burning cigarettes and matches.

- Keep fire extinguishers on hand in case your fire precautions fail.

- For Halloween, a little light goes a long way. Conversely, too much gloom can invite missteps and falls. Strive for a balance, but always place safety first, clearly lighting locations such as stairs that invite accidents.

- Take care that decorations don't have sharp edges or points.

- Be sure large decorations are securely attached to walls and won't fall upon partyers.

Halloween Collectibles

The commercially made decorations and Halloween display pieces have always been a bit on the flimsy side. This means that few survive from year to year, especially since they often pass through the hands of destructive children. Consequently, Halloween-related objects in good shape are rare and invite collection.

Collectors class Halloween collectibles into three periods. The first runs from 1900 to the beginning of World War II in 1939. During this era, Halloween was celebrated primarily with parties.

Commercially made decorations were imported from Germany and sold in higher-priced retail stores. Tin party favors meant to contain hard candy are valued collectibles from this period. These were often pumpkin-headed figurines or cats perched atop pumpkins. Rattles, horns, drums, clickers, candy carriers, and lanterns are other desirable collectibles from this time. Made from inexpensive steel, tin, papier-mâché, pressed cardboard, and other fragile materials, they are scarce. Rarer items from this era have drawn prices in the thousands of dollars.

The second period, from the end of the war in 1945 to 1960, was marked by the advent of trick-or-treating. Collectibles from this era include costumes, treat bags, jack-o'-lanterns, and noisemakers. Most of these objects were made by American companies using paper, tin, and pressed paper pulp. Japanese companies also entered the decoration market, selling less expensive items. This period's collectibles are usually less costly than prewar collectibles. Baby Boomer collectors, however, seeking mementos from their childhood, are expected to drive prices up.

The third period runs from 1960 to 1965. Halloween collectibles from this time include costumes linked to television shows, movies, and rock groups such as the Beatles. The end of this period marks the end of most collectors' interest. Plastic became the predominant material, workmanship became poor, and mass production eliminated scarcity. Prices for items from this era are consequently low.

Those wishing to collect Halloweeniana are advised by experts to begin with inexpensive items. Unlike some collectibles, such as coins or stamps, there is much leeway in what is considered good condition. Items with minor signs of use are actually favored by some collectors, who like to imagine a child from years gone by playing with a treat bag or tin pumpkin lantern.

The growth in Halloween collecting has created a market for fakes. The materials used in old decorations are very inexpensive and easy to reproduce. New collectors are advised to learn as much as they can before buying, and even then, buy only from reputable sources.

11

BRING HALLOWEEN TO YOUR HOUSE AND YARD

Nighttime is dark so you can imagine your fears with less distraction.

Calvin, in the comic strip *Calvin and Hobbes*,
by Bill Watterson, July 1994

Decorating the exterior of your house for Halloween can enliven the holiday for your whole neighborhood. Here are some simple, inexpensive outdoor decoration ideas.

OUTDOOR DECORATIONS

BATES MOTEL SIGN

A nifty decoration can be made by creating a sign for the Bates Motel, the roadside hostelry made infamous by Alfred Hitchcock's *Psycho*.

Using one-by-sixes, build a two-foot by three-foot frame. Cut a two-by-three-foot section from a sheet of quarter-inch exterior-grade plywood. Nail this to the frame. Cut the ends of two eight-foot two-by-twos into points. Attach these to the frame so that the sign can be erected on your lawn. Paint the frame flat black on the outside and yellow inside.

Obtain a two-foot by three-foot piece of Plexiglas and a sheet of paper of equal size. Carefully draw the letters of BATES MOTEL on the paper. Beneath this, in smaller letters, draw VACANCY. Place the plexiglas over the paper sign. With a grease pencil, trace the letters onto the Plexiglas. Flip the Plexiglas over and carefully cover the letters with masking tape. Spray-paint the Plexiglas flat black. When completely dry, remove the masking tape. The letters should be clear upon a black background.

Purchase a battery-powered lantern. The lantern will make the sign's letters glow. Some lanterns are equipped with blinker switches so that they can be used to warn of dangers such as a car stopped on the road. A blinking lantern will make the sign seem more realistic.

Cut a circle in the plywood so that you can have access to the light to turn it on and off and to replace batteries. Cut a larger circle from another sheet of plywood to cover the opening. Drill a hole through the top of this and through the plywood of the sign over the opening. Pass a bolt through. The circle of plywood can be swung aside to access the lantern.

Use sheet-metal screws to secure the Plexiglas to the frame. Drill holes larger than the screws around the edges of the Plexiglas and into the frame. Don't put too much pressure on the drill; this may crack the Plexiglas. Don't overtighten the screws, also to avoid cracking.

A small signboard can be added to the hotel sign that lists motel features such as B/W TV, CHEAP RATES, CONGENIAL STAFF, and HOT SHOWERS.

To Plug or Not to Plug

Using battery-powered lights in outdoor decorations is safer than using lights plugged into wall outlets. They pose less danger of shock or shorts and won't overload your home's circuits. If you must use lights that plug in, take sensible precautions.

- Use only Underwriters Laboratory (UL) approved products.
- Use low-wattage bulbs to avoid overheating decorations that might melt or burn.
- Never string together extension cords. They can become overloaded and may pose a hazard of shock.
- Don't cobble together lights. Amateur workmanship can be dangerous.

- Only plug lights into ground fault interrupt (GFI) outlets. These help prevent shocks.

- Never use electric decorations in rainy weather or in damp areas where they may become wet. Joined extension cords, in particular, can be dangerous if the join comes into contact with water.

- Don't run wires where passersby can become entangled or trip over them.

- Children may be tempted to toy with decorations. Place them safely out of reach.

- *Always* unplug electric decorations before handling them. Even something as simple as changing a bulb can be dangerous under some circumstances.

EYES

A pair of eyes gleaming from the darkness can be produced using a flashlight, a soda can, flat black spray paint, some red cellophane, and black duct tape. Cut the top off an empty soda can. Poke two holes in the can to simulate eyes. Spray-paint it flat black. Tape the cellophane over the holes, and tape the can over the end of the flashlight. Switch on the light and position it to effect in a bush, under a porch, or perched in a tree.

Another way to simulate eyes in the dark is with a string of small-bulbed, exterior Christmas lights. Replace the bulbs with red ones. Take a section of the string with two bulbs. Pinch the cord between the two bulbs and, using electrical tape, secure the loop together. This will bring the bulbs close enough together to look like a set of eyes. Repeat with the rest of the string and hang in a bush. It will seem as if a small horde of demons is lurking there.

HANGED MAN

This is essentially just a scarecrow suspended from a tree limb. Hang the "body" high enough so that viewers won't be tempted to pull it down. Don't use a hangman's noose. Wrap the rope in an unclosed loop simulating the real thing. A real noose may encourage viewers to foolishly try it on, with disastrous results.

The hanged man can be enlivened by tying stout fishing line to its knees and elbows. The limbs can be made to twitch by pulling the lines.

A simple indoor hanging effigy can be made using a pair of pants, some socks, and a pair of shoes. Stitch the socks onto the pants and stuff them with newspaper. Attach the shoes to the socks with glue or stitches. Old sneakers work well—the thread will easily pass through them. Leave a shoe untied with a lace dangling for a bit of realism. Suspend the pants from the ceiling next to a window. Lower the shade in the window to conceal the top of the effigy. From outside the window, looking in, it will appear that someone is "hanging around" inside.

An even simpler indoor hanging effigy can be made by cutting a silhouette from black paper and taping it to a large sheet of thin paper. Attach the result to the window so that it appears to be a window blind. A blind pull attached to the bottom can help create this illusion. When lit from inside, it will appear that a hanging body is casting a shadow upon the blind.

Every Halloween, someone is injured or killed while pretending to be hanged. Never attempt a fake hanging with a live person. It is simply too dangerous. Use a dummy. A little effort can produce a very lifelike—or in this case deadlike—figure to dangle from a rope. Remember, you don't need to make a realistic head or hands. Those executed by hanging usually have a bag put over their heads and their hands tied behind their back. The rest of the body is simply stuffed clothing and a pair of shoes.

LAWN SILHOUETTES

Exterior-grade plywood can be used to create cutout lawn decorations. Ghosts and black cats with high-arched backs are good subjects. Battery-powered lights can give them a baneful stare.

LUMINARIES

A luminary can be made using a coffee can. Draw a jack-o'-lantern face on the can. Fill it to an inch from the top with water. Place it in the freezer. Once the water has frozen, punch holes in it with an awl, tracing the design. Let the ice thaw and dry the can. Spray the can inside and out with primer. When this is dry, spray-paint the interior of the can with yellow gloss paint. When this is dry, spray the exterior with orange gloss paint. After this dries, use a brush to paint the inside of the facial features gloss black. Light the can luminary with a votive candle.

MUMMY

Fashion a life-sized dummy by stuffing a pair of pants and a shirt with newspapers. Fold the mummy's arms across its chest. Make a head with a trash bag also stuffed with newspaper. A pair of boots can be used for feet. Use duct tape to join the body parts to a six-foot board "spine." Wrap the mummy in strips of cheesecloth.

SCARECROW

Scarecrows are easily constructed from old clothes and hay. Set a headless one upon a bale of hay and place an electrically lit jack-o'-lantern in its lap. To give visitors a shock, you can set the headless scarecrow against a fake wall with two holes cut in it, so that your arms can pass through and into the scarecrow's sleeves. Wear gardening gloves and glue bits of hay to protrude from the scarecrow's cuffs. Place a bowl of candy in the scarecrow's lap; when someone reaches for a piece, take a grab at them. Alternatively, you can pass out candy to trick-or-treaters as the headless scarecrow.

Costumes saved from earlier Halloweens can be used to make effigies. Stuff them with newspapers and add shoes, gloves, and a stuffed trash-bag head.

SKELETONS

A simple skeleton can be constructed with white cardboard and elastic cord. The diagram featured in this chapter shows one design. It produces a skeleton that is about six feet tall. The measurements can be altered to create a larger or smaller skeleton. A pair of elastic bands can be used to attach the lower jaw so that it will bounce up and down as if chattering. The arms and legs are connected using stouter elastic. Light plywood, painted appropriately, can be used to create a more durable skeleton.

A rather grotesque skeleton can be made using tree branches, a small pumpkin, a saw, wire, and a power drill. You'll use the drill to put holes through the branches so they can be secured together with the wire. The branches need not be symmetrical or smooth; in fact, the odder they are, the more grotesque the results. Bent ones for arms can make the skeleton appear to be gesturing. Bent leg branches can give the skeleton a humorous pair of bow legs. Start by making a cross with two branches to serve as the basic torso. Add a short crosspiece for hips. Arms and legs are made by joining two branches at their ends. Hang arms and legs from the crosspieces. Pieces of branch with lots of offshoots can be used for hands and feet. The small pumpkin serves as the skeleton's skull. Hang the branch skeleton where the wind will set it rattling.

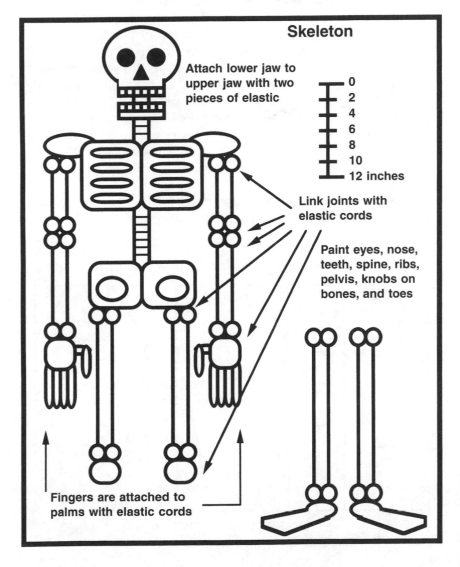

Skeleton

Attach lower jaw to upper jaw with two pieces of elastic

0
2
4
6
8
10
12 inches

Link joints with elastic cords

Paint eyes, nose, teeth, spine, ribs, pelvis, knobs on bones, and toes

Fingers are attached to palms with elastic cords

SIMPLE COFFIN

A simple coffin (see diagram) can be made from three sheets of four-by-eight plywood or from cardboard sheets of the same size. When made from cardboard, duct tape will suffice to hold the coffin together. After construction, the coffin can be painted black on the outside and white or red on the inside.

When made with plywood, use three- or four-inch strap hinges to hold the coffin together. After connecting all the sides, line them up over the top. The bottom is then laid on top of this and lined up. Screws can then be run through the bottom to hold it to the sides. Next, flip the box over and place the lid on it. Use strap hinges on one of the longer sides of the coffin (C–D or F–E on the diagram). When everything is attached, duct tape can be used to cover any gaps. When everything is secure, paint the coffin as above.

For those with more carpentry skills, angles can be cut on the ends of the side pieces that allow a snug, finished appearance. Properly done, the coffin can look very professional and could actually be used for a burial.

At a party, a coffin can serve as a novel way to serve food or can contain a prop cadaver. Its ominous appearance alone can add a chill to the festivities.

Cutting Diagram for Simple Coffin

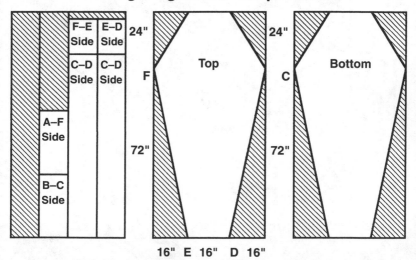

Three sheets of 4 × 8 plywood or cardboard

A Politically Correct Coffin

ENVIRONMENTALLY FRIENDLY CASKET

"Swiss engineered, recycled cardboard, no trees must die when you do. Mahog.-type fin. No tool assembly. Use for storage or Halloween while alive. $199, while supplies last."

A classified ad placed in 1994
in the *Washington Post*

SPIDER'S WEB

A spiderweb can be made using string by tacking up three lines that intersect at a single point. Then, starting near the intersection, run a spiral of string outward. Knot the string to the cross lines as the spiral passes over them. The size of the web is determined by how far apart you set the initial tacks.

Build a Spider's Web

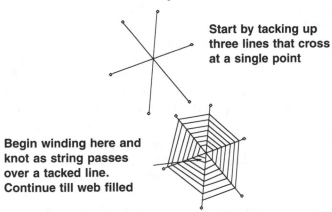

Start by tacking up three lines that cross at a single point

Begin winding here and knot as string passes over a tacked line. Continue till web filled

HAUNTED HOUSES

The largest display created for Halloween is the "haunted house." As mentioned earlier, during the nineteenth century, it was common for well-to-do families to create haunted houses through decoration. A cellar might be hung with creepy rags and lit with dim candles. Somber music might be played on a gramophone while hidden hands rattled chains or shook skeletons. A parlor might receive similar treatment, then be used for a costume ball. Some families invited trick-or-treaters inside to enjoy the terrors, then be rewarded with a treat. Haunted houses faded during the first half of the twentieth century but have been revived.

Civic groups commonly turn old houses or empty warehouses into haunted houses, selling tickets to raise money for charity. Large sums are often raised; indeed, creating haunted houses has become a minor industry that insiders refer to as "dark amusements." Fog generators, spooky lighting, sophisticated sound systems, elaborate props and decor, and dozens of actors dressed as monsters and victims are used to produce terrifying Halloween experiences. Ghosts dart from behind doors. Witches busily brew potions. Monsters lumber and groan, while homicidal maniacs spring forward brandishing hatchets.

Many haunted houses feature dungeons where mannequins are tortured. Sometimes real people wearing elaborate makeup serve as victims. One common device is to present a blood-spattered mad scientist operating on a victim. This is done by cutting a hole in an "operating table" large enough for the victim's chest to pass through. The victim is positioned so that his body is exposed from under the arms up. His lower body is hidden under the table by white sheets. A dummy body is laid out on the table so that it seems to be the victim's lower body. A hospital gown and sheets cover the substitution. When visitors to the haunted house pass by, the mad doctor chops and saws at the dummy body, which is splattered with blood. The doctor can reach inside the dummy and pull out yarn soaked in ketchup, soup bones, and fake organs dripping phony gore. The victim can scream and flail his arms while the doctor works. A squirt bottle filled with ketchup can be surreptitiously squeezed from inside the body to provide ghastly fountains of blood.

Haunted houses once featured madhouses, wherein insane killers taunted visitors. Concern for the mentally ill has made this rare; instead, prison cells and execution chambers are now popular. In them, a phony electric chair might buzz furiously, causing the lights in the room to flicker and dim when a condemned man is electrocuted.

Peter Wing of Stamford, New York, a community eighty miles north of New York City, uses items scavenged from garbage dumps to construct his "Frankenstein's Fortress," which features a haunted library, a witches' forest, an opium den, a Transylvanian graveyard,

ROOM TO LET

and Frankenstein's laboratory. "Stuff that you picked out from a Dumpster has that trashed-out look that you can't get with new materials," Wing told the Associated Press in 1999. "Death and decay is unsettling—and that's what we're going for here."

Wing's haunted house enjoys the support of Stamford's government. The eighty actors who play monsters and victims are all members of the city's youth recreation program. It gives these kids a positive Halloween activity that diverts them from more destructive Halloween pranks.

Some religious groups have set up haunted houses to persuade young visitors to avoid behavior the group condemned. Called Hell Houses, they depict graphic scenes associated with abortion, AIDS, suicide, drunk driving, drug abuse, and, recently, school shootings, such as that at Columbine High School. During the Clinton administration, at least one depicted Bill Clinton and Monica Lewinsky misusing the Oval Office. The controversy over these houses is discussed in chapter 5.

SUGGESTED AMATEUR HAUNTED HOUSE FEATURES

Professionally constructed haunted houses can involve expensive special effects, sound systems, lights, and machinery. A discussion of their creation is outside the scope of this book, which is intended for amateurs. In addition to the decorations described previously, the amateur haunted house builder can try some of the following suggestions for scenes, devices, and stratagems. Remember, if not carefully executed, some of these can cause injury. No endorsement or guarantee of their safety is given by the author or publisher.

DEVICES AND STRATAGEMS

- Cover the walls in a room with a fluorescent design. Dress a helper in dark clothing with a dark ski mask. Paint the same design on the helper's clothing. Light the room with just black lights. Have your helper stand still against the wall. He will blend into the wall design, and visitors to the room can be surprised when he jumps forward.

- A portrait with eyes that follow visitors is a haunted house staple. It can be constructed by photocopying an old photo and enlarging it to portrait size. Glue it to a sheet of thin plywood and add a frame. Cut out the eyes. Glue a matching pair to a strip of plywood. Mount it behind the eyeholes so that a helper can move the eyes to follow visitors. An amusing variation is to use a portrait of two people or of a family complete with pet, all of whom have eyes that watch visitors.

- Place stereo speakers on the roof of the house and play the sounds of a thunderstorm. Their location will make the storm sound very realistic. Lightning can be added to the storm by stationing strobe lights set up to fire at random intervals by the windows.

- A masked maniac with a roaring chain saw can be very frightening. The effect can be safely produced by removing the chain from the saw. Paint a black rim on the blade. With the motor making a ferocious buzz and the maniac jumping up and down, few will notice the lack of a chain.

- A ghostly effigy can be made to swoop past a visitor by hanging a cable painted black at a descending angle along the path you want the effigy to take. Suspend the effigy from a pulley. Pull it up to the high point of the cable and release it when visitors are near. Test the device to be sure it doesn't strike visitors. Remember, some visitors may be taller than you expect.

- Hang an opaque curtain, then set up a light source to cast shadows upon it. You can stage a bit of drama behind the curtain that the light will reveal. For example, you might have an old woman sitting in a chair knitting. A maniac sneaks up behind her with an ax and brings it down on her head. Actually, the woman is a dummy with a durable block of wood for a head—one that will withstand multiple whacks from a rubber ax. The knitting hands are those of a helper crouched low and safely out of the way of the ax. Alternatively, the maniac can grab the woman's hair and lop off her head—which is actually a dummy head with a wig securely attached.

- Have an accomplice go into the house with the other visitors, reacting as they do to several exhibits. Then suddenly a masked maniac leaps out and grabs him. The accomplice is dragged off screaming and thrashing. The visitors will believe that they, too, might be carried off. You may have the accomplice reappear later in another exhibit as a victim.

     Another similar trick is to have the maniac stab the accomplice with a rubber knife. A plastic bag full of fake blood can be hidden under the accomplice's clothing to spurt gore when the knife blow is delivered.

     Don't use a child or a woman for the abducted accomplice, as the other visitors may try to rescue the abductee.

- A floating ghost with a talking head can be created by placing a platform large enough and strong enough to support a body at head level in a closet. The platform is painted black to conceal it. A helper with his face made up to look spectral lies on the platform with his head and arms extended over the edge toward the closet door. His torso and legs are concealed under a black sheet. His head and arms are covered with cheesecloth to look ghostly. The material is positioned to dangle down to within a couple of feet from the floor. A fan is positioned to make the cloth billow, revealing that no body is below the head. A black light can make the cloth glow and make the black sheet seem blacker. The ghost can bellow and wave his arms.

- Have a helper dressed as a monster extend a bowl of candy to visitors. He-she can be very friendly. When a visitor accepts and reaches into the bowl, the monster can say, "I hope you enjoy that!" and pat the visitor on the head with a third arm while companionably holding the visitor's shoulder with a fourth. The illusion is accomplished by using a set of fake arms attached to a harness under the monster's clothing. These hold the bowl, leaving the monster's real arms free to reach out and surprise the visitor.

- Purchase a radio-operated toy car. Remove the auto body and mount a plastic jack-o'-lantern in its place. Install a battery-powered light in the jack and place it near a pile of similar jack-o'-lanterns. When someone stands nearby, move the motorized jack slightly. This will spook the bystander. When he takes note of the movement, make the jack leap forward toward him and chase him. The toy can also be disguised as a small monster.

- A bat can be transformed into a vampire using an electronic camera flash. A helper, costumed as a vampire, is concealed by wrapping a large cape around himself. Another helper dangles a rubber bat in front of the cloaked vampire. When the flash is fired, the bat is pulled away and the vampire opens his cloak. The flash will conceal the switch.

- A mirror and lights can be used for a more complex transformation that is often featured in carnival side shows. Construct an L-shaped room. Place two identical coffins at the two ends of the L. Put a monster effigy in the one on the top and a helper in the one on the right of the L. Place lights near the floor at both ends. Close off the ends with glass, leaving a square at the angle. Erect a third sheet of glass at a forty-five-degree angle in this square. The glass should run from the inside angle of the L to the outside corner of the L. A fourth sheet of glass is set up to block visitor access to the inside of the L. It provides a window into the room from the bottom of the L. The helper's part of the room is lit. A third helper, disguised as a mad scientist, throws a switch, whereupon there is a shriek; the lights illuminating the helper fade while the lights illuminating the monster brighten. This turns the diagonally suspended glass into a mirror that reflects the monster. It will appear that the helper has become a monster. Carnivals commonly used this setup to transform a pretty girl into a gorilla—actually a helper in a costume who would leap at spectators.

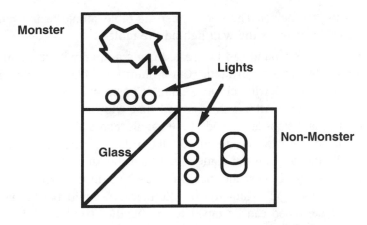

Monster-maker

Viewer **When the lights are on in the monster side and off in the non-monster side, the non-monster is seen. If the lights are on in the non-monster side and off in the monster side, the monster is seen.**

- A simpler mirror trick is to mount a piece of glass in a mirror frame on a fake wall on one side of a dimly lit corridor. With no light behind the glass, it will appear to be an ordinary mirror reflecting guests. Behind the wall, station a helper dressed as a ghost. Be sure that the wall behind the helper is identical to the wall opposite. Put a light attached to a dimmer switch by the feet of the helper. When guests pass by, the helper can turn up the light. This will make her image appear to be standing behind the guests—but if they turn, they'll see no one there.

- Another mirror trick can be used to position a severed-yet-alive head upon a table. A piece of plywood is hung from under the table at a forty-five-degree angle slanting away from the viewer. A mirror is attached to the plywood facing the viewer. A hole is cut in the table, and the helper is positioned on the plywood so his head pops through. The mirror will reflect the floor, concealing the helper. The floor under the table should bear a pattern that matches the wall behind the table.

- A fake knife wound can be created using a knife with a collapsing blade and a squirt bottle. Cut a blunt knife blade from cardboard. Paint it with chrome paint. Construct a hollow knife handle from quarter-inch plywood that will contain the entire blade. Place stops at the end of the handle, and add a collar to the blade so that it won't fall out. Stretch a thick elastic band inside the handle to push the blade out. When the knife stabs a body, the elastic will allow the blade to slide back in the handle then push it back out. Paint the handle black. A squirt bottle filled with fake blood can be taped to the handle. The knife wielder squeezes the bulb when the knife strikes the victim. Care should be taken to not strike too hard, in case the knife blade jams in the handle. Don't strike the victim anywhere near the face.

- The walls of a room can be made to come alive using a large rubber sheet. Cut an opening in the wall. Cover the hole with the sheet, securely fastening it in place. Paint the sheet to match the wallpaper. A helper can then press his hands and face against the sheet from the other side of the wall, making it appear that a spirit is trapped in the wall. Use a railing to keep visitors from touching the wall or poking the helper.

- Another wall effect can be achieved using a sheet of thin fabric. Hang it over a large opening in a wall. Place a powerful light behind the wall and dim the lights on the visitors' side of the wall. Position helpers behind the wall so that the light will cast their shadow upon it. They can enact a murder or some other horrific event that supposedly happened in the haunted house. Use a railing to prevent visitors from touching the wall and discovering that it's made of cloth.

Combination Scares

A scare can be intensified by combining it with another shock or shocks. An obvious combination is matching a suddenly appearing apparition with a scream. A scream matched with turning out the lights is another combination scare. An air compressor and air hose can produce a combination scare by squirting visitors behind the knees as an exhibit startles them (be sure to never point the hose at visitors' faces; debris might be thrown into their eyes).

A subtle secondary scare can be given by placing a sheet of foam rubber upon the floor by an exhibit. Cover the foam with a sheet of plywood. Viewers will feel a sense of unease as the floor gives under their feet. The unease turns into a scare when a hidden helper slams a mallet against the plywood, sending a shock into the viewers' feet as the primary exhibit startles them.

HAUNTED HOUSE SCENES

- By the entrance of the house, construct a cemetery with a variety of plywood tombstones bearing humorous epitaphs. Scatter skulls and bones about. Dress helpers as grave robbers and have them pull a coffin from a shallow grave. It can then pop open, revealing another helper dressed as a corpse. The corpse charges the visitors after "killing" the grave robbers.

  Fresh graves can be simulated by laying a three-foot by six-foot sheet of plastic on the ground. Mound potting soil upon the plastic. After Halloween, you can easily transfer the dirt from the plastic sheet to a wheelbarrow.

- A room in the house can become a mad scientist's laboratory. Furnish it with white furniture and any odd device that can be found. Float fake body parts in pickle jars. These can be made using pink rubber, tissue paper, red and blue yarn, and other everyday objects. The water can be made repulsively murky with soap.

  A fake head can be set in a large glass pot placed on an old hot plate. Don't turn on the hot plate or even plug it in. Run the hose from an aquarium aerator into the pot to make bubbles. They'll make the water look like it's simmering. Place a small red electric bulb under the burner. Its light will make the burner appear to be active. A little dishwashing soap in the pot will make the water foam disgustingly.

A helper dressed as a Frankenstein-style monster can be strapped down on a tilted table. Wires and tubes can be linked to him (perhaps a set of jumper cables can be attached to the creature). At a suitable moment, the scientist pulls a switch, the lights darken as circuits buzz, and the monster springs to life to attack his creator and menace visitors.

- Construct a mad dentist's office. The dentist can use a variety of terrible tools—a power drill, hedge trimmers, a hammer, a chisel—on the mouth of a dummy.

- A funeral parlor can be constructed using a coffin set on a table with lots of phony flowers surrounding it. Organ music plays, but it can't drown out a tape recording hidden inside the coffin. This plays a recording of a helper pounding and demanding to be let out. A helper dressed as a ghoulish funeral director can use a tape to measure visitors for a coffin.

- A circus knife-throwing act can be performed. Tie a lovely assistant to a target and have a blindfolded knife thrower hurl blades at her. This can be done by hanging a paper target over a piece of plywood with holes cut in it. Fake knives made from stiff cardboard are mounted in sleeves attached to the back of the plywood, so that a blow from a mallet will cause them to pop through the paper at spots all around the assistant. The mallet blow will sound like the knife striking the target.

The knife thrower stands with his throwing arm away from the spectators and fakes a throw. He can do this by tossing the knife backward as he rapidly swings his arm or by not releasing the knife at all. Faking the throw is easier than you might think, because the spectators will look at the target, wanting to see if the assistant was struck, and not at the thrower. The thrower uses rubber knives just in case he makes a mistake and actually throws a knife at the assistant.

The act can be spiced up by taping balloons over the spots where the fake knives will emerge. Fit a bit of wire to the knife handles. This will pop them, making the throws seem more realistic. As a finale, the knife thrower can start to sneeze and misthrow. A fake knife positioned to pop out close behind the assistant's torso then emerges. She screams as blood is squirted through her costume; the lights switch off before anyone can detect that she wasn't hit at all.

- A trio of cackling witches can gather around a cauldron made to smoke with dry ice. They can toss in odd ingredients and magically (assisted by helpers with thread) make objects leap from shelves to plop into the pot. The witches can finger visiting children, commenting on their plumpness and whether they'd cook up tender. Display a few frogs in a glass case labeled BAD LITTLE BOYS AND GIRLS. If possible, dress the frogs in doll clothes to heighten the suggestion that they were children turned to frogs.

- A zoo exhibit of a captured bigfoot can be made using two-by-twos to construct a cage. Hang a tire in it for your bigfoot to exercise with. Place straw bedding on the floor. Include a large food bowl filled with bones. Scatter a few of these around the cage. A zoo guide describes how the ferocious creature was captured at the cost of dozens of lives. He also describes the creature's diet, which includes lots of raw meat. While he does this, a zookeeper shoves a meaty bone toward the creature, which suddenly roars and grabs the zookeeper's arm, tearing it off. It then smashes open the cage and charges the crowd. Of course, the arm is phony. With a bit of costume engineering, you can also give the zookeeper a phony head that the bigfoot rips off. The keeper can then run about flailing as the bigfoot tosses his head at the crowd.

- A corner of your yard can be set up as a UFO crash site. A farm supply store can sell you a large cattle watering tub that you can add pie plate portholes to, flip over, and tilt into a shallow crater to simulate a spaceship (the tub can later be used as a children's splash pool). Scatter debris around the crash. Hide a strobe light behind the tub. Attach battery-powered lights to the sides of the tub. A twirling light display can be created by mounting spotlights on a rotating table and having a helper turn it back and forth. Hide the table and helper under the tub. The light will spill out. Play a recording of beeping electronic sounds and aliens gibbering. Dry-ice fog helps create mystery. Flop several alien bodies around, ready for autopsy. Dress a small child helper as an alien with a ray gun who can zap an accomplice mixed in with your guests.

SÉANCE SILLINESS

A haunted house can host a spooky séance that is made entertaining with the tricks that phony mediums use to gull suckers. First, set up a room for the séance. You'll need a round table surrounded by old-fashioned chairs. Hang windows with long cheesecloth curtains. Darken the lights. Burn a little incense to give a mysterious smell to the air and to cast some twining streamers of smoke. Dress your medium in sober garb—a dark suit for a man or a pale, flowing dress for a woman.

Visitors are invited to join hands at a table and invoke the dead. The medium can use monofilament thread to make objects move. Helpers can swing cheesecloth ghosts at the participants or create spirit voices using hidden speakers. While the medium's hands are holding the hands of participants to either side, he can make the table jump, using hooks attached to his elbows. A hair dryer set to cold and a length of dryer hose can send shivering breezes around the ankles of the participants. The sound of the hair dryer can be masked with spooky music or by hiding it behind a wall. Answers given with taps can be produced by signaling a helper who uses a knocker tied to a string to make the table bang out the correct response.

Have an accomplice mix in with the participants to solicit information from them earlier in the evening. This can be passed on to the medium, or the accomplice can signal answers to a helper during the séance. For example, the accomplice asks a teenager if he goes to the same high school as the accomplice's son. Later, the medium can claim to have a vision of an animal, which turns out to be the mascot of the high school. A little preperformance research can obtain a list of mascots for local schools. The medium can even claim to see a happy or sad animal by being aware of which high school teams won their last sporting events.

A surprising amount of information can be gathered from visitors without their catching on. You can have them sign in with the name of their home town and then check the phone book for their address. A guide can ask them the name of their next of kin. You can observe them arriving and examine their automobiles, which may contain items you can link to them or have out-of-state license tags. You can have a guide jokingly ask them if their parents know they're visiting the house with their girlfriend or boyfriend. You can even make visitors wait a few moments before entering the house and simply eavesdrop on their conversation.

The medium can use leading questions or twist answers to make himself appear powerful. For example, he can claim to see romance in the room and ask if someone has made some transition in a romantic relationship. In a crowd, this is almost always true. If no one says yes, the medium says he sensed a longing for romance and predicts that he sees it coming. If someone says yes, he can claim to have sensed this and, based upon the respondent's behavior, offer general observations about him or her. If the respondent is there with a date, the medium can say, "I see someone thinking of a romantic trip." One member of the couple is likely to have considered some sort of travel.

The medium can ask the participants to think of an important question that can be answered yes or no; he will transmit this to the spirits for their counsel. After urging everyone to focus all their mental energy, the medium can respond with answers such as, "Yes, but only if that is what your heart truly wants"; "yes, but not in the way you expect"; or "no, or only after difficulty." The answers are apt to be correct, because they are both positive and negative at the same time.

HAUNTED HOUSE CAUTIONS

- Review your insurance coverage. It may need to be increased or altered.

- Don't frighten young children. Halloween should be fun for them, not terrifying.

- Be mindful of objects that might trip visitors, or poke them, or fall upon them. Darkness can turn an otherwise easily avoidable danger into a trap. Pad edges with foam. The foam can be painted black to hide it. Use black duct tape to seal cords and ropes to walls or to the floor so they won't snare visitors. Lighting narrow areas is a good solution. Safety is better than a bit of atmospheric gloom.

- Devices that are meant to pop out in front of visitors should be carefully designed and tested. You must be sure they don't skewer or bump visitors. They should never project into areas where visitors may be standing.

- Axes, knives, or other weapons used in sketches should be made of rubber or cardboard.

- Monitor and control all your helpers. They may become overly excited and behave inappropriately.

- Monitor your visitors. Rowdiness, alcohol use, horseplay, or combative behavior can be dangerous in a confined area. Don't be afraid to ask troublemakers to leave, or to shut down your house if necessary. If your haunted house gets a reputation as a trouble spot, you will invite more trouble and discourage decent visitors.

- Count visitors as they enter and as they leave. Be sure no one stows away.

- Don't use live animals. They are unpredictable, and the experience may be unpleasant for them.

- Don't use props that can decay or become germ-infested. Everything should be clean and sanitary.

- Helpers who will be exposed to loud noises need ear protection. Don't overdo the sounds you subject visitors to, either.

- You should have a standby, battery-powered lighting system so that your house can be cleared if the main power fails. Helpers should have flashlights so they can guide visitors to exits.

- Carefully review all props, devices, and decorations for fire dangers. If there's any risk, don't use them. Prohibit smoking. Don't use candles, even in jack-o'-lanterns. A risk that might be acceptable on a front porch or a kitchen table isn't acceptable in a house full of people. Pyrotechnic devices, such as flash explosives, should not be used.

- Make sure there are multiple fire escape doors and check that there is more than one exit route from any spot inside the haunted house. These exits and paths should be clearly marked with lighted signs and reflective tape. Practice fire drills with your helpers so that they will know exactly what to do if danger arises. If there are narrow or congested points in the house, rearrange the house's features to eliminate them.

SUGGESTED HAUNTED HOUSE READING

- *The Complete Haunted House Book* by Tim Harkleroad.
- *Give Them a Real Scare This Halloween* by Joseph Pffiffer.
- *Haunted Attraction,* a magazine for haunted house builders (P.O. Box 451, North Myrtle Beach, SC 92597).
- *How to Run a Financially Successful Haunted House* by Philip Morris.

12

HALLOWEEN FOODS

[Wednesday has set up a lemonade stand.]
Girl Scout: *"Is this made from real lemons?"*
Wednesday Addams: *"Yes."*
Girl Scout: *"I only like all-natural foods and beverages, organically grown, with no preservatives. Are you sure they're real lemons?"*
Pugsley Addams: *"Yes."*
Girl Scout: *"I'll tell you what. I'll buy a cup if you buy a box of my delicious Girl Scout cookies. Do we have a deal?"*
Wednesday Addams: *"Are they made from real Girl Scouts?"*

The Addams Family (1991)

Food is an important part of any holiday celebration. Halloween is no exception. If a regular dinner is to be served, any of the favorite dishes served at Thanksgiving are appropriate, especially those that can be given a Halloween twist. Orange, yellow, bloodred, and black foods are best—for example, yellow squash; orange yams; carrot and raisin salad; black bean, corn, and tomato salad; dark pumpernickel bread, cheeses, and red beets. Non-Thanksgiving fare can also be given a Halloween twist. Italian dishes have thick red sauces. Mexican dishes have orange cheeses, red peppers, black olives, and fiery spices that seem devilish.

For younger diners or for playful adults, the dishes can be given Halloween name tags corresponding to their appearance. Carrot and raisin salad can become CARROT AND BEETLE SALAD. A bowl of spaghetti and sauce can be topped with a shelled hard-boiled egg "eyeball" and dubbed SQUIRMETTI. A pupil for the eye can be made by cutting a shallow dimple in one end and inserting a brown M&M with the lettering to the back. Another novelty dish can be made by cutting the head and feet from a rubber chicken. Place them under a grilled chicken breast and serve it as ROAD KILL CHICKEN or THE CHICKEN WHO DIDN'T MAKE IT ACROSS THE ROAD. Your imagination will provide lots of horrific names.

For the strong of stomach, food coloring can be used to give food bizarre hues—blue mashed potatoes, for example, or green slices of ham. It's surprising how sickening ordinary foods dyed an unnatural shade can be; you may want to go easy on the food coloring. Here are many food items and beverages that can be put together for your Halloween party.

SNACKS

MAGGOT DIP

Mix a spoonful of cooked brown rice into ordinary onion dip. Sprinkle a few grains on the top of the dip before serving.

MASHED MARTIAN DIP

Stir a few drops of green food coloring into bean dip. Add finely chopped red and yellow peppers and two-inch pieces of green onion.

UNNATURAL NACHOS

Prepare nacho cheese sauce as indicated on the label. Pour a jar of chunky salsa or a can of spicy stewed tomatoes into the cheese. Add a bit of green food coloring and stir. Repeat until a nice shade is created. Serve with blue taco chips.

JACK-O'-LANTERN SANDWICHES

Use a jack-o'-lantern cookie cutter to cut slices of bread. If the cookie cutter cuts eye-, nose, and mouth holes, use the cut slices as sandwich tops. Prepare bottom slices of bread by using a knife to trace around the cookie cutter. If the cookie cutter doesn't cut holes through the bread, cut them with a sharp knife.

Fill the sandwiches with any filling. A slice of American cheese makes a good topper for the filling; its yellow color will show nicely through the holes in the bread.

Other Halloween cookie cutters can be used to make sandwiches of different shapes.

JACK-O'-LANTERN PIZZA

A pizza can be given a Halloween look by using yellow cheese slices cut into triangles for eyes, nose, and mouth. American cheese is the most obvious choice, but there are other varieties of yellow cheese that are more flavorful. Pop the pizza under the broiler for a couple of minutes to melt the added cheese.

WITCH HANDWICHS

Purchase a package of pizza crust mix. Prepare it as the box directs and roll it out flat. Place your washed hand on the flat dough and, with a knife, trace your hand, cutting away the excess dough. Place the "hand" on a greased baking sheet. When all the dough has been used up, bake the hands at the temperature the box instructs but for less time—the hands will bake quicker than a pizza crust. Check them often to avoid burning.

When the hands are done, allow them to cool, then use them as you would bread to make sandwiches. Well-chopped chicken or tuna salad works well. You might also try raspberry jam. The red jam gives the handwich a gory appearance.

DEAD LADY FINGERS

Roll store-bought pretzel dough into finger-sized cylinders. Press an almond into one end of each cylinder to serve as a fingernail. Bake as indicated on the package.

SWEETS

NIGHT CRAWLER PIE

Make a chocolate pudding pie using a premade graham cracker crust. Insert several gummy worms in the pudding. Leave enough space on top for a quarter-inch layer of crushed chocolate cookies. Be sure to have a couple of the worms peeping up through the "dirt."

Chocolate Roll Bat

Cupcake Spider

Whipped Cream Ghost

Ice Cream Witch

Oblong Cookie Grave

At Halloweentime, gummy bugs and spiders may also be available to bury in the pie.

GRAVEYARD CAKE

Purchase or prepare a cake iced with dark chocolate frosting. Cover the top of the cake with crushed chocolate cookies to simulate the dirt of a graveyard. Mound dirt crumbs to simulate graves. Push oblong vanilla cookies into the frosting as tombstones. Use a tube of black decorator icing to write R.I.P. on the cookie. If you have a delicate touch, you can write other inscriptions on the cookies, such as YOU'RE NEXT or SEE YOU LATER. Don't use the names of any of the guests; some might be upset or feel you're tempting fate.

Bones and skulls can be added to the graveyard using white decorator icing. Draw bones mimicking skeletal arms or legs on the surface of the cake as if they are protruding from graves. Sprinkle cookie dirt over part of the bones to suggest they are partially buried. Skulls can be formed by drawing a horizontal 8 for the eye sockets. Draw a rounded cap on top of this, then draw several vertical lines under the horizontal 8. These will form the skull's teeth. Fill in the upper part of the vertical lines.

Whipped cream ghosts can be added to the graveyard using aerosol whipped cream. Pile up a narrow conical heap, then use two chocolate chips to make eyes.

CHOCOLATE BATS

Chocolate bats can be made using chocolate-covered chocolate cake rolls, a dark-colored fruit roll, a small tub of prepared dark chocolate icing, a tube of red decorator icing, and a tube of white decorator icing.

The cake roll serves as the body of the bat. To form bat wings, cut a circle from the fruit roll. Cut straight across the circle, then cut curved pieces from the round side of the half circle. This is to create the scalloped bottom edge of the bat's wings. Use the chocolate icing to glue the wings to the flat side of the chocolate roll. To create ears for the bat, make two cuts with a knife into either side of the "head" of the bat. Insert one of the curved pieces earlier cut from the half circle into each cut. Use a bit of the chocolate icing as glue to secure the ears. Finish the bat by drawing two beady red eyes and two white fangs.

CHOCOLATE SPIDERS

Chocolate spiders can be made using store-prepared chocolate cupcakes. The best kind are those that are iced with dark chocolate and dusted with chocolate sprinkles. If you can't find cupcakes with sprinkles, buy some sprinkles in the cake decorating section of your grocery. Also purchase a package of black licorice and a tube of red decorator icing.

Using a knife, poke six holes around the base of the cupcake. Insert pieces of licorice to form the spider's legs. Bend them so that they appear to be supporting the spider. Draw two eyes on top of the cupcake with a tube of red decorator icing. If there are no sprinkles, add them to simulate the hair that covers the back of a tarantula.

The spiders should be served with the licorice giving them a natural spider stance. Try placing them on a bloodred napkin on a platter.

ICE CREAM WITCHES

Using an ice cream scoop, scoop out a nice round ball of lime or orange sherbet. Place it on a waxed-paper-covered platter. Push two chocolate chips, point first, into the ball as eyes. Push a third, point out, in the ball as a nose. Alternatively, a kernel of candy corn, point out, can serve as a nose. Using a tube of black decorator icing, draw a smile (or frown) and scraggly hair on the ball. Add a sugar cone as a witch's hat. Store in the freezer until served.

JACK-O'-LANTERN CAKE

A rounded, dome-shaped cake can be baked in a microwave using a microwave-safe bowl. Follow the directions on the package. After the cake has cooled, remove it from the bowl and place it on a plate. Cut a jack-o'-lantern face into it. Ice it with orange frosting. Use one of the pieces cut out to make a stem. Ice this with milk chocolate frosting.

BUG BUTTER COOKIES

Simple bug cookies can be made with a bag of store-bought chocolate cookies, small pretzels, a tube of black decorating icing, and a jar of crunchy peanut butter. Glue the cookies together with a dab of the peanut butter. Break the pretzels into one-inch lengths. Insert the pretzel pieces into the peanut butter to form legs. Use the black icing to give the bug some beady eyes.

SQUID EYE PUDDING

Make some lemon pudding. Portion it out into serving bowls and chill. Serve with a scoop of whipped dessert topping. Use a melon baller to produce a round, eyeball-shaped scoop. At the center of the scoop, place a brown M&M to serve as the squid's pupil. Using a tube of red decorator icing, trace a few bloodshot veins on the eye.

BAT CAKE

Bake a nine-inch, circular yellow cake using orange juice instead of water. Tint it orange with food coloring. Slice a rectangle from the center of the cake by making two cuts across it about an inch and a half apart. This will be the body of the bat. Cut a small square from the center of the top of the body, then clip the square stubs to points to form bat ears. Take the two crescents left, and set them on either side of the body to form wings. Scallop the lower edges to make them more batlike. Cut a small square from the bottom of the torso to form legs. Ice the cake with dark chocolate frosting. Make a set of eyes with dots of red icing.

CANDIED OR CARAMEL APPLES

Choose ten unblemished, firm apples. Granny Smith apples are a good variety for candying. Remove their stems and wash them well. Insert a stick into the apple where the stem used to be. Mix 2 cups granulated sugar with $\frac{1}{2}$ cup corn syrup and $\frac{3}{4}$ cup water in a saucepan. Place the saucepan on a burner set to low or medium low. Stir until the sugar is completely dissolved. Let the mix continue to cook for 30 to 45 minutes with an occasional stir. The mix is ready when a candy thermometer placed in it reaches 275 degrees.

Quickly stir 6 drops red food coloring and 1 teaspoon of vanilla into the hot mix. If you wish, 1 teaspoon of cinnamon can be added to the mix. Immediately begin dipping the apples into it, using the sticks to avoid burning your fingers. Place the dipped apples, sticks pointing up, on a greased baking sheet or a sheet covered with waxed paper. Wait 15 to 30 minutes for the candy mix to cool and harden. Children can be easily burned making the apples or eating them too soon. An adult should supervise them closely if they participate in the preparation.

Caramel apples are prepared in a similar way, but you coat the apples with caramel instead of candy. Unwrap a 14-ounce bag of caramels. Place them in a microwavable bowl with 2 teaspoons of water. Microwave on high, stirring every minute, until they are melted. Remove the melted caramel and dip the apples in it (the apple can be rolled in chopped nuts). The caramel is very hot; let the apples cool 15 to 30 minutes before eating.

Candied and caramel apples can be given a Halloween touch by cutting a jack-o'-lantern face into the skin of the apple with a paring knife before coating them.

TRADITIONAL POPCORN BALLS

Put 2 quarts popped popcorn in a large pan. Keep the popcorn warm by placing the pan in a 200-degree oven. Put 1 cup granulated sugar, $\frac{1}{4}$ cup butter, $\frac{1}{2}$ teaspoon salt, $\frac{1}{3}$ cup light corn syrup, and

⅓ cup water in a saucepan. Place the saucepan on a burner set to medium. Stir the mix constantly until it comes to a boil. When it's boiling, stop stirring and let it cook until it reaches 270 degrees on a candy thermometer. Remove the saucepan from the heat and stir in 1 teaspoon vanilla.

Take the popcorn from the oven. Slowly pour the hot syrup mixture over the popcorn, periodically stirring with a large spoon. Continue until all the popcorn is coated. When the coating cools to a touchable temperature, lightly grease your hands with butter, then form the popcorn into balls. You should have enough coated popcorn to make a dozen balls. Place the popcorn balls on a sheet of waxed paper to cool. Wrap the popcorn balls in orange cellophane and tie with black ribbon.

"Bloody" popcorn balls can be made by adding red food coloring to the syrup mixture.

QUIVERING SLIME

Make a bowl of green gelatin. Put a third of it aside in a large bowl and pour the rest into individual serving bowls. When the gelatin is about to solidify, add gummy bugs to the serving bowls. Take the large bowl of reserved gelatin and, using an electric mixer at a low setting, mix it into a froth. Pour this over the individual servings and let the gelatin solidify.

PUMPKIN GOOEY GLOP

Place 4 cups vanilla ice cream, ⅔ cup milk, 1⅓ cups pumpkin puree, ½ teaspoon ground ginger, ½ teaspoon ground cinnamon, 2 pinches allspice, and 2 pinches mace in a blender and blend till smooth. If your blender is too small, halve the measures. Pour in glass bowls and sprinkle with miniature chocolate chips or raisins.

CRUNCHY FROG CHOCOLATES

Inspired by a Monty Python sketch, these candies are simple to make. Gather 12 ounces of chocolate chips, 1 teaspoon grated chocolate, 1 cup whole, cooked cranberries, and 2 cups broken pretzels (the pieces should be no longer than an inch). The cranberries serve as frog "innards" and the pretzels as frog "bones." The chocolate must be softened, then rehardened. This is done by zapping it in a microwave for 2 minutes, stirring, then rezapping it for 15 seconds and stirring more. Repeat the short zaps till the chocolate is very soft. Mix in the cranberries and pretzels. Stir in the grated chocolate. This will cause the melted chocolate to reharden. Before this happens, press the result into frog-shaped candy molds. The molds can be found at stores that sell candy-making supplies.

The tang of the cranberries and the salty pretzels mixed with the chocolate provide a pleasing and distinct taste. A sweeter treat can be made using whole raspberries instead of cranberries.

CHOCOLATE SPIDERWEB

Melt chocolate in a microwave, as described in the Crunchy Frog recipe. Using a pastry bag with a small-ended tip, pipe four or five lines crossing at one point upon a sheet of waxed paper. Draw a spiral on top of the crossed lines. Let the web cool, then remove it from the waxed paper. Use it to garnish a bowl of ice cream or other Halloween treat.

DECORATING COOKIES OR CUPCAKES

Cookies or cupcakes, prepared by yourself or store bought, can be given a quick Halloween guise using tubes of decorator icing. Spiders can be drawn on white-iced cookies with black icing. A white cookie with a black icing pupil with bloodshot red lines made with red icing can be served as an "eyeball." Orange icing can be used to draw jack-o'-lantern faces.

Spiderwebs can be put on cookies by icing them with white frosting, then piping a spiral of chocolate icing upon this (warm the chocolate icing in a cup of hot water before using it). Take a knife and, starting at the center of the cupcake, draw the knife tip to the outer edge of the icing. Repeat to create the spokes of a spiderweb.

A simple but charming spider can be put on a cupcake using M&Ms and a tube of chocolate icing. Draw four crossing lines for the spider's legs, then place the candy, letters down, on the intersection of the lines.

Another decorating technique utilizes stencils. Using carbon paper, the outlines of Halloween icons such as jack-o'-lanterns, black cats, and witches can be transferred from newspapers, magazines, or cards to an unfolded manila folder. Place the folder on a cutting block and use a sharp craft knife to cut out the design, turning the transferred drawings into stencils. Place the stencil on top of a chocolate-iced cupcake that has been chilled in the refrigerator. The cold should stiffen the icing so the stencil won't stick. If this doesn't work for the icing you're using, try lubricating the underside of the stencil with a shot of cooking spray.

After the stencil is in place, put a bit of powdered sugar in the crease of a piece of folded paper. Lightly sprinkle the sugar over the stencil. Carefully lift the stencil away so that surplus sugar won't dribble. A nice image should be produced. If it's smudged, sprinkle more sugar over the cupcake to form a background for a second attempt using a contrasting color of sugar. Cake-decorating sections of grocery stores contain tinted sugar.

Orange, red, or black sugar on white icing, yellow on orange icing, and other combinations can produce a great variety of images. The stencils can also be used on un-iced cupcakes, cookies, cakes, pies, and even nondessert foods. A bowl of bean dip, for example, can be enlivened by leveling it with a knife and stenciling a jack-o'-lantern face of chili powder upon it.

CREEPY ICE

Buy a pair of latex gloves that do not contain talcum or other powder. Wash thoroughly with soap and hot water. Rinse well. Fill with raspberry juice and tightly tie off the wrist opening. Freeze. To use the ice, dip the glove in hot water till the ice slides out free. Place in a punch bowl.

ORANGE OOZE

Mix 1 cup orange yogurt, 1 cup orange juice, and 2 cups orange soda in a blender. Pour into ice cube trays and freeze. To serve, place the frozen cubes into a blender, adding ⅔ cup orange soda for each tray of cubes. Blend until smooth but not runny. Serve with an ice cube at the bottom of each cup to help keep the ooze cold and thick.

Red ooze can be made using raspberry yogurt, raspberry-cranberry juice, and raspberry soda. Green ooze can be made using lemon yogurt, lemonade, and lemon-lime soda.

Brain Food

The mail-order firm Johnson Smith Company of Florida offers for sale many "traditional" novelties such as rubber chickens, X-ray glasses, and itching powder. One item in its inventory, however, is a truly unusual product. It's a "heavy-duty" and "dishwasher-safe" gelatin mold that allows you to fashion realistic brain-shaped desserts. The mold, which is priced at $11.98, comes with a recipe for gelatin of an appropriate brain color. The company's catalog claims that the mold is "great for Halloween or anyone who likes brain food." Johnson Smith also offers kits that allow clever cooks to make gelatin molds of their own hands and faces.

BEVERAGES

PUMPKIN MILKSHAKES

Mix a small can of pumpkin pie filling, ½ cup milk, 1 teaspoon cinnamon, and ½ gallon vanilla ice cream in a blender. Serve with a dab of whipped cream on top.

ORANGE PUNCH

A pleasing orange punch can be made using 2 quarts of orange sherbet, a 12-ounce can frozen lemonade concentrate, and 2 1-liter bottles lemon-lime soda. Put several spoons of sherbet into a punch bowl. Add the lemonade concentrate and 1½ cups cold water. Stir, adding the rest of the sherbet as the mixture smooths. To preserve its fizz, slowly add the soda by pouring it down the side of the bowl. Gently stir to mix the ingredients. Keep the punch cold by setting the bowl on a tray of ice. Putting the ice in the punch will make it watery. Place a second bowl of ice cubes by the punch for those who like to have their punch on the rocks.

DRACULA'S SWEET, COLD-BLOODED PUNCH

Mix 8 cups cranberry juice, 6 cups sparkling apple juice, 1 package lightly sweetened frozen raspberries, and 6 orange slices. Chill and serve using the Creepy Ice described on page 243.

DRACULA'S SPICED, HOT-BLOODED CIDER

Combine 10 cups apple cider, 12 ounces lightly sweetened frozen raspberries or blackberries, and 2 to 3 cinnamon sticks in a large pot.

Bring to a boil, then reduce the heat. Simmer, covered, for 10 minutes. Remove from the heat and strain through cheesecloth. The mixture should be served warm. If it was prepared beforehand, reheat it. This recipe makes 16 five-ounce servings. For those who like a spicier taste, 2 or 3 cloves can be added before boiling.

Serve the cider in glass punch cups. Place several "red hot" candies in the bottom of the cups. The warm cider will melt the candies, and it will look as if there's a puddle of blood at the bottom of the punch cup.

SOME ADULT BEVERAGES

There are many cocktails and punches that can be served at Halloween. A bit of rum can be added to the punches described above, or you could try one of the novel potions below.

WITCHY GINGER PUNCH

Mix 2 liters chilled ginger ale with 2 liters chilled sparkling cider and 2 cups rum. Add a fistful of raisins.

TOXIC WASTER

Pour 1 ounce Midori and 1½ ounces gin over ice, then fill with Mountain Dew. Mix a drop of blue food coloring with corn syrup in a soup bowl. Take a glass and dip its rim in the tinted syrup. Twist slowly and remove gently. The blue goo will drip a bit then set, making a nice creepy garnish to the drink (dripping blood for other drinks can be made using red food coloring). Serve under a black light to make the drink glow poisonously.

ZOMBIE

In a cocktail shaker, mix 1 ounce apricot brandy, 1 ounce light rum, and 1 ounce dark rum. Add 1 ounce lemon juice, 1 ounce lime juice, and a dash of grenadine. Shake well, then strain into a highball glass filled with ice. Add orange juice, leaving room for 1 ounce Demerara 151-proof rum. Float this rum into the glass by gently pouring it in over an upside-down spoon. Garnish with a cherry, an orange slice, and a wedge of pineapple. Dust with a teaspoon of powdered sugar.

MONKEY BRAINS

Fill a small shot glass with red Curacao (about ¾ ounce). Float ¾ ounce of Bailey's Irish Cream into the glass. It will billow like a small brain in a jar of blood.

BLACK CAT

Combine 1¼ ounce tequila and 1¼ ounce Amaretto in a lowball glass.

HALLOWEEN MARTINI

Combine 1½ ounce vodka, 1 ounce Grand Marnier, and a splash of orange Curacao in a shaker. Serve chilled.

HOT MULLED CIDER

Peel 5 apples and stud each with 4 whole cloves. Place in a large pot, adding 2 or 3 cinnamon sticks and the zest of an orange. Pour 1 gallon apple cider into the pot and warm the mixture on a low setting for 1½ hours. Don't allow the mixture to boil. Add 1 or 2 cups rum according to taste. Serve warm.

HOT SPICED WINE

Buy a jar of mince pie filling. Combine 1 cup of this with 1 cup of raisins and 2 bottles of red wine in a large pot. Warm until the mixture starts to bubble, then turn the heat down but not off. Stir occasionally. Serve warm with bits of apple floating upon each serving. For those who don't like "lumpy" drinks, strain the mix through a sieve. For a spicier brew, mix in more mince pie filling.

13

HALLOWEEN PARTIES

The Zombies were having fun, the party had just begun.
The guests included Wolfman, Dracula and his Son.

"Monster Mash," by Bobby "Boris" Pickett

A party is an excellent way to celebrate Halloween. For children, it can serve as an alternative to trick-or-treating or as an after-trick-or-treating activity. This can help minimize the mischief your children get into without spoiling their holiday. For adults, a party is a good way to share the fun kids have and to socialize.

A Halloween party should always feature costumes. While traditional Halloween costume parties provide ample opportunity for guests to demonstrate creativity in the outfits they choose, a particular theme for your party can help your guests more easily concoct a costume. All the decorations described earlier in this book can be used. A theme can also suggest decorations, foods, music, and activities. Be sure that you make a note of the theme in your party invitations. Here are a few themes.

ADULT PARTIES

BARN DANCE

Country is the theme. Decorate with bales of hay and farm implements. If you can, rent a cow for the night, and hitch it outdoors where guests can feed it fistfuls of hay. Be prepared for cleaning up after the animal and keeping it safe from playful children or drunken adults. Play country, bluegrass, or rockabilly music. Simple square dancing can be a fun party game, or you can try a few of the country steps popularized in the 1980s.

BEACH PARTY

This provides an excuse for girls to wear bikinis and guys to look at girls in bikinis. You can simulate a beach indoors. Palm trees, beach towels, a life guard stand, and sun umbrellas help create the mood. Play surfer music, have a limbo contest, and set up a big-screen TV to screen beach movies starring Frankie and Annette. Serve hot dogs, corn on the cob, hamburgers, and the like. Don't use a charcoal grill indoors. It's a flame hazard and produces poisonous gases. Grill the food ahead of time and rewarm it for serving.

DISCO NIGHT

Rent a disco ball and crank up the Bee Gees. If you hire a caterer, dress the waiters in leisure suits and the waitresses in pantsuits. Have a "Worst Use of a Man-Made Fiber" contest to reward the guest who shows up wearing the biggest polyester crime. Decorate bowls with a photocopied likeness of Jimmy Carter and fill them with varieties of peanuts. Paste BILLY BEER labels on cans of beer. Have disco-savvy guest teach disco steps, then stage a disco dance contest so your older guests can relive their Travolta moments.

HAWAIIAN LUAU

A luau party makes a nice celebration for warm or cold climates. In warm areas, guests can wear their best Hawaiian shirts, shorts, sandals, and swimsuits. In cold areas, guests just wear their luau duds under warm coats. The summery wear makes a nice contrast to the cold as long as the place where the party is held is toasty warm.

Leis, inflatable palm trees, beach towels, sun umbrellas, lawn chairs, and grass skirts help make the party. A tiki god statue can be made out of cardboard. Serve tropical drinks in hollowed-out pineapples with little parasols. Play Hawaiian music. Screen Michener's *Hawaii* (1966) or Elvis's *Blue Hawaii* (1961). Stage a hula contest. Roast a pig.

HIPPIE HAPPENING

The theme is centered on the counterculture of the 1960s. It gives Baby Boomers a chance to relive their youth and younger folks a chance to enjoy the activities Baby Boomers enjoyed. Decorate the party area with 1960s posters (black lights and strobe lights can be fun). Play 1960s rock. A few miniskirted, caged go-go girls are a nice touch. Serve blue Kool-Aid with brownies and other munchies. A little fluorescent body paint for face painting can make a good party game, as can 1960s trivia games.

SCI-FI NIGHT

Rent as many flashing lights as you can afford. Hang sheets of silver Mylar from the walls. Suspend beach balls spray-painted various colors from the ceiling to simulate planets. Add cardboard circles to simulate planets like Saturn. If you hire a caterer, dress the waiters and waitresses in alien masks. Serve eggnog and snacks dyed green, orange, or other bright colors. Black lights will add a glow to everything pale. Play European techno rock on a turntable set at a low speed or high speed. Hardly anyone will be able to figure out the lyrics—tell your guests it's Martian hip-hop.

SOCK HOP

Simulate a high school sock hop from the 1950s. Stage it in a high school gym. String crepe paper and set up a punch bowl on a folding table. Display posters of Elvis, Pat Boone, James Dean, Tuesday Weld, and other stars from that era. Rent a jukebox and play golden oldies. As with the Disco Night party above, have someone who is familiar with period dances teach guests the old moves. Make sure you play a few slow ones. A classic, high-finned car can make a nice mood setter. A drawing can be held to see which couple gets to drive it to the local lovers' lane.

TOGA PARTY

This is the classic college theme party. Play classic rock and the soundtrack for *Animal House*, which includes such hits as "Shout," "Dream Girl," "Let's Dance," "Hey Paula," "Shama Lama Ding Dong," "Tossin' and Turnin'," "Twistin' the Night Away," and "Louie, Louie." Serve tubs of iced beer in long necks. Expect a food fight, so serve the least messy foods you can in an easily cleanable area.

CHILDREN'S PARTIES

Children prefer a traditional Halloween costume party. This allows them to wear whatever outfit strikes their fancy. For younger children, who can't attend evening parties, a home can be given a nocturnal feel by hanging black curtains over windows. The adults who host the party should also dress in costume. Children enjoy seeing adults they know dressed as vampires, witches, or other Halloween monsters. Care should be taken to not scare younger children.

CHILDREN'S PARTY GAMES

The traditional Halloween party games—pumpkin carving, pin the tail on the donkey, and so on—are perfect. Here are a few other ideas:

- Bobbing for apples is a Halloween favorite. Place a washtub or children's splash pool on a plastic tarp and fill it, using buckets, with water up to four inches from the top. Water is heavy, and you should place the tub where you won't have to go far to fill it or empty it. Remove the stems from several apples and float them in the water. Players compete to remove an apple using just their teeth. To avoid head banging, let only two or three players compete at any one time. Provide plenty of towels and extra apples.

- Pumpkins, Pumpkins, Pumpkins is played by choosing a player to stand before the other children and answer every question put to him with the word *pumpkin.* The child answering must keep a straight face. If he smiles or laughs, he is replaced by the child who produced the reaction. Keeping a straight face can be difficult when asked questions such as "What do you put your hat on?" or "Your girlfriend is as round as a . . . ?"

- Ghost-story telling is a fun activity. Before the party, prepare an age-appropriate ghost story. Gather the children in a circle in a darkened room, then slowly regale them with your story. Don't be afraid to be dramatic or comic. Tie your story to local history and local sites. One popular type of story relates the depredations of an ax murderer. He kills several people and hunts a young couple. The couple escape but the killer isn't caught and continues to lurk in the dark waiting for more victims. In fact, he's been reported out tonight. The climax can be given a scary jolt by having an accomplice jump out of the darkness with a plastic ax and a light under his face.

One form of ghost story for children is told by blindfolding the children and passing ordinary objects through their hands while describing them as the remnants of a horribly murdered man. A boiled egg, for example, can be described as one of his eyeballs. A pot of cold macaroni can be his diced brains. A can of sliced peaches can be chopped kidneys. A plastic bag filled with gelatin and covered with cooking oil can be his torn-out liver. Pumpkin innards can be shredded intestines. Strips of uncooked bacon can be gobs of flesh. A torn-up latex glove can be a skinned hand. Glue "fingernails" cut from a plastic milk jug to the fingers of the glove for more realism. Chill everything in the refrigerator overnight to make it all extra creepy.

- Play Vampire Tag in the backyard. Label a tree on one side of the yard CHURCH, and a tree on the other side CASTLE. Select one child to be the first vampire. When the first vampire touches a child, that child becomes a vampire, too, unless he is touching the church tree. The church-touching player is only safe for a count of thirteen, which he must shout. The vampire is not allowed to touch the player while the player is counting. New vampires chase after the other children. When only one child is left, the game shifts. The leftover child becomes the fearless vampire hunter, and he runs after the vampires—who are safe when touching the castle tree. When only one vampire remains, the game switches again. This continues until everyone is too tired to continue. The kids can refresh themselves with bloodred punch.

- Stage a costume contest with categories such as "Miss/Mr. Uncongeniality," "Deadest," and "Most Horrid." Paper sashes bearing these titles make nice awards. Bring a Polaroid camera to the party and snap pictures of all the costumes. Parents are usually urged to give an award to each child, but this undercuts the value of winning for the children. Most kids who lose won't be upset, and those who win will have a nice Halloween memory.

- Skeleton Scamper is played by drawing several skeletons on white cardboard and cutting them out. Cut off the skeleton's head, legs, and arms. Discard most of the cutouts for one part so that that part will become key to winning. Hide the pieces in a room where there is nothing delicate that might be destroyed by rampaging kids. Send the children racing to find all the parts necessary to build a skeleton. For older children, the skeleton can be divided into more parts. An effective accompaniment to the game is a recording of the song "Dem Bones," with its lyrics of "the neck bone's connected to the head bone" and so on. When the song ends, the collecting ends and the kids assemble their skeletons. Give prizes for complete skeletons, but also award a prize for the "fastest-running" skeleton—the one with the most legs.

- Jacko is a version of Bingo. Take an ordinary Bingo set and replace the letters on the cards' columns with those of the word *Jacko*. The easiest way to do this is to place a sheet of tracing paper over one of the Bingo cards. Draw the letters of *Jacko* over the letters of *Bingo* so that they will match in size and position. Also draw lines matching the lines that enclose the Bingo heading. Make several photocopies of the tracing, clip out the Jacko heading, and glue it over the Bingo heading. You needn't change the balls that are drawn; just remember to substitute *J* for *B* when you draw a *B*, an *A* for an *I*, a *C* for an *N*, and a *K* for a *G*.

- Skull and Crossbones is played like Tic-Tac-Toe. The children are divided into two teams. One team is the Skulls, and the other is the Crossbones. Questions are posed to a member of each team; if the question is answered correctly, that member gets to place a marker for his team on a square of a three-by-three grid. The first team to draw a line diagonally, horizontally, or vertically wins. For young children, the questions can be as simple as, "What's round and orange and has a grin?" Harder questions can be given to older kids. Horror movies make good subjects for the latter. Examples are: "In the movie *Psycho,* where is the young woman killed?" "What horror hero said 'I don't drink wine.'?" and "How do you kill a werewolf?" (The answers are a shower, Dracula, and a silver bullet.)

- Mummy Run is a good indoor party game. In a large room, arrange chairs in two opposing rows as far apart as the room will allow. Divide the players into teams and place them by the chairs on one side of the room. Give each team a roll of inexpensive toilet paper. The Run is conducted like a relay race. The game begins by taping the end of the toilet paper to the starting chairs with a piece of masking tape. At the shout of "Go," a player from each team races across to the opposing chair, trailing a length of toilet paper. When he gets to the opposite chair, he winds the paper around the chair and returns to his starting chair, where he passes the roll to another player. If the paper breaks, the team must return to the starting chair, secure the paper again, and start again. The first team to make thirteen unbroken spans wins. Tear several pieces of masking tape for each team in case they need to retape the toilet paper to the starting chair.

- Pumpkin Head is another indoor relay race. It uses plastic jack-o'-lantern treat buckets with the handles removed. The children are divided into teams and race while balancing the jack-o'-lantern on their heads. If it falls, the racer must restart.

- Feed the Monster is a game that combines drawing with throwing. It requires an even number of players. To prepare, take a cardboard box that is about twenty-four inches on each side, or larger. On the side of the box, cut a mouth lined with pointy teeth. Seal the box, then paint it to look like a monster. You can make cardboard arms with clawed paws or use Styrofoam spheres and dowels to give the monster eyestalks. Prepare a smaller, second box to hold the monster's food. Label it MONSTER CHOW or PEOPLE TO GO. Obtain a plastic jack-o'-lantern. Draw an empty gingerbread man shape on a sheet of paper. Make photocopies of this figure on lightweight cardboard.

  Play begins by giving one copy of the blank figure to each child. Place slips of paper with the children's names into the plastic jack-o'-lantern. Draw the names two at a time to pair up the children. Using markers, the children draw a likeness of the child they were paired with on the blank figure. Cut out the figures, then label the back of the figure with the name of the child depicted. The figures are placed in the food box. The slips of paper with names are returned to the plastic jack-o'-lantern. The coordinator of the game draws a name, and that child is placed at the head of the monster feeding line. The coordinator draws another name, placing that child next in line. This continues until all the children are lined up.

Monster feeding now starts. The first child draws a figure from the food box and, from a distance, tries to toss the figure into the monster's mouth. If he is successful, the child corresponding with the figure is considered "eaten" and steps out of line. He stands behind the monster, where he now helps the monster growl and demand food. The successful thrower draws another figure. If he misses, he goes to the back of the line. If a child draws his own figure, he returns it to the food box and goes to the back of the line. Drawing continues until the food box is empty, then the misses are gathered up and put back in the food box. Eventually, only one child will remain with his the only figure in the food box. He is the only survivor and the winner.

While the game is a bit complex to set up and play, children enjoy drawing caricatures of their friends, trying to feed them to the monster, and making monster growls.

- Sunlight is a version of the game Redlight. One child is selected as the Vampire Hunter and turned away from the other children, who are all vampires. They charge toward the hunter while he counts to ten. At ten, he turns and yells "Sunlight." Any vampire who is caught moving must return to the starting point. If the Hunter is tagged before he finishes counting, he becomes a vampire and the tagger becomes the Hunter.

- Centipede Tag is played outside in a limited area, such as a baseball diamond. When the person who is It tags someone, that person becomes the Head of the Centipede. He is It, and the former It is now part of the Tail of the Centipede. The Tail must hold the hand of the Head. As a team, they now pursue the others. Only the Head may make tags. A tag doesn't count if the chain of hands is broken at the time the tag is made. In the heat of play, a child may break through the centipede. He must take the hands of the children he separated. A child who moves outside the area of play is considered tagged. The centipede can get quite long, and kids enjoy running in a great chain. Play continues till all have been tagged.

- Lend A Hand is a version of Hot Potato played using a "hand." The hand is made by stuffing a glove with newspaper and stitching it shut. It can be made a bit more fanciful by dyeing it green and gluing felt fingernails to it. The children are arranged in a circle sitting. While a tape of a Halloween tune, such as "The Monster Mash," is played, the children pass the hand to the player to their left. The music is stopped at random intervals; whoever is left holding the hand is out and he must leave the circle. Play continues until only one child is left.

PARTY MUSIC

Collect the music that you will play before the party. Organize the records, disks, or tapes that you will play so that you can find what you want in a dim room. Have the music playing before your guests arrive. Play instrumental music and slower tunes at the beginning of the evening. Gradually the music can grow more compelling and boisterous. Play popular tunes that your guests can enjoy. At the peak of the evening, play the most pulsating music. As the party fades, play less energetic music. Slower, gentler tunes help signal that it's time for your guests to leave.

A few Halloween-appropriate tunes are:

- "Attack of the Fifty-Foot Woman"—The Tubes
- "Bad Moon Rising"—Creedence Clearwater Revival
- "The Blob"—The Five Blobs
- "Boogie Fever"—The Sylvers
- "Boogie Oogie Oogie"—A Taste of Honey
- "The Creature From the Black Lagoon"—Dave Edmunds
- "Creature With the Atom Brain"—Roky Erickson and The Alien
- "Devil Went Down to Georgia"—The Charlie Daniels Band
- "Disco Inferno"—The Trammps
- "Elvira"—Dallas Frazier
- "Full Moon"—Elvira
- "I Put a Spell on You"—Screamin' Jay Hawkins

- "I Was a Teenage Werewolf"—The Cramps
- "I'm Your Boogie Man"—KC and the Sunshine Band
- "Le Freak"—Chic
- "Little Demon"—Screamin' Jay Hawkins
- "Love Potion #9"—The Clovers
- "Martian Hop"—The Ran-Dells
- "Monster Mash"—Bobby "Boris" Pickett and the Crypt Kickers
- "The Purple People Eater"—Sheb Wooley
- "Spooky"—Classics IV and Dennis Yost
- "They're Coming to Take Me Away Ha Ha"—Napoleon XIV
- "Thriller"—Michael Jackson
- "The Time Warp"—from *The Rocky Horror Picture Show*
- "Toccata and Fugue in D Minor"—Bach
- "Twilight Zone"—Neil Norman/Cosmic Orchestra
- "Werewolves of London"—Warren Zevon
- "Witch Doctor"—David Seville
- "Witchy Woman"—Eagles

Many television series have evocative Halloweenish themes. These include:

- *Alfred Hitchcock Presents*
- *Dark Shadows*
- *Kolchak: The Night Stalker*
- *The Munsters*
- *The Outer Limits*
- *The Twilight Zone*
- *The X-Files*

Several movies also have themes that can give you the shivers. A few are:

- *The Addams Family*
- *The Amityville Horror*

- *The Exorcist* ("Tubular Bells")
- *Ghostbusters*
- *Halloween*
- *The Omen*
- *The Outer Limits*
- *Psycho*
- *The Rocky Horror Picture Show*
- *Rosemary's Baby*
- *The Shining*
- *Vertigo*
- *X-Files*

This music can be run down on the Internet. Often, there are compilations that include several songs on one disk.

PARTY INVITATIONS

Halloween party invitations can be made with simple construction paper. Bats can be cut from black paper or ghosts from white paper and folded into an invitation so as to pop out when opened.

A coffin-shaped invitation can be made using a piece of black paper and piece of white paper. Fold the two in half together. Cut a coffin shape from the paper using the crease as one side of the coffin so that it can be opened to reveal the text of an invitation. Glue the black and white paper together and draw a vampire lying inside. His arm can be extended onto the lid to appear to be holding it open. Write the text of the invitation on the inside lid.

A pull-out jack-o'-lantern invitation can be made by folding a piece of orange paper in half. Cut a pumpkin shape from the paper. This produces two identical shapes. Glue the two shapes together, putting glue only near the edges. Slice off the top of the pumpkin to make a lid. Cut a rectangle of yellow paper. Put a drop of glue on its top and tuck this inside the lid. The rest of the rectangle will carry the text of the invitation and will be tucked inside the pumpkin's body. Using a brown marker, color the pumpkin's stem. Draw a jack-o'-lantern face on the pumpkin with a black marker.

A pull-out grave invitation can be made using brown paper and gray paper in a similar way. The brown paper is folded and cut into an oblong grave mound, producing two identical shapes. The shapes are glued together at the edges. An upward curve is cut across the top of the joined mound shapes. The gray paper is cut into a tombstone with a long tail. This is glued onto the upward curve, with the tail extended below the curve. The text is written on the bottom of the tombstone. It is tucked inside the grave. A black pen can be used to put an epitaph on the tombstone.

The pull-out grave invitation can be embellished by adding a coffin made as described above.

More elaborate invitations can be made by photocopying Halloween-related drawings or photos. Set the image behind a black construction-paper frame, and glue to the front of a card formed by folding orange construction paper. Images of monsters, spiders, or witches work well.

Martha Stewart suggested an interesting invitation in a Halloween issue of her decorating magazine. She used rubber mold mix to make a mold of her finger, then filled the mold with plaster to make a plaster finger. She tied a black string around this white finger and nestled it on a bed of moss in a small white cardboard box. The inside lid of the box urged her guests to not forget to attend her party.

Spooky Parent-Child Party Activities

Parents and children can make some nice Halloween memories by spending time together during the days before the holiday. A few fun activities are:

- Rent a horror movie and pop some corn.
- Go to a pumpkin patch and select a few for jack-o'-lanterns. Go home and carve away.
- Bake Halloween cookies.
- Put a blanket over the kitchen table and stage an in-house camping trip. Turn out all the lights. Climb under the table with a flashlight and tell ghost stories. The teller holds the flashlight under his chin to increase spookiness.

- Stand side by side in front of a mirror and have a face-making contest.

PARTYING CAUTIONS

- Keep fire extinguishers on hand.

- Too-loud music can do more than annoy your neighbors—it can damage hearing permanently.

- Take care serving alcoholic beverages. With more and more adults celebrating Halloween, alcohol abuse during the holiday has become more widespread. This abuse can be especially dangerous when drinkers take to the road. Children darting through the streets are hard even for sober drivers to avoid. Party planners should remember that they have a moral duty to prevent injuries and may be legally responsible for drunk drivers leaving their festivities. The old adage "Friends don't let friends drive drunk" should be recalled, and party givers should closely monitor their guests.

- Alcohol can also increase the likelihood of accidents. Dim lighting, entangling decorations, and drunken partyers don't mix well. Again, you can wind up in legal difficulties.

  In addition to safety issues, while drinking may make you feel like the life of the party, it can make you the bore of the party, the laughingstock of the party, and the loser of the party.

Boos Spoiled by Booze

A few years ago in Tichigan Lake, Wisconsin, Otto Ashpole and his twenty-two-year-old wife, Mary Ann, went trick-or-treating in a rather different way. Instead of asking for candy, they asked for liquor. They apparently received quite a few such treats, for Mary Ann tripped over a landscaping railroad tie, fell, and smashed the glass she was carrying against her neck. The jagged fragments tore open her throat and she bled to death.

CIVIC CELEBRATIONS

All across America, cities and institutions sponsor Halloween events. The Key West Fantasy Fest and the Greenwich Village Halloween Parade are two examples of celebrations intended for adult audiences. Georgetown, in Washington, D.C., hosts its own Halloween carnival, which features prominent politicians in costume. In Salem, Massachusetts, there is an annual Haunted Happenings celebration that includes a psychic festival, a "Pumpkin Patch" ham-and-bean supper, and lectures by the Witches' League for Public Awareness. Other communities stage carnivals featuring Halloween-related activities, such as jack-o'-lantern carving contests, cornfield mazes, hayrides, and pumpkin-pie-eating contests. A few big-city cemeteries offer Halloween tours and concerts. Many historic sites that are purported to be haunted offer tours and Halloween festivities.

Zoos often stage Halloween festivals. Staff members dress in costume, and exhibits of scary animals are featured. The Hogle Zoo in Salt Lake City stages an annual Boo in the Zoo program that rewards costumed children with treats and displays of snakes and millipedes.

Some Halloween civic events are meant to serve special causes. Charity costume balls are traditional cause-related events. Some community groups sponsor coffin races, wherein coffins mounted on wheels or carried by running pallbearers compete to carry a "body," sometimes a live compatriot, across a finish line. Police underwater rescue teams compete in underwater jack-o'-lantern carving. Pumpkins are sunk in an icy pond, and the divers demonstrate their skills by finding and carving faces upon them under water. Blood drives often capitalize on associations with vampires. UNICEF, which collects money for international children's programs, is the most notable organization that uses Halloween to support social causes.

He Wants Your Blood

Ottomar Rudolphe Vlad Dracul Kretzulesco, fifty-eight, is the heir to the title of Vlad Dracula, the historical figure on whom Bram Stoker based his fictional Dracula. Like his ancestor, he is interested in collecting blood. His use of it is different, however. Prince Otto is a Red Cross volunteer. In 1999, from his castle outside Berlin, he hosted a blood drive dressed in a black cape. More than eight hundred donors turned up to give blood to Dracula's heir.

Prince Otto is not a biological descendant of Vlad. He was adopted by the last heirs, two elderly noblewomen, one of whom, Katarina Olympia Princess Kretzulesco Caradja, did her own good deeds during World War II when she helped American POWs escape the Nazis. Otto plans to establish his castle as a vampire theme park. He already has a hearse and coffin museum and a bar that features bloodred wine. He also sells T-shirts, souvenirs, and vampire-related music.

Homecoming?

While many towns stage Halloween events associated with local legends, history, or geographic features, one town hopes to turn Halloween into a local industry. Civic boosters in Hell, Michigan, a community sixty miles west of Detroit, want to make their town the capital of Halloween. Hell's shopkeepers already make a tidy income selling souvenir T-shirts and postcards to those who have gone to Hell.

"I'll admit the irony, but this has got to be bad for business."

14

THE FUTURE
OF HALLOWEEN

*We seem to have a compulsion these days to bury
time capsules in order to give those people living in
the next century or so some idea of what we are like.
I have prepared one of my own. In it, I have placed
some rather large samples of dynamite, gunpowder,
and nitroglycerin. My time capsule is set to go off
in the year 3000. It will show them what we are
really like.*

Alfred Hitchcock (1899–1980), *Alfred Hitchcock Presents*

HALLOWEEN'S CHANGING IMAGE

Halloween now is second only to Christmas in terms of money spent, with, according to the National Retail Federation, nearly $6 billion expended on candy, costumes, decorations, and holiday items. More than 65 percent of American homes display Halloween decorations of some sort. These figures might suggest that the holiday is secure, but this isn't the case. Several serious challenges have been made to Halloween that may limit it, alter its character, or destroy it as it has been celebrated in the past.

The 1970s and 1980s brought changes in Halloween. Greater urbanization and social mobility eroded neighborly associations. It became common for people to not know their neighbors, even after living next to them for years. Parents grew uneasy about letting their children roam the streets unattended to knock on strangers' doors and gather treats that might be tainted. While nearly all the stories of razor blades in apples or drug-laced candy were urban legends, a tiny few were true. These were more often linked to purposeful murder rather than to random attack, but they still terrified parents.

Some of the poisoned Halloween candy rumors can be traced to a Halloween 1964 incident in Greenlawn, New York, a suburban Long Island town. Housewife Helen Pfeil grew annoyed at the many older teenagers who rang her bell to ask for treats. She thought the holiday should be reserved for small children. To make her point, she gave out treats that were more trick than treat to the older children. In little paper envelopes, then the popular way to hand out treats, she enclosed such prank treats as dog biscuits, steel-wool pads, and ant traps marked POISON. The kids who received these items complained to their parents, who called in the police. Pfeil was arrested for passing out the arsenic-filled ant traps. She plead guilty to a lesser charge and was given a suspended sentence.

Vandalism returned to Halloween in an uglier form during the 1970s. Childish pranks were replaced by criminal actions. Young children were harassed by older children, who stole their treats. Homeowners were wise to turn on all their exterior lights and put away yard items. Windows were more likely to be smashed than soaped. Instead of bonfires, vandals burned derelict buildings. In some cities, Mischief Night became Devil's Night, with hundreds of buildings set ablaze. Thousands of citizens were placed in danger and millions of dollars were lost in property damage.

In response to vandalism, Halloween was more carefully monitored by the authorities. Official trick-or-treating times were established. Many cities imposed curfews for Halloween and Mischief Night. Police increased street patrols and called up reserves and volunteers to bolster their street presence. In Detroit, for example, a city that has been particularly plagued by Devil's Night fires, thirty-five-thousand volunteers join police to patrol the city's streets in a citizen-police effort called Angel's Night. Their effort paid off by greatly reducing the number of fires set.

Parents have begun to limit the number of homes and the areas their children visit for trick-or-treating and accompany their children to ensure their safety. Hospitals commonly volunteer to X-ray the treats to detect foreign objects. Newspapers and television news programs broadcast long lists of precautions that can make Halloween safer. Some families have stopped trick-or-treating altogether, substituting Halloween parties, hosted by parent groups, schools, churches, and even shopping malls.

Another change in Halloween has come in the age groups celebrating it. Baby Boomers, who had enjoyed Halloween as children, began to celebrate it as adults. Elaborate and expensive costume parties for adults are now commonplace (the costs involved in adult participation are a principal factor in the growth of Halloween as a commercial holiday). Some businesses stage large-scale office Halloween parties, with entire floors decorated to a theme and all employees costumed. Ironically, in a reversal from the days when parents were invited to school to see their children in costumes, employees' children are sometimes invited to visit the decorated offices and see their parents in costume.

Adult Halloween celebrations often have a sexual component. While fun for the adults, who get to indulge themselves, the alteration of the holiday into an adult carnival similar to Mardi Gras in New Orleans excludes children (at least, one hopes they are excluded). One of the most notable of these adult carnivals is the annual Fantasy Fest held in Key West, Florida. Nudity, mitigated by body paints, is almost mandatory. The revelry is fueled by large quantities of alcohol.

Another adult Halloween carnival began in the early 1970s in New York's Greenwich Village. Theater artist Ralph Lee dressed his children and his friends in grotesque masks of his own design, then led them in a parade to Washington Square Park, where they put on a play. By the 1980s, as many as 100,000 people were joining him in his parade and 250,000 spectators were turning out to watch. The artistic neighborhood produces ornate, witty, and irreverent costumes. Today, the Greenwich Village Halloween Parade has become a predominantly gay celebration. Halloween has often been labeled Gay Christmas. Supposedly, the costume parties held on the holiday gave gays an excuse to dress in otherwise unacceptable costumes and openly enjoy themselves. The Greenwich Village parade certainly features outrageous getups. Notable costumed participants have included the Fashion Police, handing out on-the-spot clothing citations, witches on stilts, the foursome from *The Wizard of Oz* with a male in Dorothy-drag and a poodle as Toto, the Big Apple Corps Gay and Lesbian Marching Band, regiments of fairy godmothers, and Moses on Roller Skates.

West Hollywood stages a Halloween parade similar to Greenwich Village's. Dubbed the West Hollywood Halloween Carnival, it attracts as many as 250,000 people. Events include costume contests and "Drag Races" down Santa Monica Boulevard in which all contestants must wear two-inch stiletto heels. The highlight of the carnival is the crowning of an honorary mayor who presides over the festivities. These mayors have included comic Judy "The Aphrodite of the Accordion" Tenuta, actress Kathy Kinney of *The Drew Carey Show*, and Elvira, Mistress of the Dark.

When adults are busy celebrating Halloween, they commonly leave no one at home to answer their doors to children trick-or-treating. Once it was unusual to spot a dark, locked house on Halloween; today it has become commonplace, and even the majority trend in some communities. Communal children's activities are a poor substitute for the door-to-door adventures enjoyed by children in earlier years.

Compounding these sociological changes, there are organized groups actively seeking to neuter Halloween's wilder aspects or ban it altogether.

RELIGIOUS OPPOSITION TO HALLOWEEN

While all religions dislike the gorier and more demonic elements of Halloween, different religions have different views of it. Generally, the Catholic Church has little problem with it. This makes sense, as Halloween is linked to All Saints' Day, a Catholic holy day. The Eastern Orthodox Church has similar views. Liberal Protestant churches also have little problem with the holiday, considering it a traditional, secular holiday. The Church of Jesus Christ of Latter-Day Saints has no official position on Halloween other than to frown upon celebrating it on a Sunday. Jewish rabbis also have little to say about the holiday, other than to worry about it encouraging mischief and distracting children from more important activities. Wiccans and Neopagans tend to embrace the holiday as their own and use it to explain their religious views. They dislike witches being portrayed as ugly and evil. They so routinely decry this custom in the media as to make their decrying a custom of the season.

Some fundamentalist Protestant groups regard Halloween as a celebration of Satan and roundly condemn it, especially when it falls on Sunday. Some Protestants have tried to reform the holiday by removing all references to magic, witches, demons, and the like. They stage "Hallelujah" parties instead of Halloween parties. Children are encouraged to wear wholesome, nonviolent costumes. "A lot of people do see the scary costumes as the equivalent to violent behavior," the Reverend Beau Abernathy, pastor of Christ Community Evangelical Free Church in Lawrence, Kansas, explained in 1993, after his church staged a Halloween costume party where children dressed as their favorite biblical characters. "There is a dark side to Halloween. It's kind of like you don't want to play with fire. Why give them a taste of evil at that young of an age?"

These modifications are sometimes not enough, and some Protestants reject Halloween entirely, referring to Exodus 22:18, cited earlier: "Thou shalt not suffer a witch to live." These Protestants believe that even playful dabbling with witchcraft is dangerous. This is also a common view among Islamic religious authorities, who fear celebrating Halloween is too close to Devil worship.

In 1995, parents complaining of Halloween's supposed Satanic associations managed to convince the Los Altos, California, school board to cancel all Halloween celebrations in their schools. The news of this decision spread across the country; television news programs featured interviews with board members, who explained that they were just being sensitive to the feelings of offended parents. Los Altos parents who weren't fearful of Halloween's Satanic possibilities angrily protested the decision. Hundreds of parents and children, many in Halloween costumes, jammed the next board meeting. The board backed down, reinstating Halloween 4 to 0. Parents who objected to having their children attend the celebrations were allowed to keep their children home.

In 1999, Dr. Beth Willingham of Baylor University countered fundamentalist objections to Halloween as "reading too much into it." She noted that it began as a pagan rite but has been Christianized for twelve hundred years. Modern Halloween, Willingham observed, is simply a secular celebration.

SATANISM AND HALLOWEEN

Fear of Halloween is not completely unjustified. Some troubled people do use Halloween as an excuse to attempt demonic rituals. While the number of these evil worshipers is tiny, their actions and intent are disturbing. It is worth noting that several spree killers in the last decades have been self-proclaimed Satan worshipers.

Satanists can clearly be dangerous, but it isn't logical to equate Satanism with Halloween. Millions celebrate Halloween without turning murderous, and if there were no Halloween there would still be murderous people always able find an excuse to indulge their evil whims. Perhaps they'd settle on Christmas as an occasion for evildoing, celebrating Satan in opposition to what everyone else celebrates.

The answer to the Halloween and Satanism problem lies somewhere between alarm and apathy. We should be aware that evil people may take advantage of the holiday, but not allow them to terrorize us into abandoning it.

POLITICALLY CORRECT OPPOSITION

The religious opponents to Halloween have found an ally in those who see the holiday as politically incorrect and mentally unhealthy. Halloween activities sponsored by the public schools have been particular targets for these national nannies. Costumes deemed too ghoulish or too violent are banned, as are those that might encourage harmful attitudes. An evil witch, for example, is forbidden because it stigmatizes Wiccans and Neopagans. A soldier costume, especially one including a gun, is seen as advocating militarism. A vampire outfit might be forbidden as too fearsome and likely to produce psychological trauma. Dressing as a cartoon character or as a film star might be too commercial. The old standby of days gone by, the hobo costume, is viewed as insensitive to the homeless. It is common for schoolchildren to be given lists of acceptable costumes that include such things as endangered species, healthful fruits and vegetables, and the always acceptable circus clown. It is easy to see how this can drain the fun out of the holiday.

A typical example of Halloween purging was detailed in October 1996 by the *Manchester Union Leader* of New Hampshire. It reported that school officials at Maple Avenue and Bartlett Elementary Schools had decided to end their schools' thirty-year tradition of staging a Halloween parade with their first-, second-, and third-graders. Maple Avenue principal Marc Boyd said, "So many Halloween costumes are based on themes of gore and violence. We have to wonder if that's something we really want the children involved in." Instead of a Halloween party, the schools staged a bland "Harvest Day Celebration."

Another avenue of attack upon Halloween in the schools is to claim that it is a religious holiday and that religion has been banned from public schools. This rationale has been used to purge other holidays, such as Christmas and Easter.

Still another criticism of the observance of Halloween comes from the practice of charity groups setting up haunted houses to raise funds. As described elsewhere in this book, haunted houses once meant for party entertainment have become a major moneymaking enterprise. Some haunted houses have been criticized for presenting too fearful a performance. Others have aroused controversy for using displays to teach religious views.

Fundamentalist churches have set up haunted houses called Hell Houses. The Reverend Jerry Falwell, founder of the Moral Majority, is sometimes credited with the idea. In 1972, the youth division of his Lynchburg, Virginia, church, the Thomas Road Baptist Church, put on a "Scaremare." Other churches soon followed the example.

Hell Houses feature scenes depicting the horrors of AIDS, teen suicides, drunken driving, and what Hell itself will be like for sinners. They often depict what abortion clinics are like in graphic terms. In 1999, after the shootings at Columbine High School, a Hell House staged by the Trinity Church in Cedar Hill, Texas, featured a skit that began with two teenage boys playing violent computer games while planning a shooting spree. They then put on long, dark trench coats and enter a school library, where they discover a girl studying. They kill her as she prays. After the killing spree ends, the boys kill themselves. Jesus arrives to take the girl to Heaven and dispatch the boys to Hell. This presentation offended relatives of the Columbine victims, who saw it as an exploitation of their tragedy. Tim Ferguson, Trinity's youth pastor, who set up the Hell House, claimed he had to scare teenagers in order to save them from sin and prevent another school attack.

Trinity Church's Hell House receives about twelve thousand visitors each year at seven dollars a head. Production costs are said to run as much as twenty-five thousand dollars. All profits are earmarked for church missions.

Not only religious groups have been criticized for staging unacceptable haunted houses. In 1995, the Jaycees in Pasco, Washington, planned to stage a charity haunted house featuring grisly skits. These included an insane teacher hacking up students with poor grades, a deranged Santa Claus passing out disgusting gifts, and a Jeffrey Dahmer–style killer "slicing and dicing" human limbs and flambéing a human head. Irate citizens swamped the Jaycees with phone calls protesting the performances. The skits were quickly toned down or eliminated. The skit that got the most protests depicted O. J. Simpson jumping out of some bushes to slash and stab dummies of Nicole Brown Simpson and Ronald Goldman, then pausing to give a fan an autograph before dropping a bloody glove and fleeing. The Jaycees eliminated the Simpson skit.

Yet another threat to traditional Halloween is the use of the holiday for fund-raising. For many years, UNICEF has solicited donations to help children around the world. This activity has inspired a Catholic organization in Toronto called Aid to Women to use trick-or-treaters to collect money to fight abortion. In 1998, it raised more than seven thousand dollars. If more organizations resort to such fund-raising, Halloween may become politicized. For many, the holiday has always served as an excuse to promote political agendas—thousands of Nixon masks are still being sold a generation after Watergate and years after the ex-president's death.

FEAR OF VANDALISM

Aside from the religious and political opposition to Halloween, there are a substantial number of civic authorities who object to Halloween because of the vandalism and disorder that accompany it. The terrible epidemic of arson that commonly occurs on Devil's Night is the most dangerous of these disturbances. Governments rightly strive to thwart this. Unfortunately, some authorities see any disturbance as something that must be squashed. They seek to regulate the hours of trick-or-treating, sometimes changing the date of Halloween, and have even gone so far as to license children before letting them trick-or-treat. In 1997, the Bridgeport, Ohio, city council decreed that all children under the age of fifteen must register with the city and obtain an orange sticker to affix to their costume before they can go door to door collecting candy.

ARE THE DOUBTERS RIGHT?

Is Halloween too frightening for children? Different children at different ages find different things frightening. A very young child may laugh at a gory mask but cry when confronted by a tiny, fuzzy caterpillar. The key is which is understood and which seems unnatural.

The child might understand that masks are for play but never have seen a caterpillar. The latter moves by itself and might, in the child's mind, be looking for a snack.

Children can also be persuaded that something is frightening. Telling a child that the old lady down the block is a witch who turns into a cat can cause the child to screech like a banshee if the elderly woman smiles and waves hello. Halloweentime is laden with stories of witches, goblins, and horrors. It isn't surprising that a child may believe some of the stories are true or, at least, wonder if they might be true.

Psychological studies have shown that childhood frights can haunt a person far past childhood. Nightmares are the most obvious legacy, but phobias can be produced through fearful events during childhood. Clearly, Halloween can frighten, but so can many other things. A stuck Ferris wheel can create a fear of heights. A nasty teacher mocking a reciting child can create a fear of public speaking. Discovering half of a worm in a half-eaten apple can create a dread of worms (or apples). So many things can initiate a phobia that there is no way to prevent their developing. Exposing a child to a fearful thing in the context of Halloween may actually minimize damage by showing the child that the vampire or witch or whatever is just make-believe. After all, it can be pretty hard to develop a phobia of were-wolves, for example, when your kid sister is skipping along trick-or-treating dressed as one.

Adults should take children's fears seriously and listen when they want to describe their fears. A reasoned discussion may defuse fears. An adult, for example, might point out to a child afraid of ghosts that ghost stories are just stories and that no one has ever proven that ghosts exist, to say nothing of their being able to hurt the living. If the child is unpersuaded, adults can talk about solutions to the child's fears. Ask the child if closing the closet door or leaving a light on will help. One parent took a can of apple-scented air freshener, taped an ANTIGHOST SPRAY label on it, and sprayed his worried child's bedroom, saying ghosts hated the smell of apples. Even when children see through these measures, they feel reassured that an adult is taking time to make them feel better.

For the terrors of Halloween, a healthy approach would be for adults to encourage children to embrace the holiday and confront their fears. "Shielding" children from Halloween scares may be counterproductive. Los Angeles child psychologist Robert Butterworth observes, "By sheltering your kids from a 'pagan' holiday, you're actually making them dwell on their fears more. 'If Mom and Dad don't want me dressing up as something scary, these creatures must actually be all around us.'"

A Revival in Trick-or-Treating?

There is evidence that the traditions of Halloween are enjoying a resurgence. In 1999, according to the National Confectioners Association, 92 percent of children went trick-or-treating. That's a 10 percent increase over the percentage doing so a decade earlier.

SHOULD WE END HALLOWEEN?

In 1995, John Nichols aptly observed in "Nothing Scarier Than Halloween Paranoia," an editorial in the *Capital Times* of Madison, Wisconsin, Halloween is "an innocent holiday that offers a rare, guilt-free opportunity to dress weird, be mischievous, get spooked, knock on neighbors' doors, demand excellent treats and eat inordinate amounts of candy. Halloween is supposed to happen at night. Halloween is supposed to happen outdoors. Halloween is supposed to involve walking up to the doors of neighbors, knocking on them and screeching 'trick or treat'. . . If America collapses as a nation, it will not be because of a few bad apples on Halloween night. It will be because of the weight of fear and paranoia that we have piled on top of an otherwise functioning society."

A wise religious approach to Halloween was expressed by the Reverend Darlene Avery, a minister of Holladay United Church of Christ in Salt Lake City. She said: "To be a Christian, one must contemplate and come to some terms with concepts like life and death, sacrifice and atonement, good and evil . . . Halloween is a healthy expression and outlet for those experiences."

Perhaps that is the best use of Halloween, to encourage us to think about life and death, and remember those who have died. That was the root purpose of All Saints' Day, All Souls' Day, and of the Celtic

Samhain. Halloween is a good reminder of how close we all are to death, and at the same time, it urges us to rejoice like a costumed kid with a sackful of goodies and a plot for small mischief that life can be sweet and that even our fears can be fun if we have courage to face them and laugh.

There is no sun without shadow and it is essential
to know the night.

Albert Camus (1913–1960)

INDEX